Bette

Also by George Mair

The Eagle and the Dragon
Braceros: The Helping Arm
The Jade Cat Murders
Bridge Down: America's Collapsing Infrastructure
How to Write Better
Inside HBO: Cable TV vs. VCR
Lethal Ladies: True Stories of Women Who Murder for Love
Family Money: Inheritance Battles of the Rich and Famous
Star Stalkers
A Woman's Guide to Divorce
Oprah Winfrey: The Real Story

Bette

An Intimate Biography of
Bette Midler

George Mair

A Birch Lane Press Book
Published by Carol Publishing Group

A Birch Lane Press Book
Published by Carol Publishing Group
Birch Lane Press is a registered trademark of
Carol Communications, Inc.
Editorial Offices: 600 Madison Avenue, New York, N.Y. 10022
Sales and Distribution Offices: 120 Enterprise Avenue,
Secaucus, N.J. 07094
In Canada: Canadian Manda Group, One Atlantic Avenue, Suite 105,
Toronto, Ontario M6K 3E7
Queries regarding rights and permissions should be addressed to Carol
Publishing Group, 600 Madison Avenue, New York, N.Y. 10022

Carol Publishing Group books are available at special discounts for bulk
purchases, sales promotion, fund-raising, or educational purposes.
Special editions can be created to specifications. For details, contact:
Special Sales Department, Carol Publishing Group, 120 Enterprise Avenue,
Secaucus, N.J. 07094

Manufactured in the United States of America
10 9 8 7 6 5 4 3 2 1

Library of Congress Cataloging-in-Publication Data

Mair, George, 1929–
Bette : an intimate biography of Bette Midler / by George Mair.
p.   cm.
"A Birch Lane Press book."
Includes index.
ISBN 1-55972-272-X
1. Midler, Bette. 2. Singers—United States—Biography.
I. Title.
ML420.M43M35   1995
782.42164'092—dc20   94-25242
[B]   CIP
MN

Thanks to . . .
Natasha Kern, an insightful, dynamic literary agent
who makes things happen and ignited the spark
that produced this book.

Hillel Black, a talented and patient editor
whose guidance allowed me to craft a work
that you, the reader, will enjoy.

Dedicated to . . .
My father, Ludwig L. Mair, who also worked
with his hands as a fine cabinetmaker
and was the kindest and most decent man
I have ever known.

Contents

PART V / The Kipper Phase

PART VI / The Life of a Movie Star Mother

Part I

Living in Paradise and Hating It

1

The Illumination of a Star

It was a special moment in the lives of all who were in that smoky little bar in Manhattan. The place was called Hilly's and it featured a lot of young, striving talent trying to catch the brass ring of show business success by performing for nothing in hopes that something or someone would happen to boost their careers. Performers entertained the inattentive patrons who were gossiping, drinking, eating, clinking silverware and glasses and occasionally giving the person on stage partial attention.

One of the regulars was Marta Heflin, an actress in her early twenties who had a minor role in the Broadway hit *Fiddler on the Roof.* That night late in 1968 she convinced Bette Midler, a twenty-three-year-old actress friend who had played the feature role of the older sister, Tzeitel, in *Fiddler* for three years, to come with her. Bette had been in New York since 1965.

Marta did her performance and then told Bette she ought to go on stage and try out. Bette had just come to watch and listen and she wasn't ready to perform. Marta persisted and Bette finally changed from her private persona into the performing mode and moved onto the stage to sing three songs. When she began the first song, the audience chatter diminished and table noises ceased as the crowd quieted down and began to listen.

Marta recalls, "As I was watching her sing, I thought, Oh my God. Something is happening here. This is really hot because the audience just freaked. It was *very* heavy. I had no idea she could do that."

By the time Bette reached "God Bless the Child," her third number, she had the audience mesmerized, and the emotions in the entire club swelled until, at the end, the whole place exploded.

Bette remembered, "I always sang, but never seriously. I got up in front of this little audience and just sang. The first two songs weren't anything special, but the third, something just happened to me. Something happened to my head and my body, and it was just the most wonderful sensation I'd ever been through. It was not like me singing. It was like something else!"

It was the musical magic coming in. She didn't realize it fully at the time, but in "God Bless the Child" she was the child whom God was blessing at that moment, because it would change the whole direction of her career. "The song," she recalled, "had a life of its own, and the song imposed itself on me and I didn't even know what was going on. It was just what I needed to help me decide to become a singer."

That night, in the dark, noisy, initially inattentive, smoke-marbled room, Bette experienced an epiphany that would redirect her career from actress to song stylist for the next decade and start her on the road to becoming an international star.

Throughout her career, Bette has taken guidance and been an imitator or an adapter, and that's what made for the magic of that night in Hilly's. The man who guided her to explore the artistry and music of older stars and earlier music was Ben Gillespie, whom she had met in *Fiddler*.

She recalled, "Ben Gillespie was one of my oldest friends, just the most wonderful gay guy. He was a dancer in *Fiddler on the Roof*. And he introduced me to the world. He played records for me, we went to old movies together, we talked about art. I worshiped him. I was with him for three years, and he literally changed my life. He made me want to sing. I'd always sung, but I didn't really know there was something called popular music. I have never focused on it. He showed me who Marlene Dietrich was—I had *no idea* who she was. In 1966, I think it was, I went with this guy to see a Marlene Dietrich show. Burt Bacharach was her conductor at the time. And

I'm watching this woman with her hairdo and this long white fur coat. She sashays across the stage and drops this coat, and this crowd is going crazy! People are screaming! Their faces are turning red. They're crying. And I'm thinking, 'What the fuck is going on here?' Anyway, she does this whole show and *I didn't get it.* Then, at the end of the show the audience got up as one and rushed to the footlights and started pelting her with flowers. And I said, 'Wow! Check this out! This is the most amazing thing.'

"I was about twenty-four or twenty-five. Afterward I told Ben who I had seen, and then we started going to all these Marlene Dietrich movies. I saw one after another. I never saw anything like it in my life: I'd never seen so much gauze, so much glue, so many eyelashes, so many sequins, those things that von Sternberg did for her. It started out neat and then got just bizarre. But it was so beautiful. I was totally enchanted by it. And I was swept away. The more he showed me, the more exciting it became for me."

The woman who captivated the audience at Hilly's that night may have been Bette Midler performing as if she were the smoldering-voiced Marlene Dietrich singing as Lola Lola at the Blue Angel Cafe in the Berlin of the 1930s. The synergy between Bette and the audience awakened the blues artist within her.

That magical moment at the little Manhattan bar would launch the woman who would become the Divine Miss M. In ten years she went from being a not-very-pretty, not-very-lucky teenager to one of the most sought-after stars in the world today. But there is another Bette Midler, insecure, uncertain, vulnerable, studious, who is not at ease with herself and frightened of relationships with men and money.

This is her story.

2

Born in Paradise

Chesty and Ruth Midler could have chosen Paterson, New Jersey, or paradise, and, predictably, they picked paradise. Fred Midler had earned the nickname Chesty while weightlifting at the YMCA in Paterson. In the early 1940s he met and married Ruth Schindel of Passaic, and his glowing tales of the Pacific paradise he had experienced while in the Navy entranced the dreamy Ruth. The vision of a tropical paradise coupled with an easier life away from their families brightened their imaginations and they left New Jersey for Hawaii and settled in Aiea (pronounced "Ah-EE-ah") a suburb of Honolulu.

When they arrived, Fred got a job as a housepainter with the U.S. Navy, and they lived in Navy housing at 731 Seventeenth Street in part of the Pearl Harbor military complex. It was there, on December 1, 1945, that Bette Midler was born, in the Kapiolani Maternity and Gynecological Hospital in the Ewa district east of downtown Honolulu. She was the third daughter born to the Midlers, with each named after a movie star: Susan after Susan Hayward, Judy after Judy Garland, and Bette after Bette Davis, except that Ruth Midler thought that Bette was pronounced "Bet" and that's the pronunciation her daughter grew up with.

Fred and Ruth Midler were frugal and managed to get by on what Fred earned working for the Navy, but the end of the war brought a change in their housing. With the war over, a lot of military personnel came back to Hawaii, and the Midlers were moved out of the Navy compound and into two-story barrackslike units called Halauua Housing at 4083 Atlanta Street in the rural Aiea District. This meant young Bette had to transfer from the second grade and a neighborhood largely populated by military dependents to Aiea Elementary School, where the students were mostly local Hawaiian youngsters.

Bette and her sisters were among few white children in the school and the neighborhood. Her neighbors and classmates were mostly Hawaiians, Samoans, Chinese, Japanese, and lots of rough and tough Filipinos. To get some idea of Bette's childhood world, one only has to review the last names of the children Bette grew up with as neighbors and classmates: Liane, Aebisher, Agbanlog, Ahana, Ahnee, Akamu, Akiona, Aleata, Alma, Adnerson, Aquino, Pajadali, Balgos, Barros, Araki, Sharylasao, Asato, Ching, Hayashi, Martin, Miller, Yamauchi, Kudzma, Saifuku, Fujiuka, Clingenpeel, and Ichiki.

Two of her close friends were Jane Nakamura (now Jane Kawasaki) and Judy Tokumaru (now Judy Kuwabara) in Mrs. Tyau's second-grade class. Jane said that, while Bette was the only haole in the class, "I never considered her any different [from the rest of us]." In fact, Judy added, most of the class hadn't a clue as to Bette's religion: "We never knew what Jewish was." As for Bette's later talk of all the Samoans in the neighborhood, "She always mentions Samoans," Judy said, "There weren't that many. We had a lot of Filipinos and Japanese, not too many Chinese."

Beyond that, both Jane and Judy didn't understand Bette's allusions to her unhappy childhood, because that's not how they remember her. "She was always a happy person. I think she was happy on the outside. Some girls at Aiea Intermediate would laugh at Bette's hair, laugh at her clothes, laugh at her shoes." While Jane remembers Bette was ridiculed for her awkwardness at sports, that didn't make her an outcast. She usually dressed the same as the other girls in the class, according to Jane. "Bette wore oxfords like the rest of us. Her clothes were neat and clean. She always wore jumpers with a white blouse."

The Midlers later lived among the sprawling sugarcane fields. Every year after the cane harvest, the fields were torched to make ready for the next crop, and the dense smoke and ash covered every-thing in the neighborhood. Bette's mother had her hands full with the three children, keeping house, and, one of her favorite activities, reading movie fan magazines. She didn't like Aiea because as one of the few Jewish women in an alien Asian culture, she felt forsaken. However, her loud and overbearing husband insisted their life was wonderful and the envy of everyone back home in Paterson. (Their old neighborhood no longer exists. It was razed to make way for the Aloha Bowl Sports Stadium and parking lot.)

Fred worked hard and eventually moved his growing family out of the converted barracks apartment and into a freestanding house. In time, he saved enough money to buy several modest homes in the area, renovate them, and rent them out to supplement his in-come from painting and other enterprises. One of the other enter-prises was his appliance repair business. The yard of their home was carpeted with dozens of nonworking refrigerators, power lawn mowers, and other broken appliances that Fred planned to repair and sell at a profit. Ruth's clutter inside of the little house matched Fred's clutter on the outside.

Bette recalls, "The house was always littered with swatches of fabric and other things my mother meant to get to eventually. In one corner of the room were boxes and boxes of patterns that friends had given her, as well as cartons of rickrack, piping, laces and but-tons, and a magical thread box with its rows and rows of brightly colored silk threads."

Bette felt like an outsider. She said, "At the time I really hated it—I was an alien, a foreigner even though I was born there. I re-member children being so cruel. You don't forget these things." Adapting to survive, Bette tried to deny she was Caucasian, passing herself off as Portuguese, which was more acceptable than being a haole.

The nonwhites made fun of the haoles by speaking a pidgin English that was a hybrid lingo the locals used among themselves, saying such things as "Boddah you?" for "Bother you?" or "What's it to you?" as well as "I owe you money o' wot?" and, "bumbye, bambai" (by-and-by). "Brok da mout" literally means "broke the mouth" and refers to something delicious to eat, as does "ono," as in "Oh, da pupus [snacks] was so ono!" "Stink" means something similar to what it does in plain English; "no talk stink" and "stink-eye" mean talking nasty or giving someone a dirty look. *Mokes* and *kane* are names for men and *titas* or *wahini* are names for women.

The Hawaii in which Bette Midler matured had many different nationalities. In the 120 years between its discovery by Capt. James Cook in January of 1778 and 1898, the main source of prosperity for the Hawaiian Islands was their location. It was an ideal resupply port for ships plying the Pacific, and between 1820 and 1890 some five hundred ships a year from the American whaling fleet would visit Honolulu, with sailors spending $1 million annually. When the whale oil trade died because of the discovery of kerosene, farming became the main source of Hawaii's prosperity as white planters began growing sugar and, later, pineapples, and by 1900 Hawaii was supplying 10 percent of all America's sugar needs.

Since sugar and pineapple required a lot of hand labor and most of the native Hawaiians had died off from the white man's diseases, the planters imported Portuguese male laborers, but soon shifted to Chinese and Japanese workers. When the United States annexed the Republic of Hawaii in 1900, the American government declared it would exclude the immigration of Orientals. The planters rushed to bring in 70,000 Japanese male field-workers. When that supply of cheap labor proved inadequate, the planters turned to the Philippines, which, as an American protectorate, was exempt from Oriental exclusion laws, and imported 170,000 Filipinos from 1907 to 1945, when Bette Midler was born.

During many of these years, Honolulu still was dominated by the military and by sailors from ships around the world, and it continued to be, as it had been for over one hundred years, a world seaport. It became the polyglot, rough, international, paternalistic, male-dominated society that Bette Midler would grow up in.

Ruth Midler's connection to the outside world came almost entirely through the medium of the movies, which she attended whenever she could. She would follow the fortunes of its stars religiously in fan magazines. Bette also lived in a world of fantasy and daydreams, which her mother encouraged. Even if she could pass as a

Portuguese, Bette knew her own little secret, and she pulled back from confrontations with her contemporaries. She developed into a shy, introspective little girl who enjoyed her own internal world, enhanced by some of the beauty from the lush surroundings of the island. She recalled, "My first memories of Hawaii are of the oleander bushes that surrounded our apartment house. Their flowers gave off a sweet—almost too sweet—smell."

She grew up with a different sense of color and taste from children who matured on the Mainland. For one thing, there was the difference in the language of colors, with the Mainland women tending toward navy blue, beige, and gray, while in the islands those colors were only worn by older women or people in religious orders. In Hawaii, girls like Bette grew up in a yellow, orange, red, and chartreuse world of orchids, bougainvillea, and hibiscus.

Fred, meanwhile, lived in the world of the limited lower-middle class with conservative values of hearth, home, and hard work. He was pleased that his wife stayed home and cared for the house and their three girls, who arrived in close order. Fred had very strict ideas about morality and the right way to live, and he constantly tried to enforce them on his daughters. Fred's concept of a good daughter was traditional in that he wanted her to be chaste, polite, and respectful of her parents—devoted to growing up, marrying a nice young man, and having a family that Fred and Ruth could be proud of as grandparents. It wasn't going to work out that way for Fred.

The time into which Bette Midler was born saw an explosion of recorded music sparked by entertainers who had performed for American troops overseas during the war, including the three Andrews sisters, who gained fame singing songs such as "Rum and Coca-Cola" and "Boogie Woogie Bugle Boy." Bette didn't know it as a young girl, but the Andrews Sisters' version of "Boogie Woogie Bugle Boy" would become a signature song of her professional career.

In 1943, two years before Bette Midler was born, 3,600 teenage girls jammed into the Paramount Theater in New York City and lapsed into a moaning, screaming, twitching form of dementia that had never been seen before. Outside the theater another 30,000 teenagers had completely immobilized Times Square, requiring seven hundred riot police to restore order. The cause was a skinny twenty-five-year-old young man, five feet ten inches tall, weighing 135 pounds, with tousled oily hair. His name was Francis Albert Sinatra. Sneered at by adults and the media but admired by fellow entertainers, Sinatra possessed an aura and style that mesmerized his fans. Contemporary torch singer Jo Stafford explained, "Call it talent. You knew he couldn't do a number badly." He was a phenomenon not unlike what Bette Midler would become.

About that same time, Dr. Peter Goldmark invented the LP 33 rpm record disc, which would ultimately replace the fragile 78 rpm and hold ten times the amount of music that the 78 rpm did. The LP record disc and radio broadcasting were two technologies that would merge with Sinatra's and Midler's talents and make them both megastars.

3

Bette's Preteen Years

As a father and a husband, Fred would not allow any "bad" girls in his home and, to that end, tried to control the behavior of his daughters. As teenagers, the three daughters had their own ideas, which did not mesh with Fred's concept of the cloistered and demure life he wanted them to lead.

So Fred indulged in a lot of yelling. He made it clear this was his house. His three daughters yelled back. In the middle, quiet, docile Ruth tried to be the peacemaker. As Bette described it, "My father was a bellower. To get a word in you had to bellow back. It was usually us against him." Her older sister, Susan, was particularly rebellious, to the point that occasionally she would call the police to control her father's rages. Then, six years after Bette, came the joy in Fred's life—a son.

Sadly, the joy was short-lived for Fred, because Danny was retarded. Bette woefully recalled, "My father always wanted a boy and instead he got three daughters and a retarded son. So it sorta freaked him out."

The Hawaiian state health authorities felt Danny would be too much of a burden for the Midlers to raise and strongly recommended the boy be institutionalized, which incensed Fred. He did agree to a sensitive operation to cut off part of Danny's tongue, because the doctors told Fred and Ruth that it was too long, but the cure—as too often is the case—was worse than the affliction. The surgeon slipped and cut a nerve, which robbed Danny of the ability to chew or speak normally.

Devastated, Fred made a vow to care for Danny from then on. He kept the boy home and tutored him himself, which often deteriorated into a screaming session as Fred became frustrated because Danny couldn't learn fast enough. After an hour or two, Fred would yell at the boy and Danny would begin to cry. He could not understand why he had angered his father, the center of his universe.

Around the time Danny was born, Bette started school and went through two different phases: hell in elementary school and heaven in high school.

In elementary school she found out that she wasn't pretty, she wasn't nonwhite, and she wasn't Christian. All of that counted against her, and she took a lot of grief from her classmates. "I was miserable," she said. "I guess it was because I looked like I do."

Bette withdrew into her own private world of make-believe. Given her mother's enthusiasm over the lives show business people led, Bette's make-believe drew her into performing, even in the first grade, where she won a prize for singing "Silent Night." Even this prize was the source of a problem for Bette because she was afraid to tell her parents that she had won it singing a Christian carol. She knew her father would not be pleased, and it was a harbinger of the future that Bette's first stage recognition would be something that would have offended her father.

Bette remembers what it was like during those Christmas holidays. "We didn't even have a Christmas tree, which would have made us normal in the eyes of the neighbors. They were all Christians and they had Christmas trees which they decorated to death. No matter how poor a family was, they would scrape together money and give their children the most wonderful Christmases."

Probably the most fun Bette and her older sisters, Judy and Susan, knew took place on Saturdays when the older Midlers would "go to town" to do the weekly shopping. Fred and Ruth Midler would drive into Honolulu and spend hours shopping at John's Bargain Store after they had left the girls at the library. Either in the library or outside, Bette had a way of poking into forbidden territories of which her parents would have disapproved had they known. In the library she sought out books about French courtesans and ladies of the evening and soaked up all that lore and thought that world was very exciting. When she and her sisters grew older, they made sorties into the real world that was Honolulu, primarily a man's town during those years, when catering to male tastes meant big business.

So, while Mama and Papa were searching out the best buys in groceries at John's Bargain Store, Bette and her sisters were prowling around notorious Hotel Street watching other grown-ups searching out the best buys in dope and women.

"When I got very brave, I'd go out to the red-light district and walk around," Bette said. "All the sailors and people in the armed forces would go there to see a dirty movie or a bawdy show or to pick up a girl. It was a *real* red-light district and it was so wonderful! It wasn't bullshit [like] Forty-second Street or Eighth Avenue in New York. It was for real with opium dens and lots of Orientals! My mother was always trying to make sure I wasn't exposed to any of the seamier aspects of life. Consequently, I was always fascinated by the seamier aspects of life. That was the biggest influence on my life. I wanted to be with seamy people and be in seamy places."

Bette was intrigued by the bad girls wearing tight skirts, pointy shoes, and pointed bras, with a vocabulary that would make a sailor blush.

In elementary and intermediate school, Bette continued to perform whenever she could. She had found a way to gain the acceptance of her peers. She also discovered she could make her classmates laugh, and that opened a new world for her. It happened the first time when she had teamed up with classmate Barbara Nagy to perform a skit for the fifth-grade class as the duo of Herman and Oysterbee, with Bette in the role of Oysterbee.

As they began their number, they forgot their lines and fell back to ad-libbing, which Bette discovered came naturally to her. She just knew what to say and do. They had the audience laughing, and afterward, students who had hazed her before expressed a new appreciation for her talents.

A year later, in the sixth grade, Bette auditioned for the school talent show and won another prize for her rendition of "Lullaby of Broadway." In a way, that was also a foretaste of the fame to come, because in her later years on the stage, "Lullaby of Broadway" became another one of her signature numbers, performed with her backup trio, the Harlettes.

The other side of the footlights also proved a revelation to Bette, when Mrs. Seto, the school librarian, gave the young girl a ticket to a live stage performance. Sitting in the audience and gazing at the world as it appeared on the stage, Bette knew she had discovered heaven on earth.

"I looked up at the stage and there were all those shining people," she recalled. "They were dancing and singing, looking so happy. It was the most wonderful thing I'd ever seen."

She immediately fell in love with the theater and vowed that someday she would be on the stage, happy, carefree, and released from Fred's rigid rules about makeup and ladylike behavior.

Meanwhile, Ruth insisted that each of her daughters know how to sew. Soon Bette learned to run the sewing machine and make her own clothes. Ruth dressed the three girls alike from nice conservative patterns, but when Bette began to sew for herself, her design tastes seemed to be a bit wild. Bette's designs were more like Frederick's of Hollywood than the Simplicity patterns most girls wore. "Now I could make the clothes of my dreams," she remembered, "ensembles inspired by the revolutionary Mr. Frederick of Frederick's of Hollywood."

She was now in the eighth grade and coming to school in these sophisticated—tarty—clothes she made for herself. She certainly was the only eighth-grade girl to show up for class in a crimson and lilac copy of Mr. Frederick's Satin Surrender. In spite of, or perhaps, because of, the way she looked and dressed and her ethnic origin, her social life in school barely existed. She wasn't asked out on dates or invited to social events.

Classmate Judy Kuwabara didn't remember much about Bette's bellowing father, but she had nice memories of Bette's mother and of Bette's drive to perform. "She never wanted me to meet him, because she said he would scare me. I met her mom, though. She was like Bette. Very different." Judy recalled, whatever Bette may have been feeling inside herself, she was never reticent about performing in intermediate school.

"Bette was not shy at all. You know how local kids don't want to get up in front of their classmates. Bette was never like that. Any talent show that we had, she'd be up there. One time when we were in seventh grade, I remember she went on the roof of JoAnn Sato's garage and sang for us. JoAnn's mom came out to watch."

Judy lost touch with Bette after graduation, but they saw each other in 1987, when Judy read a magazine article about Bette in which she referred to "her two Aiea Intermediate School friends." When Bette next visited Hawaii, the two women got together for dinner at McCully Chop Sui, which is one of Bette's two favorite eating spots in Honolulu, along with Zippy's. During their leisurely meal, Judy observed, "She had changed. She was calmer than I'd known her before. She's kind of found herself. That was right after she had the baby [Sophie]."

That was the last time Judy would see Bette, who clearly did not want to be with her old classmates. She told Judy, "To tell you the truth, there are certain people I'd rather not see."

In intermediate school, Bette's body betrayed her in a way she hadn't expected. Every little girl thinks about breasts and when she is going to get them and what they will mean and how they will affect their lives. So, too, Bette thought about her breasts, when all of a sudden, they arrived in a womanly size which made the girls in her class envious and the boys lustfully sarcastic.

"I was a little chubbier than I am now," she recalled years later. "I had gigantic tits and I was very plain. I wore harlequin glasses. I was fairly bright and had a terrific sense of humor. I never had boyfriends until high school, and then I found myself mainly with military kids." Her parents would not let her wear a bra, because they thought she was too young, just as they believed Bette and her sisters were too young to use makeup. So young Bette became quite focused on her breasts because she was forced to go jiggling around school. This was another precursor of what her later career would involve, and so was the music she and her classmates listened to on radio stations like KSSK.

The most popular music of Bette's high school days had its prophet in a man who turned the music world on its ear during this era. He was a twenty-one-year-old Memphis truck driver who shouted, trembled, did the bumps, and set teenage girls on fire. With his first LP, Elvis Presley rocketed to the top of *Billboard*'s charts, and his singles "Heartbreak Hotel," "Don't Be Cruel," and "Love Me Tender" all topped a million copies each.

The music he popularized was born of black rhythm-and-blues melded with the songs of white backwoods country musicians and was pioneered by a black group, the Crew Cuts, in their 1954 hit, "Sh-Boom, Sh-Boom." Presley's music was developed further by the white trailblazer of rock, Bill Haley and his all-white band, the Comets, and their first big number, "Rock Around the Clock." Haley and His Comets, prophetic as they were, somehow didn't communicate the same animal magnetism to the audience that Elvis did.

The top ten songs each year during the time Bette Midler was growing up in Hawaii shifted from mood songs and ballads to the ultimate triumph of rock over pop and novelty songs. In 1950, when Bette was only five, the top song was "Goodnight Irene" by the Weavers and Gordon Jenkins, the next year it was "Tennessee Waltz" sung by Patti Page, and in 1952 it was "Cry" by Johnnie Ray. By 1954 rock and roll was making itself felt with the appearance of "Sh-Boom, Sh-Boom" by the Crew Cuts in the top ten. "Sh-Boom, Sh-Boom" would become an important Bette Midler song in later years.

Probably the busiest celebrity of the late 1950s and early 1960s was Elizabeth Taylor, with four marriages, three children, two divorces, and one widowhood—all in those ten years. Bette's ideal growing up was Debra Paget, who, along with most of the new starlets of that decade, faded into obscurity. Television was dominated by humor in the form of the imaginative, irrepressible Lucy, *The Honeymooners, Dobie Gillis, Ozzie and Harriet, Leave It to Beaver*, and *Your Show of Shows*, along with Edward R. Murrow's *See It Now* and a new concept called the television talk show, as realized by *Today* and *Tonight*. *Tonight* would in the years ahead become very important to the young Bette Midler and play a significant role in her success.

4

Heaven in High School

When Bette moved on to high school, her life changed. "The school I went to was just like any high school anywhere—like a high school in Brooklyn or Cleveland—we had rock and roll, sock hops, *American Bandstand*, the same as anywhere else. The only thing different was that all the kids were Japanese, Chinese, Filipino, and Samoan, and all the girls hated me because I had such big boobs."

It helped that her mother broke down and bought her a bra. Much to Bette's enormous relief, life got better in a hurry. Bette became a full-fledged American teenager, and, as with most teenagers, music was an important part of life. "I used to listen to the radio a lot," she said, "but always AM. Before rock and roll it was mostly white music. I didn't get into rhythm and blues until later on in rock and roll, like the early sixties. I loved the girl groups and I loved straight rock and roll: the Coasters, the Del Vikings and the Skyliners."

High school was a great maturation time for her. "I came into glory in high school. I bullossomed [*sic*]. I blossomed into a D-cup and there were finally white kids in my school. I was even popular. It was a real surprise. In high school I became a person."

She organized a female vocal trio called the Pieridine Three and began performing at school functions. Later they would start touring military bases, which gave them, and Bette in particular, experience with more mature audiences. It was a fulfillment of the dream

18

she had experienced earlier when she had gone to that first stage performance and when she and Barbara Nagy ad-libbed on stage.

The person who drew out the warm, bawdy, funny performer lurking inside Bette and who helped her mature as the public person she was going to be was Beth Ellen Childers, her best friend since they met in their junior year at Radford High. Childers said, "She was the funniest person I ever met," and Bette's memory of Beth Ellen was, "She made me believe in myself. She was hysterically loud and loved noise and a good time. She made me feel okay to be who I was. My family never made me feel this way."

As seniors the two young women experimented with makeup and even went on an adolescent shoplifting mission to a nearby mall to steal cosmetics.

"I had no money," Bette recalled. "I had absolutely nothing. I got a quarter a week for allowance. What are you going to do with a quarter a week? So my girlfriend said, 'This is what I do.' So I said I'd do it with her. But I didn't really like it. It was too terrifying. It hurt my nerves. I stopped and I've never stolen anything since. I would never, ever think of it. After my girlfriend and I took this makeup—lipsticks and hair dye—from the mall, we were on our way home with our little bags. It was pouring rain, we were in the middle of a hurricane, and my girlfriend and I got down on our knees and said, 'God, if you don't kill us in this hurricane we swear we will never do this again.' We didn't die and we never did it again. I keep my vows."

At home, Bette was getting a lot of grief from her father, who objected to the makeup, which he would flush down the toilet. One day Bette starting dyeing her hair, and this drove Fred nuts. She recalled, "He didn't like us wearing makeup and we had a curfew, some ridiculous hour like ten o'clock, and if you weren't in the house, you usually got locked out. Us sisters were always sticking up for each other and sneaking each other in the window at night."

He thought he was protecting his girls from becoming whores without knowing that they knew a lot more about whores than he did. And, in fact, they were entranced by streetwalkers, who were plentiful in the hot liberty town of Honolulu. "I was always fascinated by the local bad girls. We were surrounded by these JDs—

juvenile delinquents—and listen, I *loved* them! I used to follow them even though they wouldn't take me with them or anything. I've always liked that other side of life."

Bette was now accepted socially and began achieving recognition by being invited into Radford High School's Regents Club; she was increasingly outgoing, social, and popular and, in her senior year, was elected class president. She became involved in stage performances: the school variety show and class plays showing off her comedy talent as she did funny things with her hands, eyes, and feet, to the delight of the student audiences.

"By the end of my senior year in high school, I was crazy to be an actress," she said. "I was always working on a show or some kind of presentation. I really liked the theater better than anything else."

Bette won the lead in the senior class play, *Our Hearts Were Young and Gay*. She then confided in one of her close friends the dream that grew in her heart. She had decided that, whatever it took and however it had to be done, she was going to become a Broadway actress. The friend, Penny Sellers, remembers, "I thought she was talking from excitement, [but] she seemed so ambitious, so sure of herself."

By now Bette realized the stage made her feel happy and worthwhile. "As I grew older, all the best times of my life were when I was standing in front of an audience performing. I learned that I could be popular by making people laugh. I became a clown to win people's acceptance, and I think that's when I decided that I wanted to be in show business."

That ambition was in response to the feelings of depression she felt at home and what she saw happening to her mother under the pressure of their modest financial circumstances and Fred's dictatorial rule. Ruth had dreams, too, but they were circumscribed by her age, four children—one handicapped and requiring constant attention—and a penurious husband, a man whose autocratic and straitlaced view of the world and his role in it would not have let Ruth enjoy herself even if they did have enough money. Bette saw her mother smothered by her life and circumstances, clinging only to the fantasy world of the movies and, later, to the joy of seeing

Bette become what she, Ruth, had dreamt of being. Bette swore she wasn't going to end up the way her mother did.

At her high school graduation, Bette made the family proud as the class valedictorian, but there is no record of what she said to the assembled audience of parents and students on graduation day in 1963. There is a record of what the graduation edition of the school newspaper predicted for her:

"Bette Midler, who is considered to be one of Radford's greatest dramatists, is the president. Unknown to many is her scrawny soprano warble which can be heard while taking her Saturday night bath. Her ambition is to join the Peace Corps and, perhaps, someday become another Bette Davis."

Like many school predictions, it contained an element of the ludicrous and an element of prophecy. After graduation she went back to work in the local pineapple cannery for the third summer in a row. She said, "You see, only the middle part of the pineapple is used for slices. So I would sit there and all those sliced pineapples would come by and I would pick out the good slices to put in the cans."

She would continue to study to be an actress, at the University of Hawaii, but in the meantime she needed money. "I worked there [at the pineapple cannery] for three summers, starting when I was sixteen. I was very anxious for money because I never got a cent at home. I was on my feet for eight hours with a half hour for lunch and a ten-minute break—at $1.25 an hour."

About this time, she made her first move to adult independence and got a place of her own so that her father wouldn't know she was romantically involved with a man her age. She told her parents she had enrolled at the university, which was a long way from where they lived in Aiea, and that she wanted to live near campus.

At the university she pursued drama as she had in high school and appeared in productions of _The Typists_ in 1964 and _The Cherry Orchard_ in 1965. Drama teacher Joel Trapido directed her in both plays, and he and his wife entertained Bette in their home five years later after she had gone to New York and appeared in _Fiddler on the Roof_.

Evelyn Trapido recalls her coming to their home for dinner in 1970. "She was wearing some kind of stocking cap. I guess she didn't have time to wash and set her hair. She was her quiet self for a while, but after dinner she began cracking jokes in sort of a monologue. It wasn't until after she left that I realized she was doing her act for us."

During the next year and a half, two major things happened in Bette's life. In 1964 her best friend, Beth Ellen Childers, was killed in a car accident. Beth Ellen meant more to Bette at that point than any other person alive, and her sudden death at such a young age left Bette grieving. She was so stricken by Beth Ellen's death and so demonstrative in her grief that her mother began to think there was some romantic, sexual connection between the two girls and that maybe her daughter was a lesbian. For Bette it was a somber reminder about the fragility of life. It would be the beginning of a much closer acquaintance with death than she could ever have anticipated back then in Hawaii.

The other major event was the arrival of a Hollywood film crew and cast in Honolulu in April 1965. They were there to shoot location scenes for the movie version of James Michener's novel *Hawaii*, and the film company sent out a casting call for extras. An eager Bette came to audition and was hired for a bit part in the movie that turned out to be a big part in her life because it gave her the key that would open the door to her career. Ten local actors were selected, including Wally Chappell, who has since gone on to become director of the Hancher Auditorium at the University of Iowa, and Cecilia Fordham, who continues to act in and direct local productions in Hawaii. According to Fordham and Chappell, about 150 people showed up for the audition, which was held at the Ilikai Hotel on Wakiki Beach.

The part Bette got was that of a seasick missionary wife who spent most of her voyage from New England to the Hawaiian Islands heaving over the ship's rail. Originally it was a minor speaking part, but that ended on the cutting room floor, so her film debut consisted of Bette making unpleasant noises. She did not utter a distinguishable word. The crew shot for two months at Makua Beach near Makaha on Oahu Island, and Wally Chappell saved five thousand dollars that saw him through graduate school, while Cecilia Fordham bought a new station wagon. It gave Bette a nest egg to finance what she really wanted: a trip to New York.

Another plus for Bette was that she met the director George Roy Hill, who told her to look him up if she ever got to New York and he would try to help her. The twist of Bette's role in the movie was that she played the part of a white woman arriving in the Hawaiian Islands and used the money she earned to become a white woman *leaving* the Hawaiian Islands. Her next film appearance wouldn't come for another fifteen years. It would mark a significant change in her life.

At nineteen, Bette Midler was a young woman who had a clear vision of her life and her career and what she had to do to achieve her dreams. At a time when most young women are worrying about getting a date for Saturday night, Midler was plotting her future.

"I thought that if I had to have a career in the theater, the way to do it was to get a job on the New York stage," she said. "I mean, they don't have much theater in Chicago or Cleveland. See, I figured it was the only place to go."

After shooting the location shots in Hawaii, the film company moved back to Hollywood and took some of the locals there to help on reshoots of some scenes, and Bette was among those chosen to go. She boarded the plane in November 1965, a month short of her twentieth birthday. Her description of her departure is classic Bette Midler. "You should have seen us all in that car! Everybody cried—even my father cried, which was unusual. I told my family I was gonna be a star. I was wearing a plaid dress and I had on my first pair of nylons and a girdle with a garter belt—for a ten-hour flight. I just sat there in my cramped seat trying to imagine New York City and what a giant star I was gonna be."

It is doubtful that her father had any inkling that Bette was leaving home forever and going on to New York. At the time, he probably assumed she was just flying to Los Angeles with the rest of the movie crew and would return in a few months. In fact, the few months in Los Angeles gave her the rest of the nest egg to get her to New York.

"I was paid three hundred dollars a week and seventy dollars per diem," Bette explained about her brief time in Los Angeles with the movie company. "I lived on two dollars a day. When it was over, I took my money, my little savings pot with a thousand dollars, and I came to New York at the end of 1965. I left fifteen hundred dollars at home, just in case I had to go back or in case they had to send it to me. I was really frightened. I had to go out and get a job. I wanted the money to last. I think I still have that original thousand!"

The one thing Bette left behind when she flew out of Hawaii was a bitter feeling among many people with whom she had grown up and who thought they were her friends. One was Barbara Velasco, a physical education teacher at Radford High School, who feels that Bette has always given the world a lousy picture of life at Radford High School:

"Bette was always bubbly, always smiling, and always doing kooky things, but I remember that first interview she gave. She said she was the only haole in her high school. Well, Radford is 80 percent military [and mostly white]. I think when she first started out, she must have gotten some wrong information from her manager about how to act regarding where she was from. I'd like to ask Bette, 'Why did you forsake your background?' From the interviews she's given, it's like she never existed here."

There is a similar bitterness with other friendships and relationships. Diana Carter Anderson, Lynne Ellen Hollinger, and Bette were the best of friends in Hawaii days after they met at the Honolulu Community Theatre during a production of *Show Boat*. The show was a bomb, but the three girls formed a folksinging trio and performed as the Calico Three through their high school years and into the first year at the University of Hawaii, practicing at the home of Anderson's parents in an apartment on Date Street. They used Peter, Paul and Mary records as backup for their rehearsals and sang once a week for University of Hawaii students at the campus Hemenway Hall lounge in addition to performing several gigs at Schofield Barracks.

Diana recalls that, in those days, Bette had gorgeous legs and was obsessed with the split ends of her hair. "I remember her getting a wig," Anderson said, "and trying her best to look like Barbra Streisand, and, contrary to what you read, of the three of us, she was the one who always had a boyfriend."

They would hang out at the College Inn on the corner of Dole and University streets at the edge of the university campus, sitting in a booth and eating tuna sandwiches, sipping Cokes, playing the Beatles on the jukebox, and smoking nonstop. According to Diana, "Our university careers were undistinguished. We dropped out. Bette was not motivated to be in college. She was motivated to get to Broadway. Of the three of us, she was the most driven."

After Bette left for New York and her new life, she lost touch with Diana and Lynne Ellen except for a brief reunion in Manhattan in February 1975, when the three of them had dinner together and then adjourned to a recording studio. Anderson recalled, "We stayed in the studio until five in the morning recording the three of us singing our old songs. It was a lovely reunion. That's the last memory of her."

Not exactly. A bitter friendship-breaking incident occurred in 1988, when Bette was living in Los Angeles and ran into Lynne Ellen's dad. Diana recalls, "Bette had a conversation with Lynne Ellen's father, who lives in L.A., and according to him, she said some unpleasant things about us, that we were among those who tried to take advantage of her. Lynne Ellen and I got a little upset. It was right after Bette's miscarriage. We thought maybe she was just emotional. Honestly, we never did try to take advantage. When I was a struggling actress in New York, I had a boyfriend who said, 'Why don't you call up Bette and ask her if you can be a Harlette?' I said, 'No, I'm not going to do that.'"

Bette would later tell the Honolulu reporter Eddie Sherman that she had lost touch with her old triomates. Sherman reported that Bette said, "I don't know what happened between us, but somehow we lost our friendship."

Diana Anderson did finally hear from Bette after many years, and it wasn't pleasant. The December 1991 cover story of the monthly *Honolulu* magazine portrayed one of Hawaii's most famous natives. Entitled "Desperately Seeking Bette," the story by Marilyn Kim told of trying to understand who and what Bette Midler was by interviewing her friends, her former classmates, and both her brother and sister Susan. Diana was one of those interviewed for the article, and she described their University of Hawaii days and their singing together as the Calico Three, but said nothing that could reasonably be construed as derogatory or mean. However, Anderson's comments enraged Midler, and what happened next as told to the author by a member of the Anderson family was abhorrent to the Andersons.

About the time the *Honolulu* magazine article appeared, Diana's grandmother was dying in the hospital. That's when Bette tried to reach Diana to yell at her for the things she said in the article, which Diana claimed were all true. Bette called Diana's home and her mother took the call and told Bette that Diana was in the hospital with her dying grandmother and that it was not a good time to call.

In spite of that warning, Bette phoned the hospital and talked her way past the nurses and doctors, and the call was put through to the grandmother's room, where Diana had gone. Once connected, Bette blasted Diana unmercifully for what she had said in the *Honolulu* story. Diana and her family were stunned by what they regarded as a gross breach of common decency, and, moreover, Diana insists that even if Bette regarded what she said as uncomplimentary, it was true. At this point it is understandable that Diana does not remember Bette as being a particularly popular girl in school.

Another lost friendship with an acrid overtone involved the Malzman family. The Malzmans and the Midlers had been family friends in Paterson, New Jersey, and they all moved to Hawaii together in the forties and were very close because of their New Jersey connections, their common religion, and the isolation they felt in their community. Both Fred Midler and Mr. Malzman worked together for the Navy, and Lillian Malzman and Ruth Midler supported each other through many trying times, as well as enjoying holidays and good times together.

Lillian Malzman rails at Bette's characterization of Fred and Ruth Midler as being poor. "The Midlers were never poor. But they were frugal. Anybody that worked at Pearl Harbor made good money. They had overtime and, in those days [World War II], they'd work seven days a week. They were never poor. Fred owned houses in Manoa and Waialae-Kahala."

As for the bellowing, terrible-tempered Mr. Fred depicted by Bette, Lillian says, "I enjoyed him. He was very intelligent, very well read. He really wasn't loud. But very opinionated. And he had a short fuse. But he was very fond of Bette and she of him. When he was sick, she came down for a few weeks and cooked all this healthy food for him. It's just that he wouldn't go see her perform because she was lewd and lascivious."

Captain Irwin Malzman, Lillian's son, is Honolulu's radio helicopter traffic reporter and was a classmate of Bette's. He echoed his mother's caustic evaluation of Bette, saying that she was stuck-up and ungrateful for all the friends she had in Hawaii and bad-mouthed childhood friends who stood beside her in earlier days. Lillian believes that Bette had a crush on Irwin when the two of them attended Radford High School. "Bette was very ashamed of their [messy] living room. That's why she used to like to come to my house after school, because, one, my house was always neat and, two, because she had a crush on Irwin."

However, that didn't last, and Lillian is angry with Bette today because of how Lillian perceives Bette treated her father and friends. "She's a fair-weather friend," she says. "By that I mean I think she uses people. She was my friend when her father was sick and she needed me for different things—to take him to the doctor. [Fred died in 1986.] When I was in California, we drove up to her home and left a note that I was there and to give me a call. I never heard from her."

Lillian Malzman, like Diana Anderson, also received a sizzling call from Bette after Lillian's comments appeared in *Honolulu* magazine. Lillian remembered that Bette said a number of hurtful things to her that Lillian felt were totally unwarranted, given the long friendship between the two families.

When Bette first came to Hollywood for additional shots for the movie *Hawaii*, she and the other nine cast members who went with her stayed at the tacky Hollywood Roosevelt Hotel on Cahuenga Avenue just north of Hollywood Boulevard and around the corner from her beloved Frederick's of Hollywood. She shared a room at the hotel with Lynne Ellen Hollinger. When the shooting in Hollywood was over, neither Lynne Ellen nor Bette would return to Hawaii. Lynne Ellen would attend law school in New Jersey, and Bette was Broadway bound. The two traveled to San Francisco to connect with a friend of Lynne Ellen's from the Honolulu Community Theatre who was just getting out of the Navy, Bob Basso. The three of them took off cross-country in Basso's pea green VW van.

Eleven years later, in 1976, when Bette was appearing at Caesars Palace in Las Vegas, Basso was appearing across the street at the Flamingo Hilton. He visited Bette's dressing room but was turned away by security men, and his notes to Bette went unanswered. Basso ruefully recalled that when three unknowns named Bette Midler, Lynne Ellen Hollinger, and Bob Basso had rolled through Vegas in 1965, Bette had made him stop the van in front of Caesars Palace. Climbing out, Bette raised her arms in triumph and announced to the entire unlistening world, "Listen up, everybody. One day I'm coming back to this place and I'm gonna be the biggest headliner you've ever seen!"

It would turn out differently than Bette expected.

One place where she did return, but only once, was her old high school, in 1969 when she was appearing in *Fiddler on the Roof* but had yet to become a big star. She was invited to come back to Radford High to talk to the drama class. She had been a good student in high school, had made the National Honor Society, Latin Club, Speech Club, and the Regents Club, an all-girls community service society. However, as her tenth-grade geometry teacher from room 213, Emiko Sugino, who was there, commented, the school wasn't quite prepared for the Bette Midler who showed up.

Sugino recalled, "She wore a miniskirt outfit made of black crochet, with these large openings all over, and the top was cut low. We hugged her and I thought, 'Wow! She's so well-endowed—I didn't notice that in the tenth grade.' We were asking her about New York and then this loud voice of my principal shouts, 'Get a sweater on that girl!' Nobody had a sweater, so she had to wear the vice president's jacket."

One of her Hawaiian friends whom Bette saw both personally and professionally was Dick Mason, the set design professor she knew at the University of Hawaii. After leaving Hawaii, she kept in touch with him for several years, and they would get together a couple of times a year. In fact, she engaged Mason to design the set for her 1973 concert at New York's Palace Theater, which featured a huge high-heeled shoe in which she would walk down stairs set inside the shoe. After Midler moved to Beverly Hills, however, all contact was broken and, although Mason tried to reach Bette several times, his efforts have been rebuffed, and he is clearly hurt by the rebuke.

Mason said, "She was very talented, lots of fun, outspoken and yet, at the same time, in some ways very shy and insecure. But she's managed to overcome that or to put it in its place. She was not at all flamboyant personally. Offstage she was really quite modest and somewhat reserved. Her dress, her manner at home was sort of quiet. But as soon as the public was involved—whether it was an audience public or a party public, or someone she wanted to impress—she would become an actress. She would actually perform a part that gave her confidence to be more flamboyant, outlandish, unusual, outrageous."

Another connection with her Hawaiian experience is Jack Roe. "I remember when she was an extra on *Hawaii*," he said. "I was the second assistant director and I used to check in all the extras. She was one. She was one of the many atmosphere actors, but then she became a big star."

Later, Roe ran into Bette when he was the unit production manager on the shooting of *Divine Madness*, starring Bette. Roe said, "Actually, it was Gene Hackman who reminded me of Bette. I worked with Gene and he said, 'What about that gal that used to play the ukulele on the bus?' and I said, 'Oh, sure.' " That was Bette.

Part II

From Wahini to Manhattan Mama

5

Lean Beginnings in Manhattan

Los Angeles was just a way station on Bette's journey to New York and stardom. Bette whooshed through L.A. in a few months, finishing her work on the movie *Hawaii*, and then drove to New York with Lynne Ellen Hollinger and her friend Bob Basso.

It was a daring move because she was a twenty-year-old woman and had little money and no friends in the East. She would be seeking her fortune in a hard-hearted town that has been the sinkhole for the ambitions and dreams of thousands before her. Still, for Bette, it was also a liberating experience away from Fred's yelling and away from the specter of becoming like her mother, drained of hope and living on the edge of fantasy.

"I was very anxious to get to the city," she said. "I didn't notice that there was anything wrong with it. I didn't even notice the place. All I saw was a line of theaters: Forty-fourth Street, Forty-fifth Street, Forty-sixth Street. I didn't even *know* Forty-seventh Street! All I knew was that there were theaters there and real people on stage, and that was all I could think of."

Bette got a room in one of the city's seedier hotels, the Broadway Central Hotel, in Manhattan near the theater district. The Broadway Central was run-down and cheap (Bette's tiny room cost fifteen dollars a week). The bathroom was way down the hall. Moreover, the hotel was occupied by geeks and freaks including winos, whores, and junkies and, to complete the mosaic, had a dyke bar downstairs.

So, all in all, pretty squalid, but it meant freedom for Bette, who later said, "I loved it! My dear, it was my great adventure. So exciting. It became just another trip down life's merry road."

Her first order of business after settling into this surrealistic hotel was to find work that would provide grocery money while she looked for an acting job, because she knew that what she had saved from her very brief appearance in *Hawaii* wouldn't last forever. She scanned ads in the Help Wanted section, wandered around Manhattan in awe, and began to soak in the culture of this greatest of all American metropolises. She was like Dorothy in the land of Oz, quickly sensing that this was a place in sync with her curiosity and her personality. She liked New York. It became home almost overnight.

"I just blossomed out when I came here," she recalled. "I never felt I was home until I came here. It was all the things I wanted to be. It was like I was finally free." As, indeed, she was, for she was answerable to no one but herself.

Then came a series of minor jobs until the stage career took off. There was the typing job at Columbia University on 119th Street, supplemented by tips she received as a hatcheck girl. When that didn't work out because she never seemed to be able to connect the right customer with the right hat or coat, she tried being a go-go dancer at a bar in Union City, New Jersey. The money was good and it was a stage performance of sorts, but she vowed she would not dance topless, nor would she make herself available for screwing customers between sets. She had customers after her and she loved it, but she wasn't putting out for them. During this time, Bette sought every opportunity to plug into the stage circuit and find an acting role in the legitimate theater. She enrolled in several acting, dancing, and singing courses and began attending productions and going through the tough treadmill of the audition circuit.

Even though she didn't get roles, she was learning the jargon, the gossip, the essence of the New York theater world, which was essential. She wanted to be an actress, but her poise and her voice kept suggesting musical roles and she figured that getting on the stage was getting on the stage and, if musical roles were an avenue to get behind the footlights, then why not? She said, "If you don't have a lot of credit in serious or classical acting, they won't even look at you [for a dramatic role]. And I didn't have training when I came to the city. It was all instinct and guts."

That is the most succinct and accurate description of Bette Midler, the public artist: "all instinct and guts." Those traits would be demonstrated over and over again in her career, and, while her public personality and performance skills would be honed by training and by experience, it all was built on those rock-bottom qualities that have been the foundation of her success. "I wasn't disciplined or trained or anything," she said. "I mean I had no idea of what I was doing. I was just elbowing my way into the wing. I was so in love with it."

Making friends, she began exploring showplaces around Manhattan, starting in Greenwich Village, which had a good feel for her because it was filled with talented people who, like her, were looking for the main chance. Everybody seemed a bit of a maverick, which suited her own attitude. Beyond that, she adopted a strategy of persistence to break into the theater. Every chance she got, she registered with casting agencies, called casting directors, and would show up for "open calls," which meant you didn't have to belong to the actor's union, Actors Equity, to try out. She pounded the sidewalks and alleys of Manhattan going after every role she could. It was dreary and disheartening because of the constant rejections, and it took someone with determination to keep on going, but Bette did.

"It didn't faze me," she said. " 'Okay,' I'd think to myself, 'Go ahead, shut the door in my face! Be out to lunch! Hang up on me! I don't care. I'll be back! I was never intimidated by that sort of garbage, because I knew I was as good as anything else coming down the pike. I could sing. I could read lines."

As she prowled around Greenwich Village, some of the theatrical activities there exposed her to the more experimental theater. After attending many of these Off-Broadway productions, she felt she was as good as anybody on the stage. So she persisted and finally got a spot in a nonspeaking role for Tom Eyen's *Miss Nefretiti Regrets*, an offbeat musical comedy which had a short run at the La Mama theater. Eyen was impressed by the incongruity of this bouncy, ribald young woman from Hawaii with a lot of talent, and when he revived *Miss Nefretiti Regrets* some time later, he called Bette to see if she would play the lead as an Egyptian queen wearing a blond wig and a bikini and tottering around the stage in three-inch stiletto heels. Wow! You bet she would, because it meant that she was the lead in a New York (albeit Off-Broadway) play within a year after she had hit town.

The play lasted a few weeks, but the euphoria lasted longer, and with the onset of the summer of 1966, Bette decided to try the Catskill Mountain resorts, where a lot of New Yorkers vacationed. If she could get some parts in these summer stock plays, (which she did) it would be good experience and there was the chance that somebody important might see her.

When she returned to town, Eyen had another part for her in another Off-Broadway production. This was the Cinderella story presented in two versions: Daytimes it was geared for a children's audience and called *Cinderella Revisited*, and evenings it was for adults and called *Sinderella Revisited*. This was all part of the innovative and zany movement in the New York theater at this time, which, happily, coincided with the arrival of the innovative and zany Bette.

Besides Tom Eyen, Bette was drawn to another offbeat impresario, Charles Ludlam, who had organized the Ridiculous Theatrical Company, which Bette found quite appealing. "I got a great deal of my early inspiration from Charles Ludlam. The first thing I saw him do was *Turds in Hell*, which blew me away. It was incredible, the most incredible piece of theater I'd ever seen."

The auditions and the temporary jobs—all part of the routine for aspiring actors—continued for months. She got and quit a job as a glove saleswoman in Stern's department store after showing one impossible customer over one hundred pairs of gloves without satisfying her. Meanwhile, the one show she kept auditioning for was the hottest ticket on Broadway at the time, *Fiddler on the Roof*, which had captivated audiences since its opening in 1964, two years earlier. *Fiddler* periodically put out open calls to replace cast members, and Bette showed up every time a call went out. She had the guts to keep trying out for the show even though the vacillation of the casting people drove her bonkers.

First, they thought this woman from Hawaii looked too Jewish, which raised an interesting question, since the musical is about Jews living in nineteenth-century Russia. To confirm that point and confound the confusion, the casting people then decided that Bette didn't look Jewish enough. Finally, after eight months of auditioning, Bette got a temporary spot in the chorus; she was twenty-one and ecstatic. It was 1966 and she had made it to the Broadway stage.

Depressed when she was let go a little later because the chorus assignment was only an interim replacement, she went back to temporary jobs and the audition circuit, but then heard the role of the oldest daughter in *Fiddler*, Tzeitel, was available and called immediately for an audition appointment. She obviously knew the production and that gave her an advantage. Even better, she had been the understudy for Tzeitel's role during the time she had been in the chorus. However, before Bette showed for the audition, the casting director called her with a lesson about politics in the theater.

Bette recalled, "When the part opened up, Jerry Robbins [the musical's director] had to see all the girls up for it, but the lady who was casting didn't want me to have the job. She called me up two hours before the audition and said I didn't have a prayer. But if I didn't go in, she said, I could have the chorus job back."

Young as she was, Bette had become street-smart. She wondered to herself why the casting director felt she had to bribe her with the chorus job if the woman was telling the truth that she didn't have a chance of getting the Tzeitel role. Instantly, Bette knew something was fishy and said she was going to do the audition anyhow and hung up. She did and got the part.

In fact, the casting director had a friend in mind for the part and wanted to keep Bette away from the audition because she was too right for the role. It was a valuable lesson learned for Bette, but she probably didn't think much about it at the time, because now she was in an important feature role on Broadway—not bad for a little twenty-two-year-old from Hawaii who had only been in town two years!

With some money and a good role, Bette decided to forsake the geeks and freaks of the Broadway Central Hotel and moved to a better apartment on West Seventy-fifth Street while she reveled in her new persona as a Broadway actress. But over the next three years she gradually became disenchanted with the politics and maneuvering in the glamorous Broadway theatrical world. And like many ambitious and multitalented actors, she was afraid of getting stuck in a stereotype role that would define and limit her for the rest of her career.

"Tzeitel is a good role," she said. "I loved it for two years, but then came a *very* heavy bout of disenchantment. I felt that I was stagnating. What I thought was legitimate theater was cheap, dirty, full of politicking."

It was an important lesson and she learned it early, but perhaps didn't understand that it was not limited to the legitimate theater alone. Bette first encountered underhanded methods during the casting for *Fiddler*. Bookings into clubs and concert halls often worked that way too, and the success of record albums and movies didn't always depend on how wonderful the artist was, but rather other factors such as money, drugs, or women supplied to key people.

Beginning in her third year, Bette quietly began to look for other roles. As for the role of Tzeitel, "I saw it wasn't going to be the way I thought it was going to be. I wanted to work a lot, to grow, and the theater is a closed market. I couldn't get anything else, and the way I was brought up, I was taught you must work. But I came to New York to have a career, not to be in one show."

She did find at *Fiddler* a friend among the dancers, Ben Gillespie, who broadened her exposure to art and introduced her to blues and torch songs. She said, "He opened up the world for me. I was crazy for him. He taught me about music and dance and drama and poetry and light and color and sound and movement. He taught me grandeur. He inspired me not to be afraid and to understand what the past had to offer me."

Some of what the past had to offer her were the songs of Aretha Franklin and Dinah Washington, and, while Gillespie was her ticket to the past, the romance played out in time and he wasn't her passport to the future. Even so, she was excited by the world he and other friends had opened up for her and all the things that were going on around her in Manhattan.

Marta Heflin, for example, was an aspiring young singer who Bette worked with in *Fiddler*. She was always touring the clubs around Manhattan for open mike and newcomer nights so that she could perform and get experience while hoping an important agent or producer would be in the audience. Bette wanted to do the same thing on off nights or after *Fiddler* was through for the night, but the private Bette was reluctant to tour alone, so she and Marta teamed up and did it together.

One of the first clubs they frequented was Hilly's, and the first night they were there, Marta did her performance and urged Bette to give it a try. That was the night Bette first sang professionally before a sophisticated New York audience and learned that she was a captivating song stylist. It was the night she entranced the audience with her performance of "God Bless the Child." It changed her career focus and proved to be one of the landmarks in her life. Marta, now in awe of Bette's enormous talent, continued with Bette to play the clubs around town, going back to Hilly's regularly because the management loved them there, as did the audiences. One of the clubs they hit for talent night, on the west side of Midtown Manhattan on Forty-fourth Street, was owned by Bud Friedman and called the Improvisation or, more popularly, the Improv. The first time Bette performed, Friedman wasn't too taken by her, but that would change at another club.

6

The Tragedy of Judy

The experience with singing "God Bless the Child" had a dramatic effect on how Bette viewed herself, but a career change and everything else was pushed out of her mind in 1968, when she was twenty-three, because of what happened to her older sister Judy.

Judy had followed her lead and fled Hawaii for a new life on the Mainland, going to San Francisco to work in film with the goal of becoming a filmmaker. At Bette's suggestion, Judy had come to New York to visit Bette while she was in her last year performing in *Fiddler*. Bette felt so comfortable and secure with her sister living nearby that, after appearing in *Fiddler* for a total of three years, she decided she would quit and pursue her solo acting career.

Then everything in Bette's life stopped suddenly and tragically. Judy had been walking on a Manhattan street on her way to meet Bette when a car came rocketing *backward* out of an underground garage and slammed her against a wall. The impact was unbelievably cruel and smashed the young woman's body almost to a pulp. The police called Bette from information in Judy's purse for the tragic task of making a positive I.D. of her sister.

That trauma was followed by another when she called Hawaii and told her parents. In Honolulu her other sister, Susan, answered the phone, listened, and wordlessly gave the phone to her father. She recalled, "Bette spoke to him first and then it was passed around to all of us. It was a nightmare. I don't think my mother ever got over it."

Fred, Ruth, and Susan flew to New York for the funeral, joined by others from the Midler family in New Jersey. Marta Heflin, Bette's good friend from *Fiddler*, sat shivah—a traditional seven-day Jewish mourning period after the funeral of a close relative—with Bette. It is etched in Marta's memory how Bette, who loved Judy deeply, was so strong and in control during this tragic time.

"It was very interesting how she dealt with it," Marta said, "She didn't fall apart. She was the one keeping the family together, emotionally."

Certainly everyone was devastated by the tragedy, perhaps even more so because of the randomness of Judy's death and the freak nature of how she was killed and the gruesome result.

"It was very bad losing Judy," Fred Midler said later. "As I understand it, an auto came out of one of those indoor garages and smashed her right up against the wall. Mutilated her completely. The funeral directors wouldn't even permit us to view the body."

For most of the rest of 1968, Bette remained in a depression adjusting to the death of Judy. Her friend Marta was the one who helped her move on with her life. By this time, Marta was singing the lead in an Off-Broadway rock musical that was trying to attract the same audience that made *Hair* a smash. It was a Peter Link/ C. C. Courtney production called *Salvation*. When Marta got a chance to do her role with the Los Angeles company that was playing *Salvation*, she convinced the director, Paul Aaron, to substitute Bette for her.

Aaron described what happened at the audition. "She came in, walked down the aisle toward me and threw herself in my lap and said, 'Well, you may have seen a lot of girls before me, but you ain't never seen one the same as me.' And then she proceeded to absolutely blow me away. I thought, this is so special, so terrific, this makes me laugh, this is sexy and raunchy and wonderful. I wanted to hire her, so I had to tailor the role around her. With Marta, it was always the sex of the virgin. With Bette it was the sex of the vamp—the whole Mae West, Sophie Tucker thing she later became famous for."

She got the role, of course, and left *Fiddler* in 1969 to take it. It was the kind of new opportunity and chance at growth that she wanted. She was twenty-four.

As excited as Aaron was about Bette in *Salvation*, he quickly discovered that she was not all that great as part of an ensemble of singers. Bette worked best alone. She and others would find that out again and again. And while she was in *Salvation*, she continued to work the club circuit after hours because that really made her feel fulfilled as she repeatedly experienced the rush she felt the night she first sang "God Bless the Child."

She also dove into the New York Public Library's Lincoln Center branch with its vast collection of material from the arts and began learning about the great torch, gospel, and ballad singers. She listened to albums of Bessie Smith, Ethel Waters, and other famous blues singers, as well as show tunes from the past.

"I love Bessie Smith," she said. "I love Aretha Franklin. Gospel is some of the most wonderful music around. You get up and you can't stop. It makes you vibrate. I like torch songs and torch singers that can make you cry. Ethel Waters used to kill me. When I first started listening, I heard the stories those women were telling, they were laying incredible stuff down, their lives were fabulous lives and it was in their voices and their songs and I was fascinated by that. And there were some things I had to say about where I've been and who I've been with and the pain I know."

For Bette a new world was unveiled that resonated with what was inside her, and it showed her the way she had to go. Ben Gillespie, Marta, and William Hennessey, another cast member from *Fiddler*, would go together to see old movies from which Bette was inspired to do satires of the great old comediennes such as Charlotte Greenwood, Mae West, Joan Davis, and, ironically, considering what would happen between Bette and her twenty-plus years later, Martha Raye. Some believe that seeing all these old movies was the genesis of Bette's character as the Divine Miss M.

Bette's own explanation of that part of her life:

> [The Divine Miss M is] just a character. I *love* that character. That's the only character that I ever made up by myself. I made her up out of whole cloth. I was in New York, I saw these people, I looked at these movies, I said, "This is

what I want to be." And that's what I became. That's what
I made up.

But then I didn't want to get stuck in it, like how John
Belushi did with his character. I didn't want that character
to run my life. I wanted to be able to go away somewhere
and be quiet, be by myself and have a life. I really did want
that more than anything. I never exactly put it in those
words, but I really wanted to be who I always was. I mean,
I didn't think that anybody would buy what I had to say
when I was just myself, because really I'm kind of a bore.
But that character, there was nothing boring about her. She
was lively, she had red hair, she swore, she wore dresses cut
down to here, everybody *loves* that. Who wouldn't want to
be that? But that wasn't what I was. I was never that. Not
for a second. But I put it out and people were charmed by it.

She also continued to sing at places like Hilly's, where she would
appear voluntarily without a bra, similar to her appearance at Aiea
Intermediate School in Hawaii, but minus the embarrassment. A
singer named Baby Jane Dexter, who worked Hilly's, described why
Bette became increasingly popular with that audience. "Bette sang
'Am I Blue' and she sang 'Happiness Is a Thing Called Joe.' She
used to wear this red velvet dress, and she wanted to be a Helen
Morgan type. She sang only slow songs—nothing fast—all slow ballads. And she would fondle her tits while she was singing and emot-
ing. I gave her the worst advice that there ever was, which was to
put a bra on!"

Bette kept singing for free and fondling her tits at Hilly's and
the Improv and that finally led to her first paying part-time job as
a professional singer. That was an improbable gig as the opening
act for a Caribbean performer by the name of Johnny Barracuda in
the African Room on West Forty-fourth Street. She was earning
fifty dollars a night. Bud Friedman, the owner of the Improv, came
to the African Room one night to catch another singer, Roz Harris,
with whom he had a management contract. That's when he experienced Bette wearing a black velvet gown and singing "Am I Blue"

in a throaty blues rendition that knocked Friedman back on his heels and, once he recovered, sent him rushing backstage to sign her to a one-year management contract.

During this period in her career, she continued to spend time at the Lincoln Center Library for the Performing Arts listening to other singers' records and picking what she liked and what suited her voice and her style. She drew from old songs that still appealed to today's emotions and crafted them into the style she was developing as a singer. In short, the little girl who reinvented herself as the class clown in Aiea Intermediate School so that she would be accepted and then reinvented herself into a stage actress at Radford High School for the same reason and then reinvented herself upon her arrival in Manhattan into a musical actress that got her the role in *Fiddler* had just reinvented herself into what would become one of the superstar pop singers in America.

7

Bette and the Baths

In the spring of 1970, Bette received one of the most important telephone calls of her career. It was from Bob Ellston, a teacher with whom she had studied at the Herbert Berghof Studio in Manhattan, and he said, "Listen, I know this guy who runs a steam bath and it's a very popular place for homosexuals to go and gather, and he's looking for entertainment. Would you like to work there?"

He told her the owner of the Continental Baths had caught her act at the Improv one night at Ellston's suggestion and loved her performance. Bette leapt at the chance because it was a fascinating new challenge and Continental Baths proprietor Stephen Ostrow told her he would pay her fifty dollars a weekend for a one A.M. show on Friday and Saturday starting in July 1970. That sounded good to Bette and she took it, because *Salvation* had closed in the middle of April and she wanted another job.

Steve Ostrow had come up with a good commercial idea by treating a previously neglected clientele with respect. Most major cities in the world have places where gay men gather to meet, relax, and have encounters, but because gay activities are frequently illegal, these gathering places tend to be tacky and hidden. The proprietors need not make them pleasant or clean because gay men do not have a lot of choices. Ostrow's idea was to create an attractive meeting place for gays, particularly since the attitudes in New York toward homosexuals had become more liberal.

So Ostrow, a bisexual with both a wife and a male lover, created the Continental Baths in the basement of the Ansonia Hotel at Broadway and West Seventy-fourth Street. It was a clean steam bath facility with pool, "sun deck," videos, dance floor, and secluded areas upstairs reserved for private encounters. The Continental Baths was a warehouse-sized space covered with white tile and it boasted piped-in music and crowds of men wearing only big white towels wrapped, twisted, and draped around their naked bodies. When you came in, if you wanted a steam, you took a right; if you sought a private encounter, you went upstairs; and if you wished to hear the entertainment, you descended to another area downstairs.

The place set aside for entertainers to perform was primitive by show business standards and not much better than putting on a show for houseguests gathered in a patio at home. It consisted of a small area of the dance floor, and when Bette appeared for her first show, a couple of dozen gay men wrapped in towels were sitting on the dance floor waiting for her to entertain them. She did several ballads which were politely received but did not make a big impression, and she wasn't sure just which way to go. Billy Cunningham, her accompanist on these early shows, had been the piano player when she did an open mike set at the Improv. He clued her in as to what might work in this setting. He suggested that she try out her wildest stuff, chat up the audience, and let her hair down.

By the following weekend, Bette and Billy had worked up a bunch of jokes, some patter, and arrangements of campy songs of the 1950s. She appeared wearing a black lace corset and gold lamé pedal pushers and delivered self-deprecating jokes that had touches of Jewish, gay, and female humor. She launched into a new set of musical numbers including "In the Mood," "Don't Say Nothing Bad About My Baby," and "Chattanooga Choo-Choo."

In between numbers, she would talk with the audience about getting her hair done, and radio music in the 1950s that she grew up with in Hawaii, and tell jokes designed to make these gay men, haunted by the daily prejudice they faced because of their sexual preference, feel better about themselves.

"Ah, Fire Island. Health spa for hairdressers," she would say with a grin. "I was going to perform there, yunno, at Cherry Grove, but they just couldn't find any room for me in the bushes, honeest!" referring to the notorious homosexual lovemaking that went on in the underbrush common on the Island. They loved it. And they loved her because she was the heterosexual woman who accepted them and their lifestyle and was empathic to what it was to be gay.

Critic Rex Reed encapsulated what was happening at the Continental Baths at a Bette Midler performance: "Magic is in the air. Magic that removes the violence of the cold, dark streets. The insecurities, the hates, the fears, the prejudices outside vanish in a haze of camp. It's Mary Martin asking if we believe in fairies. Yes. We Do. Clap harder. And the Jewish Tinker Bell is right there in front of you. Twinkling, glittering and making soft musical chimes of peace."

With the encouragement of friends like Ben Gillespie, Bill Hennessey, and pianist Billy Cunningham, Bette honed her performances and got wilder and wilder. She did, after all, have to compete with those private encounters going on in the rooms upstairs. She became more cutting and flamboyant and created a new Bette on stage before the delighted eyes of her audience. She became the brassy, brazen, bawdy broad whom her audiences would christen the Divine Miss M, the penultimate satire of the operatic diva and the reincarnation of Mae West and Sophie Tucker.

As part of this transformation, she also broadened her singing repertoire to include brighter, upbeat songs from the past, such as "Honky Tonk Woman," "Boogie Woogie Bugle Boy," "Great Balls of Fire" and "Sh-Boom, Sh-Boom," which she had first heard on a hit recording by the Crew Cuts over AM radio in Hawaii back in 1954 when she was nine years old.

She would reminisce with her audience, "Remember AM radio? Oh, my dears, AM. That's where it was all at. You didn't have to think, just listen. What fabulous trash! Remember girl groups? The Shirelles, Gladys Knight and the Pips? Okay, I'll be the leader and you be the Dixie Cups." Then she would launch into "Chapel of Love," leading the delighted audience in a betoweled, old-time singalong—shades of Mitch Miller!

At the end of the first month of weekend gigs at the Baths, Bette—the understanding Bette, the chic, campy Bette, the outrageously zany Bette, the raunchy and talented Bette—had won the most loyal audience in America. Those entertainers who have a strong gay following know that these fans will always be there for the entertainer. Bette knew it too. She said, "As an audience, gay men are spectacular. They're very warm, very responsible. They are the most marvelous audience I've ever had, because they're not ashamed to show how they feel about you. They applaud like hell, they scream and carry on, stamp their feet and laugh. I love it."

What had originally been slated as a two-month stint for Bette was extended again and again and ended up lasting twenty-eight months, with some other performances elsewhere in between. But the Baths launched her singing career in a way that would resound over and over for her. "My career took off when I sang at the Continental Baths in New York. Those tubs became the showplace of the nation."

Bette had, as we said, re-created herself as she had once managed to do in school in Hawaii, as one of her biographers, Mark Bego, observed in an earlier work, *Bette Midler: Outrageously Divine*. Bego wrote, "She would prance around on stage in platform shoes with a towel wrapped turbanlike around her head, pretending she was Carmen Miranda on speed. Bette Midler was discovering herself and her audience was discovering her ability to make them laugh at her crazy behavior and eclectic choice of songs. Just like she had done years before in grammar school, Bette was learning to bury her feelings of insecurity and unattractiveness in the laughter of others."

Her reputation spread like wildfire in the trendy New York gay community, which is always fascinated by what's new and what's in, and Bette Midler was both of those to her audience and, in some respects, to herself. "I was an ugly, fat little Jewish girl who had problems," she said. "I was miserable. I kept trying to be like everyone else, but on me nothing worked. One day I just decided to be myself. So I became this freak who sings in the tubs."

As usual, the rest of the world saw her in a different light. Certainly both Steve Ostrow and her short-term agent, Bud Friedman, were as happy as a mother and father at their child's high school graduation.

After those first weeks of bonding at the Baths, the touchstone between her and her audience became the song she used to close her show, "I Shall Be Released," by Bob Dylan. It is a song of freedom, of rescue from oppression and bias. It is a song of great relevance for dominated women, for tyrannized minorities, for gay men who are trying to cope with their lives. It was a song of such poignancy that her audience listed to it in rapt, tear-streaming silence and, when she came to the final note, leapt to their feet cheering. This explains why she became their Divine Miss M and why those gay fans spread the word throughout the entertainment and media community of Manhattan about this shining, crazy, randy entertainer who made you laugh and cry and yell.

Meanwhile, Bud Friedman at the Improv, who was a powerhouse in the Manhattan club scene, was promoting Bette too, because she deserved it and because it was good business for him. He succeeded, for example, in getting her on *The Tonight Show*, where Johnny Carson took an immediate liking to Bette because of her lack of pretension, particularly on her second appearance, when she sang "My Forgotten Man" from out of the 1930s and startled everyone with her style and delivery.

Sitting on the couch, she then told Johnny that she was the only girl singer in America who sang in a men's Turkish bath or health club. Johnny responded quizzically, "You're not putting me on, are you? I've never heard of such a thing. They don't have anything like that at my health club. All we have is a guy with the trained duck."

"It's true," Bette answered without specifying it was a gay health club. "They all sit in front of me and when they love me, they throw their towels at me."

"That's better than a big hand, I suppose."

"And when they give me standing ovations, all their towels fall to the floor." And then she told him about her beginnings and how tough it was working in the pineapple factory. "They didn't even pipe in music. They've found that when they pipe it in to chickens, they lay better and faster and bigger."

It was a perfect lead-in for Johnny, who threw the audience into uncontrollable laughter with "Don't we all!"

She explained in greater detail later that "working at the Baths allowed me a chance to really stretch out and grow in a way I had not been able to before. I was able to work with a piano player and drummer every week, and I didn't have to pay for it. And I had a big, built-in captive audience. I mean, where were they going to go? They were practically naked!"

On subsequent appearances on *The Tonight Show*—she made a total of seven during the next two years—Bette and Carson would banter lines back and forth, often double-entendres, that would send the audience into hysterics. Once she got into her hobby of raising houseplants and noted that she had a Venus flytrap: "I don't have any flies, so I gave it bacon. It spit it out! A *Jewish* Venus flytrap, I suppose."

That kind of clever exchange along with her singing talent guaranteed Bette repeated invitations to the couch on Johnny Carson's show and gave Bette the kind of national exposure invaluable for her career. Still, she had to keep looking for other work, too, because the fifty dollars per weekend could hardly keep her going.

At the Baths, pianist Billy Cunningham was leaving for a better job, and he recommended a slim musician who worked in the CBS mail room and did pickup spots all over town. He had just written a successful McDonald's commercial jingle. His name was Barry Manilow, and he was amenable to working the Baths as long as he didn't have to take his clothes off. When they first met, Barry and Bette were at odds, but that changed quickly.

"Somehow it seemed like Bette and I were not going to get along," Barry said. "We couldn't understand what the other was into. But of course, later we worked together on the stage act and in the studio and we connected beautifully. She chose the tunes, I arranged them."

It was the beginning of a dramatically important professional relationship for both of them and, ultimately, a long friendship.

In October 1970, when Bette was twenty-four, she made her first big appearance outside of New York, at Mr. Kelly's in Chicago as a warm-up act for comedian Jackie Vernon. Vernon became known for his explanation of how to end the controversial Vietnam War: His plan was that America should just announce that it had won, pack up all its troops, and go home. "Who's going to argue?" he asked.

Her appearance in Chicago made her tone her act down a little out of deference to the presumed straight-arrow audiences in the Midwest. Bruce Vilanch, a reporter for the *Chicago Tribune* who later quit the newspaper to become a writer for Bette, was there and reported on the impact Bette had with her act:

"She came out of the kitchen—which is what she did in those days—and she was wearing a shirt without a bra. It was a political statement not to wear a bra, but in Bette's case it was a terrorist act. The shirt was unbuttoned to the waist and tied in Belafonte fashion. She also wore tuxedo pants with a cummerbund and Spring-o-Lator shoes, which were like wedgies but had a thin heel so you could defy gravity. She had all this hair, with an orchid stuck in it. She came out through the kitchen singing "Sh-Boom, Sh-Boom" . . . and shaking everything she had. All through the room you could hear forks dropping and people choking on ice cubes."

She didn't do Carmen Miranda or Mae West or any gay jokes and tried to keep herself under control, but that didn't last long. She set the tone from the minute she appeared and then sang a variety of songs interspersed with a paean to Frederick's tacky fashions with his blow-up bras and trashy panties. The Midwestern audience belied its reputation by enjoying Bette's performances and showing it. It was a good sign, because if she was ever going to be a big star, she would have to do tours and television in front of people just like those at Mr. Kelly's.

Then it was back to the Baths for another eight weeks, which actually extended into the new year of 1971. All the while she continued to try out jokes, routines, and songs like "C. C. Rider," "Surabaya Johnny," and the lewd "Long John Blues" as part of developing her act, while enjoying the adoration of her audiences. Bette described the way she massaged the classic popular songs of the earlier part of the century.

"That's really my thing, " she said. "I watch things, then I twist it around to get another view, then give it back to them and make them see it in another way that they never saw before because they were so busy taking it seriously. I can't take any of it seriously."

And the word was getting around. Bette was no longer only playing to a score of men sitting on the floor wrapped in towels, and she was no longer being just Bette; the character of the Divine Miss M was coming more and more to the fore. The character, said Bette, "was a tortured torch singer on the foggy waterfront, wrapped up in her own sorrow and fur neckpiece. I never remember her until she shows up. She has a life all her own and that's very nice, as long as she doesn't mix in when I'm talking to the grocer or the taxi driver. I don't let her into my regular life."

More and more people were showing up, and to Ostrow's amazement, straight couples were coming to see and hear the Divine, so some nights there was a line waiting to get in. Bette at the Baths had become the hot ticket attracting power brokers and movers who came to see the wild new entertainer. Audiences regularly began to include Helen Gurley Brown and David Brown—she the editor of *Cosmopolitan* and he the famous movie producer; rockers like Mick Jagger with his Bianca; and albino artistic sensation and trendsetter Andy Warhol.

Peter Dalls, famous theatrical lighting director, expressed his mystification. "I really didn't know what she did or that she had such a cult following. All I can remember is this girl steps out into a seamy basement and people start screaming and cheering and crying. It was the most incredible thing and she hadn't even done anything yet. Then she proceeded to deliver a show that warranted all that."

Ostrow allowed straight couples into the Baths but requested that the ladies leave after the show. There were, after all, still those encounters going on in the rooms upstairs.

Bette's appearances on *The Tonight Show* exposed her to the national public and to booking agents and producers. She was also becoming known through the theatrical grapevine, so it wasn't a surprise that she got an out-of-town offer from a director of the Seattle Opera Company, which was about to stage the Who's rock opera, *Tommy*, and wanted Bette to play the Acid Queen. It sounded like another of those challenging, expanding experiences, and she went for it. The central part of the role had her jumping out of a box wearing a G-string and bra to sing the Acid Queen's song.

She relished part of the role because Midler was not the Victrola type of performer who just cranks out whatever song is required at the moment. She was an intelligent singer who needed to understand the lyrics and get inside the spirit of the song. "I'm the gypsy," she sang, "I'm the Acid Queen, pay before you start. The gypsy, I'm guaranteed to tear your soul apart."

One of the things she didn't like about the part was that, to introduce the song, she had to jump out of a box on stage and she was always bumping and bruising herself. Also, she didn't enjoy the rigid and repetitive nature of structured stage plays with big casts. She preferred performing as the star alone, which had been evident from her previous experiences.

However, she did enjoy singing "Acid Queen" because it was a song that had meaning for her. "I really loved that number. As we visualized it, it had nothing to do with drugs, but was about the pervasiveness of female sexuality in American life. This Acid Queen was like all the negative forces of female sexuality, all the things that drive boys to be homosexuals and frighten men and make them run away. Larger-than-life female sexuality. Suffocating."

While she loved the concept of the Acid Queen and the show *Tommy*, it would be the last tightly scripted show she would do.

That was in May 1971, and in July she was back at Mr. Kelly's in Chicago—this time opening for Mort Sahl, whose comedy theme was that extreme right-wingers and extreme left-wingers were all the same in that they wanted the people to pay taxes, shut up, and do exactly as they were told. The only difference between the two extremes, Sahl said, was that the left-wingers insisted we all be grateful too.

As with all good performers, Bette was sensitive to what would work with each audience, and she didn't think "Acid Queen" would succeed with a Mr. Kelly's audience. However, her Mr. Frederick's of Hollywood would, because that wasn't threatening. "I mean, when people go to see a singer at Mr. Kelly's, they don't expect to see some demented lady take off her clothes and expose her body to them and shriek this incredible song at them. They just are not ready for it."

While in Chicago, she had something good and something not so good happen. By chance she met Michael Federal, a young bass player appearing in a local production of *Hair*, while she was visiting a local TV station. Within minutes of their being introduced, he asked her out. Mindful that he might not understand who she was, she asked him to come see her perform first and then, if he still wanted to date her, she would go out with him. He was impressed with her act, and not only did they go out, but he became her lover and they went to New York together.

Her disappointment came as a result of a benefit performance that didn't turn out well and that angered her perfectionist nature. The Chicago columnist Irv Kupcinet sponsored an annual cruise on Lake Michigan for disabled veterans, and Bette agreed to be part of the entertainment. She had to work with a pickup band of musicians who had never played together before and who apparently weren't very good individually or collectively. Bette rehearsed with them and they barely got it together.

During the performance they were a disaster, and it upset Bette because it made her appear to be second-rate. So at the end, she said, "I want to thank you all for being such a patient audience. I thought you were wonderful. I'm glad you're having such a wonderful time. And to this band, I'd only like to say one thing, 'Fuck you!' "

The incident in Chicago did have one salutary effect in that Bette realized she needed her own band to ensure the strongest stage presentation she could make. When she returned to New York, she put one together with Michael on bass, Kevin Ellman on drums, and Barry Manilow on piano. Bette and her new band went back to the Baths, where she continued to pack the place. One woman journalist, Marie Morreale, who was a bit apprehensive about going to an openly gay sex club, was surprised at what she found when she attended one of Bette's performances.

Morreale wrote that she knew people who had attended Bette's performances and they believed this was the place to see and be seen because Midler was an extraordinary entertainer. Morreale wanted to go because it was the in-thing to do, and it was possible to tread this previously forbidden territory of male homosexuality since the Baths had decided to let women hear Bette Midler. It became an unusual date, like seeing the movie *Deep Throat*. Then Bette emerged on stage, and Morreale was bowled over.

There was a decadent feeling about it, because it was a new policy: letting women in there. It was like entering a taboo area. You felt like you were on the cutting edge of something new and then, all of a sudden, to see this sort of bosomy, crazy, campy kind of person. She was different than anyone I had ever seen before and she had a different kind of in-the-know, sarcastic, cutting humor. Her act was total fun for fun's sake. She was unbelievable. Here is someone who didn't give a shit about the rules. She was breaking the rules with her material and you were breaking the rules by being there.

After that run at the Baths, five years after arriving in Manhattan from Hawaii, she was invited on September 20 to play at one of the hottest clubs in town, Downstairs at the Upstairs on West Fifty-sixth Street. The twenty-five-year-old Bette appeared at the club, but the audience didn't. A hurricane had swept through the area, and the Jewish holiday Rosh Hashanna was being observed. The first few nights Bette appeared, there were more waiters than customers. On the third night a total of five customers showed up. Bette didn't want to go from being the sold-out Queen of the Baths to the Flop of the Downstairs, and so she called on her Baths audience to rescue her. She took out an ad in *Screw*, a licentious tabloid read by the gay populace, announcing, "Bette from the Baths at the Downstairs."

Three nights later the place was filled with wall-to-wall Bette fans, and her two-week stand was extended to ten, with Johnny Carson and Truman Capote among the patrons who came to see this new show business phenomenon. Some other people were there who could be important to Bette's future. Both recording executives, they reacted in opposite ways to Bette's performance. One was Clive Davis, then the head of Columbia Records, who had been encouraged to catch the Midler show by one of his colleagues. Davis came, saw, and left. What he thought, no one knew, because he said nothing to anybody. Paradoxically, weeks later a promoter named Aaron Russo from Chicago would also recommend Bette to Clive and he would turn her down a second time.

But somebody who was not about to ignore her was a Turkish-

American entrepreneur by the name of Ahmet Ertegun, a recording genius. Friends also urged Ertegun to experience Bette Midler at the Downstairs at the Upstairs, and it was an extraordinary occasion for him:

> She was unlike anybody I'd seen before. People of all types—grandmothers, couples, drag queens—everybody was screaming and jumping up and down on tables for this woman. She was doing everything: fifties greaseball stuff, swing era nostalgia, current ballads. You could discern a great wit there. She was trying to seem raunchy and tasteless and exude a certain elegance and she pulled it off. What she had was style. She was overwhelming.
>
> I couldn't believe that a young person like her could not only understand those old musical styles so well but capture the flavor of the periods and make them a part of herself. It was the wittiest musical performance I'd ever seen. It was striking to see such innate elegance and good taste in someone who superficially appeared not to have elegance or good taste. You know, she never embarrassed on stage.

Ertegun was a legendary character in the record business who cofounded Atlantic Records in 1948 and made a fortune selling it to Warner Communications in 1968. Atlantic Records would later become Warner-Electra-Atlantic. In between, this fan of blues and jazz made lots of other people wealthy when he signed them to recording contracts, among them, Crosby, Stills, Nash and Young; Ray Charles; Wilson Pickett; Led Zeppelin; and, of course, Bette Midler. He is referred to in the music business as G. R. M., or Great Record Man. He can identify not only a hit song but, more important, a hit performer. The sole criterion of a hit performer is not taste, musical training or sophistication, or intelligence. It is the ability to create music that the public wants and needs. The talent is probably visceral.

As author Fredric Dannen describes Ertegun, "He had Great Record Man written all over him. He was jaunty, and bald, and had

Bette Midler's yearbook photo at age eight, when she attended Mrs. Tyau's second-grade class in Aiea Elementary School in Hawaii. (*George Mair*)

Radford High, the school Bette attended in Hawaii where she took her first theatrical steps. (*George Mair*)

The home in Hawaii where Bette's parents, Fred and Ruth, lived before they died. (*George Mair*)

Bette with Ahmet Ertegun, her recording mentor from Atlantic
Records, Cher and record mogul David Geffen. (*Peter C. Borsari*)

Bette in a limo with Aaron Russo, attending a tribute to Johnny
Carson. (*Peter C. Borsari*)

Bette with boyfriend, Peter Riegert, who would later costar with her in the TV version of *Gypsy*. (*Peter C. Borsari*)

Bette being presented with a rose-topped cake at the party
celebrating the premiere of *The Rose*. (*Peter C. Borsari*)

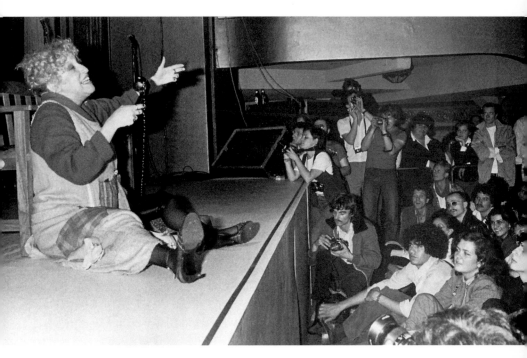

Bette performs for a Paris audience in 1978. (*Jean Louis Atlan/Sygma*)

Bette performing in another of her unusual costumes. (*Jean Louis Atlan/Sygma*)

Bette autographing her book *A View From A Broad* in a New York bookstore, 1980. (*E. Spatz/Sygma*)

Bette poses in front of a bookstore display of *A View From A Broad*, 1980. (*E. Spatz/Sygma*)

Bette and Barry Manilow welcome in the New Year of 1983 at the
Universal Amphitheater in Los Angeles—to the surprise of the
audience. (*Peter C. Borsari*)

a goatee and shone as a raconteur. He could order a bottle of wine from a headwaiter in perfect French, then turn to his jazzman dinner guest and slip into black jive. Ertegun was one of the original characters of the record business, but the one with the most class."

This man would shape Bette's musical career. He immediately offered her a recording contract, because he knew that if he could capture her on disk, he would have a winner. Bette was flattered and excited because she was still, in her mind, a struggling new artist. So a deal was made. Her appearance at the Downstairs at the Upstairs was a personal Rubicon for Bette and she crossed it on the shoulders of her loyal fans from the Baths and with the help of friends like Barry Manilow.

The certification that she was now serious, big-time entertainment came when she was noticed by the national newspaper of record, the *New York Times*, in a review by critic John S. Wilson, who pronounced that Bette Midler had a wonderful voice, wit, and an expressive face. He felt constrained to say in his professional pundit's voice, "However, with all of her divergent musical styles she never clarifies what she is trying to do."

Bette is a multifaceted artist equally at home with the blues, ballads, rock, and comedy. The very mention of her act in the *Times* was significant. However, the niche problem arose again and in a more serious context when Atlantic Records began working on her first album. The record producer had to decide which category would be right for her.

8

Bette and Barry

The interaction between Bette and Barry Manilow turned out to be professional chemistry. At the time they first performed together in public in 1971 at the Continental Baths, Barry reflected, "Actually we were both nobodies." Which wasn't exactly accurate, since Barry was well known in New York music circles as an arranger and was beginning to write songs on his own. Bette, of course, had been in a Broadway hit and had a roller coaster few years working the club and lounge scene. But that night, the two of them experienced magic between them and the audience, and, more importantly, between each other. Barry recalled that mystical evening:

"I was crying at the ballads, laughing at her jokes, playing my tail off at the piano! I was feeling this energy four feet from me—a comet, a meteor." Afterward backstage, he looked at the elated Bette and wondrously asked, "Waaa, wow, how did you do that?"

Barry grew up in a family with grandparents substituting for his father, who had deserted his twenty-two-year-old wife when Barry was two. Grandmother and grandfather filled Barry's life with music from Russia. At age seven they gave him the instrument of their youth, an accordion, on which Barry learned to play Russian folk songs along with "Tico Tico" and the inevitable "Lady of Spain." By the time Barry turned thirteen, two new elements came into his life that would push forward his musical taste and career—a piano and a stepfather, Willie Murphy, who came fully equipped with piles of albums featuring show tunes and a variety of popular musical artists. The teenager Barry gobbled it all up. The high point of the year occurred when his stepfather took him to a Gerry Mulligan concert. Manilow was stunned. "I'll never forget it. It was the biggest thing in my life." For six years the only live music the young Manilow had heard was the accordion. For the first time, he was exposed to the mellifluous sounds of a baritone saxophone.

From then on, music became the core of his life, but he assumed that he could never earn a living as a musician. So after playing Manuel de Falla's "Ritual Fire Dance" in a competition at Brooklyn's Eastern District High School and being voted the best musician in school, Barry got a job in the CBS mail room. Meanwhile, he studied advertising at City College of New York but soon switched to the New York College of Music because he loved music more than anything else. He eventually studied at the Juilliard School of Music. At his day job at CBS, he was offered a promotion to the position of TV film editor, but he turned down the opportunity so that he would be free to continue puttering around with his music, putting musical groups together, writing jingles and theme music.

Finally, in 1967 his nighttime music fun and his daytime CBS job fused and he was made music director of a WCBS-TV talent series entitled *Call Back!* The work required him to compose sixteen musical arrangements a week from rock and roll to opera. This assignment served as the springboard to the position of music conductor and arranger for Ed Sullivan specials. He was known around the Manhattan musical world as a quick and facile arranger who was easygoing, flexible, and available to do any kind of commercial work. He wrote compositions ranging from toilet bowl cleaner and insurance commercials to original music for Off-Broadway musicals. He evolved a concept for writing commercials that worked well for him.

He said, "It's a craft writing a jingle because you have twenty-eight seconds to get the message across, and that's a whole lot different from writing a pop song. I usually write about ten jingles, and the one I remember the easiest is the one I hand over to the company that wants it."

Barry launched his own singing career with commercial jingles and soon was raking in a lot more money singing commercials than writing them. His most famous at the time was the "You Deserve a Break Today" jingle for McDonald's. He was also substituting for the regular pianist at the Continental Baths, and that's where he met Bette. His overwhelming reaction to her performance was made greater by his conviction during rehearsals earlier in the day that Bette was going to fall on her face. He thought her music needed work, but she had the presence and the energy that would turn her into a real star.

It seemed impossible that those two gigantic egos could be on the same stage, much less become musical partners, but they did for the next four and a half years. At the beginning, Barry turned to cleaning up and tightening her repertoire of songs. He quickly realized that one of the phenomenal things about Bette was her versatility. Bette was a blues singer, a rock-and-roll artist, a ballad crooner, a jazz and scat singer—she could adapt to the song and the age and the moment. This incredible versatility was her strength, even though a little while later it would almost destroy her most important musical record album.

Barry went to work retooling and refining Bette's songbook, taking selections from different times to showcase her range and adaptability. He selected a mellow group of songs from the 1920s and melded it with swinging numbers from the 1930s and 1940s, then added campy songs of the 1950s and iced the repertoire with rock and roll from the 1960s. The assemblage was made fresh by Bette's interpretations and Barry's sophisticated arrangements. The result had Bette backed by Barry on the whimsical "Miss Otis Regrets" and the bright show tune "Lullaby of Broadway" along with the brassy, loud "Boogie Woogie Bugle Boy," the breathy, sultry "Do You Wanna Dance?" and the knock-down, throbbing, show-stopping, "When a Man Loves a Woman." The audiences yelled, swooned, listened in bewitched silence, and were on their feet at the end of every performance, while the critics proclaimed the genesis of a new form of multicultural popular music spanning popular American taste.

The result was invitations to concert tours and TV appearances and heady talks of rich recording deals. It didn't happen all at once, but it was coming, and Bette moved forward with enormous help from Barry, who didn't want to sacrifice his own career in order to make Bette's. The conflict and accommodation between the two strong-willed performers became evident from the start of their relationship. After her reputation pushed her to the forefront of the music buzz in New York and she was offered the appearance at the Downstairs at the Upstairs club, the two egos and two careers collided. The Downstairs was a place that music movers and shakers frequented, and a successful appearance there has been the beginning of many recording contracts and concert tours.

Bette accepted the opportunity, and she wanted Barry to be with her on the piano and write her arrangements for her. It was a key gig, and she wanted to do it in the best way possible. Barry, on the other hand, did not want to live in Bette's shadow, and he refused to appear with her unless he could sing some of his own songs. He wanted to do whatever he could to help her success, but he had his own career too. Bette readily suggested that he offer a twenty-minute session of his own material in the very middle of her show. It was a generous offer and a mark of mutual respect between the two performers of a dimension that only other artists can fully appreciate.

The club appearances, *The Tonight Show*, the Continental Baths, led inevitably to the Atlantic Records deal, and here again the clash came between Bette and Barry. Bette was signed to a good record deal by Ahmet Ertegun, and it was big money, a big record company, with big men making big deals. They knew they had signed a major talent, too, but there was one disastrous weakness amidst all this wonderful bigness—they didn't know what to do with the Divine Miss M!

Atlantic's number-one producer's first question concerned the niche in which Bette belonged. Was she to do a pop album? Or perhaps a rock album? Or maybe blues? Or boogie woogie? Or golden oldies? Or folk? The only things not considered were opera and Gregorian chant. Bette sang it all. The Atlantic crew labored and sweated for eight months trying to put something together that worked.

At the early stages of the project, Atlantic asked Barry to write all of Bette's arrangements, which he eagerly did because it was his first crack at the big-time world of commercial recording. To his dismay, when he had completed the scut work of writing the arrangements, all the big shots said, "Thank you very much and good-bye." Barry was stunned and hurt, particularly because Bette stood mute while the Atlantic people humiliated him.

Eight months later Ahmet Ertegun had had enough. His people couldn't seem to save it. That's when Barry quietly slipped Ertegun a tape of the enormously successful concert he and Bette had performed at Carnegie Hall which Barry had arranged and produced.

"I managed to get a bootleg tape of [the Carnegie concert] and played it for Bette," Barry said later. "She just freaked out. Then Ahmet Ertegun heard it and said, 'Yes, that's what's missing from the album. Can you fix it?' And I said I'd try. We went back to the recording studio and ended up rewriting nine songs. The album came out half produced by me and half by Joel Dorn."

When Ertegun heard the Carnegie Hall tape, he immediately realized that Manilow had the magic to capture the Bette sound the way it should be presented. It was a tribute to Barry's love for and devotion to Bette, and to his professionalism, that he took a deep breath and pushed all the pain and hurt behind him. Bette would say later, "Barry made it special," and in days after its release, *Bette Midler: The Divine Miss M* went gold—500,000 copies sold—as the public bought up every copy they could find. The earlier rejection by Atlantic without interference from Bette still lingered in Barry's heart, and in the end he finally had to confront Bette and ask the question, "How could you let me leave?" She told him that it was her first record album, so much rode on it, and, simply put, she was scared—terrified. It wouldn't be the last time for the Divine Miss M.

The one thing that Bette enjoyed about being busy was being busy. As she made appearances around the country, she wanted to create a troupe for herself and to have Barry Manilow as her music director, even if he wanted more and more to be on his own. She continued to entice him to stay for just one more tour or just one more concert or just one more something, and it would stretch out until it turned into several years. The two of them put together a band and went on tour around the country with Bette performing her outrageous act to crowds that had rarely seen anyone like her, and by July they were back at Mr. Kelly's in Chicago.

The tour went well, but the audiences were not always sellouts. However that was not the case when they returned to New York. In October 1971 they opened to wall-to-wall crowds at the Downstairs at the Upstairs club on West Fifty-sixth Street, and even though there was a strong gay element in the audience, it was basically a straight group, proving that Bette appealed to straights as well as the gays at the Continental Baths. Again, the critics didn't know how to define Bette except that they were convinced she was good and they loved her. Their original two-week engagement was extended to ten house-packed weeks.

9

Farewell to the Baths
and Hello to Vegas

In February 1972, Bette returned to the Baths for her "farewell" appearance, although she had already made several "farewell" appearances at the Baths. The Baths had helped launch her, had assured her success by putting her together with Barry Manilow, and had seen her through some lean times. Every time she did a show, the patrons, her original fans, dropped their towels, jumped on stage to dance with her, and screamed they wanted to make love with her.

But now Bette was a star and commanded a price beyond what Steve Ostrow could fairly pay, and in some ways, she had transformed the Baths from a relaxing haven for gay men to a showplace. Some nights more straight men and women than gay men came to the place when she performed. In one review of Bette, columnist Rex Reed estimated—perhaps a little too enthusiastically—that there was a line of three thousand people waiting to see her performance that night. In any case, it was time to say a *final* farewell so that both Bette and the Baths could get back to being what they were. Bette, of course, is not the only female star to attract gay audiences. Other dramatically popular singers have had big gay audiences, including Jane Oliver, Liza Minnelli, and Judy Garland.

Johnny Carson once again helped by showcasing her on his late-night shows, making her known to millions of Americans who probably saw her for the first time as they stared through their toes at the TV screen. As a result, Bette was getting booked to appear around the country, and for a lot more than fifty dollars a night. She needed to go on tour to take advantage of the national exposure she was getting.

So at the beginning of 1972, she put her entourage together and created a touring musical ensemble as she prepared to play clubs and colleges in Philadelphia, North Carolina, Boston, and every place in between. She created a band and a backup singing trio she named the Harlettes, featuring Melissa Manchester, Gail Kantor, and Merle Miller. The band was led by Barry Manilow, and she had Bill Hennessey and Peter Dallas along too. As a writer, Hennessey would customize her dialogue for each occasion, and Dallas handled lighting, as he had done earlier for pop singer Lauro Nyro.

Later Dallas would talk about how tense those early bus tour trips were for Bette and the group. "It was real hard and you were dealing with a very insecure woman and things were happening much faster than they should have been happening. Sometimes there was just a lot of blind terror at work."

One of her more notable out-of-town appearances occurred when she warmed up the crowd in the Congo Room at the Sahara Hotel in Vegas for her friend and mentor Johnny Carson, in April 1972 when she was twenty-six. He sensed the Vegas crowd would love her.

She recalled, "He asked me to open his show in Vegas for him and I was pleased to do it for him because he had been very good to me. Really good. The more consistent I became, the more he warmed up to me. I like working for him. He's a professional with an astonishing kind of professionalism. He gives the same caliber performance every night."

Carson was still so enamored of her talents twenty-two years later that he wanted her to close for him on his last *Tonight Show*.

Carson's discerning eye regarding talent proved right again in 1972 as she filled the stage with her new, bigger Barry Manilow band, the Harlettes, and a stream of outrageous costumes, jokes, and songs. The audience cheered and applauded and her new act worked—sort of.

For people who don't know Vegas, it is hard to understand that amid those showgirls falling out of their costumes on stage, Wayne Newton leaning into the microphone singing "Danke Schön," and women throwing their room keys on the stage for Tom Jones, Las Vegas audiences are really very square, very family-oriented Middle America. They feel they are being just a tiny bit naughty coming to Las Vegas for a few days away from Ames, Iowa, and Tyler, Texas. They look forward to a glimpse of the glamour and excitement and an iota of sexual suggestiveness just to make them feel wicked, but they really don't want anything too crass or too blatant.

On stage, Bette was crass and blatant. She made her early reputation as the trashy lady who poked fun at American hypocrisy and confusion about sex. Subtlety was not Bette's middle name, nor were polite euphemisms for anatomical parts of the human body. In her acts, Bette didn't refer to her bosom or breasts or "up here," nor did she speak of the derriere or the tush or the bum. When Bette was talking to her audiences about tits and ass, she flat out said "tits and ass" or, sometimes, she would use her favorite alternative for "tits," "knockers." So when she opened for Carson and said she was going to shake her tits a lot on one number, dentures in the audience were almost swallowed and it knocked on their derrieres some of the straight ladies and gentlemen who had paid a lot of money to get into the Congo Room.

While focusing on Bette Midler's style relative to her audience in Las Vegas, it might be worth discussing another unusual aspect of the audiences who are almost religiously devoted to her. Unlike many performers who have had a magical connection with their followers, Bette's devoted fans have not included teenagers or the young set. Even when she performed at various military installations as part of the Pieridine Three trio while growing up in Hawaii, the audience was relatively more mature than the early audiences of Sinatra or various rock groups like the Beatles, Led Zeppelin, and the Rolling Stones.

Bette's core audience began with young adults, mostly young professionals—the so-called yuppie generation. This group did not include the older generation who preferred Bing Crosby or

Lawrence Welk. Bette appealed to the sophisticated, urbane, young crowd and would be big in most cosmopolitan settings. That's why she is popular in New York, Chicago, Philadelphia, San Francisco, Los Angeles, and Colorado, but would probably not do well in Iowa, Nebraska, or Georgia, which is why she rarely toured there. And, of course, she is wildly greeted on college campuses where young people are being trained for yuppiehood. Thus, the blue-dyed-hair-and-polyester-leisure-suit crowd that frequents Vegas are not her kind of people.

Variety reviewed her appearance in what she flippantly called "the Congoleum Room":

"The debut of Bette Midler is a startling change from the norm. Her first words, and there are plenty in the thirty minutes, lay it on with candor as she describes herself as 'the last of the truly tacky women.' That could be possible, in costume only. The tie-around blouse and black slacks are certainly bizarre, although not too far from *Harper's*, yet cannot hide a whale of a voice. The texture and thrust are somewhat triangularly electric from Streisand to Joplin to West."

A few weeks later, in May 1972, with Vegas behind her, Bette appeared at the Bitter End club in New York, where she introduced one of her songs with "This next number is for the divine dick—you know, Nixon," with the rest of her patter in the same tone. She was reviewed this time by a *Newsweek* critic.

"Next to the likes of Lainie Kazan, Lena Horne, or Dionne Warwick, Bette Midler is an ugly duckling . . . . Yet, somehow it all comes together to make her one of the freshest, most captivating of the new girl singers. Bette Midler is—to use one of her favorite expressions—'hot.' "

In her tours earlier in the year, Bette was not singing to full houses in clubs and colleges. She and the booking agents attributed the failure to sell out her shows to the fact that she needed a record album to really establish her credentials with her potential audience, because then her songs would be played on radio stations all around the country. Even so, her recognition was building, and at this point in 1972, she and Barry decided on a bold stroke that underscored how much courage—or at least bravado—they had about their careers. They knew they were popular in New York, particularly with the gays and the straight night crowd from entertainment, media, and business that was always desperate to be at the cutting edge of what was "new," "in," "hot," and "big." They decided to capitalize on their New York popularity. For their next concert, they weren't going to play Biloxi, Mississippi. They would self-propel themselves on a rocket to the top and play New York's fabled Carnegie Hall!

"The first time anyone has ever played the revered Halls of Carnegie without having made it big on records," said Bette proudly. "From the steam baths straight to Carnegie Hall. Can you dig it?"

With more chutzpah than sense, Barry and Bette rented Carnegie Hall to give their own concert and immediately set to work putting together an amalgam of songs and jokes that had worked at the Continental Baths, on the road, and on *The Tonight Show*. They also decided, even though they were running out of money, that they had to hire a backup group for Bette that they initially planned to name the Bang-Bangs but ended up calling the Harlettes. "I called up my friends who sing and I had them all down and we sang together. I wanted to pick up people who I could really get along with."

The first one chosen was a singer Bette had heard at many of the small club dates that Bette had played and whose voice and attitude was right. Her name was Melissa Manchester, and she would go on later to stardom of her own. Melissa, in turn, recommended another singer by the name of Gail Kantor, and the three women had lunch at the crowded Wolf's Deli at the northwest corner of Sixth Avenue and Fifty-seventh Street, down the street from Carnegie Hall, and worked out their deal. Finally, the third member of the Harlettes was Merle Miller, whom Barry brought in from his connections. This was the birth of the Harlettes, which, through several incarnations and changes in characters, would be Bette's backup group and comedy foil for years to come.

The whole time, they were terrified that no one would show up for the concert and they would be humiliated or that everyone would show up for the concert and they would still be humiliated. It was both a gamble and a stroke of genius. When the night of June 23, 1972, finally arrived, it was a Standing Room Only crowd and, if they were going to be humiliated, everyone would know it.

Bette told the audience several times how nervous she was, but she and Barry went ahead and performed anyhow with a display of Bette's range of style and emotion that electrified the audience. From some black scat singing she worked into Bessie Smith's "Empty Bed Blues" and slid into a touching portrayal of Helen Morgan's "Something to Remember You By." From there the moods and melodies varied from the jumping "Boogie Woogie Bugle Boy" to "Moon of Manakoora" and the driving "Delta Dawn" that had the audience toe tapping one moment and sentimentally dreamy the next. The comedy patter was amusing, but the music was the focus for both Bette and Barry. As had become routine with the two, Barry had a segment of the concert for himself, opening the second act with the help of one of the Harlettes, Melissa Manchester, and Michael Federal.

The two emotion-filled hours ended with Bette singing "Chapel of Love" and the audience exploding into a roaring, cheering, standing ovation that brought her back on stage. The hall was filled with calls for her to perform each person's favorite song. After the tumult quieted down, Bette displayed her mastery of her art. She knew that night her audience included many of her longtime, loyal fans from the Baths. She said to them in a soft voice, "I'll do a song I stopped singing, but you've been very kind to me. I don't understand it, but I appreciate it."

With that the lights dimmed to feature Bette standing alone and raising her arm to the audience. "This song is from me to you," she said, and she sang "I Shall Be Released" with such intensity and depth of feeling that she, too, was crying at the end of it along with everyone in the audience. The hall erupted with another standing ovation, and at that moment, everyone in Carnegie Hall shared a rare bonding experience of understanding and love. It was one of Bette's most electric moments communing with the people who loved her and supported her.

In the weeks that followed, twenty-six-year-old Bette did the free Schaefer Beer summer festival concert in Central Park with a lot of other artists. That was August 16, 1972, and her reaction was one of joy and fulfillment. "I thought I was in a newsreel. It was like the Marilyn Monroe newsreel, you know, when she was in Korea. It was just exactly what I thought I was. I was the happiest I've ever been in my whole life."

The next month, she went back to Mr. Kelly's in Chicago for her fourth appearance. It went fine, but some other things were not going well, particularly with the managers she now had, who called themselves Artists Entertainment Complex but should have called themselves a more descriptive term such as Artists Entertainment Simple-Minded. They only saw the superficial veneer in Bette and her stage presentation; they didn't understand what was going on inside this woman, what she wanted to be and what she wanted to achieve in her career. Artists Entertainment Complex wanted to push her as a Las Vegas lounge act in some major strip hotel where she could entertain noisy drunks. It didn't happen, but what did happen was Aaron Russo.

Part III

The Modern Musical Svengali

10

Enter Aaron

The man who would shape Bette's life and career for the next seven years, Aaron Russo, seemed to have come out of nowhere in 1972. A stocky dynamo, with heavy eyebrows and a goatee, Russo arranged to meet Bette through a mutual friend and regaled her with stories of his prowess as an agent and promoter and his dreams of making her richer and more famous than she had already become.

By this time, Bette was no longer living with Michael Federal and had moved to a four-room apartment on Barrow Street in Greenwich Village from the West Seventy-fourth Street apartment they had shared. Barrow Street was a place she loved and in which she would stay for the next several years.

"The place likes me," she said. "I knew as soon as I walked in the door, it was glad to have someone here. The guy before me didn't do a thing. It was filthy and ugly and had not been painted in twenty-five years. But I'm trying to make it comfortable, like a home. I've never really had a home. I lived in one place for five years, but I had no furniture. I had a rug on the floor and I had some mattresses."

Besides the new place and new furniture, there was this new man, Aaron Russo. Many things have been said and written about Russo and, in particular, about his relationship with Bette during the seven years they were together. He was disliked by a lot of people, respected by a few, and adored by none we could find. Before

Bette connected with him, friends and associates gave her dire warnings that he was a user, an exploiter, and an opportunist. Her record mentor Ahmet Ertegun was particularly vocal in warning her against Russo. However, no one ever said that Russo was lazy or stupid, and what Bette needed was a man in charge: someone who was savvy and energetic and got things done and took care of business on a daily basis. That was Aaron Russo.

Russo was a New Yorker who first went into his parents' lingerie business until he decided it was boring and wasn't going to take him into the world of entertainment, which captured his imagination. He first became involved in show business working for a New York nightclub called the Electric Circus and then left Manhattan and sought his fortune in Chicago in the late 1960s. By 1968 he was owner of a rock club called the Kinetic Playground and was getting into talent management and record promotion. He used the club as a way of meeting new talent while watching for the main chance.

Like millions of other Americans, Russo first became aware of Bette from watching *The Tonight Show*. He made a mental note that this woman was a real talent and that he could go far if he ever teamed up with someone like her. As we saw before, he impulsively called a recording entrepreneur to whom he had an entrée, Clive Davis, and recommended he sign her to a recording deal. Nothing came of that. Russo's reaction to Davis's reaction was that Davis and the whole recording business were nuts because Bette Midler would be pure gold if she was managed right. But she was not being managed right. She had the contract with Artists Entertainment Complex but was prepared to junk it. At this point in Russo's career, his club, the Kinetic Playground, was on the road to failure, and he decided to become a commodity broker.

Two years later Russo was in New York with his wife, Andrea, and they decided to catch the Bette Midler performance at the Bitter End. Again he reacted as he had when he had seen her on the small screen. She was a hot number who would go places.

How he managed the next step was absurdly simple. He talked his way backstage to meet her, as many an admirer had done in the past, and began hanging around and being helpful as an errand boy and fan and soon became part of the entourage that milled about her. One of the Harlettes would later recall, "He really was seeking to ingratiate himself with the band and the girls." In some ways it was the right moment for Russo to arrive on the scene, because Bette needed and wanted someone like him.

"We met and it was instant love and devotion," she recalled. "He's a lot like my father. He's a bellower and in that way he intimidates people, but he's a real softie underneath."

Later Russo and Bette would say that the thing that brought them together was that they both had the same goal, namely, to make Bette a star of major dimensions. They were both in love with the idea of Bette as the luminary superstar—the word "legend" was frequently used.

There was a small problem about Russo becoming Bette's new manager. She already had the management contract with Norman Weiss and Michael Liebert of Artists Entertainment Complex. That was when Aaron first demonstrated his ability and style. He had her write Weiss and Liebert terminating their services, and when they threatened to sue for breach of contract, Russo faced his first challenge. Instead of urging Bette to fight the lawsuit with the attendant expense, hassle, and bad publicity, Russo quietly went to Artists Entertainment Complex and made a deal.

Russo pointed out that if Bette turned out to be a failure, why would they want to represent her? On the other hand, if Bette became a star making a lot of money, she could afford to fight them. She could also influence other clients to leave them, and they would have nothing after her contract expired anyhow. So the solution was not to get Aaron Russo out of their lives, but to bring him into their world. Russo convinced Artists Entertainment Complex to make him one of their agents, and that way, Russo managed Midler as she wanted and Midler stayed as an AEC client as they wanted. It worked.

Opinions vary as to why the tenuous introduction blossomed into a brief love affair and a long-term business connection. Some thought that Bette was exhausted from having just come off a tour around the United States and Canada. Others thought it was because Russo charmed her with his sense of humor and his total devotion. Still others believed that she was tired of being lonely and wanted a permanent relationship at the moment Russo walked into her life.

Clearly, Russo was bold and full of energy, and, whatever the reasons, Bette suddenly put her body and her career literally in Russo's hands. It was as if she had unexpectedly turned her whole life over to a present-day musical Svengali. She totally acquiesced and he took over and ran her life, making virtually every decision, including paying her bills, collecting her fees, controlling her mail, phone calls, and appointments, making all arrangements, making deals, and focusing her energies where he thought they belonged. When she gave Russo power over all her affairs, he began to drive out those who questioned his ability or who might bad-mouth him to Bette, and there were plenty of people ready to do that at the beginning of his reign over the Midler career.

One of the first was Charlotte Crossly, of Bette's backup group, the Harlettes. She knew at lot about Russo from her days in Chicago when she frequented the Kinetic Playground and was friends with performers there. According to Charlotte, Russo was universally disliked and regarded as a real son of a bitch, opinions she passed on to Bette. Charlotte and Bette met for the first time through Michael Federal in August 1971, while Michael was still Bette's boyfriend. Charlotte and Michael knew each other from *Hair* in Chicago. He introduced the two women at a New York party, and when Melissa Manchester left the Harlettes to pursue her own career, Charlotte enthusiastically replaced her because she admired Bette and was almost in awe of Barry Manilow, who would be going on tour with them.

"When you work with Bette, you become her friend," she said. "She's interested in you. She's sensitive to you because she wants you to be sensitive to her. And Barry was just a genius. He wrote beautiful charts, and they got along very well, creatively. He and Bette communicated well, because they like the same things. Of course, there was a lot of other negative stuff going on with them too. She really couldn't control him the way she could other men."

Norman Kean, who was associated with Mr. Kelly's in Chicago, was fascinated by the creative rapport between Bette and Barry.

"She needed a musical support to bring her up to her best energy level and mental level. Barry provided that for her. It was quite amazing, really. She could communicate with him by just waving her wrist or moving her shoulder [and] he would immediately know just what she needed. It was like his antennas were wrapped around hers . . . that's why it was so sensational to see them work together."

But now there was Aaron, and the curious aspect was not only his role as her lover while he was still married to his wife, Andrea, but how, when their romantic affair ended, Bette clung to him as her general factotum in charge of everything except romance. The breakup of Bette and Aaron's affair didn't save Russo's marriage, since he became consumed with running Bette's career. Even those who thought Russo overbearing and rude had to admit that he did convert Bette's previously scattered energy by concentrating it where it was most effective and by broadening her exposure.

His first big booking for her would also become one of the most talked-about performances of Bette's life, her New Year's Eve concert at New York's premium arts venue, Lincoln Center. Many people who attended cannot remember all the songs on the program, but everyone recalls that Bette appeared in the spotlight and, at the stroke of midnight, released a catch on her dress which dropped away to reveal her bare breasts to the audience.

And there was the later widely circulated story that Bette had originally wanted a marijuana joint taped to the underside of each of the three thousand seats in the auditorium so that she could invite everyone to light up. Russo and her attorney convinced her this plan was so outrageously illegal that it could not be ignored by authorities. She was just buying herself a one-way ticket to jail.

The next major project on the agenda as directed by Russo was the creation and release of her first album, *The Divine Miss M*, which was an immense success, along with two singles, "Do You Want to Dance?" and "Boogie Woogie Bugle Boy," the pounding hit originally done by the Andrews Sisters in World War II just before Bette was born. As noted earlier, the production of the record album *The Divine Miss M* was in limbo and Ahmet Ertegun was trying to get it produced in a way that would create the same excitement on the recording that Bette delivered in her club dates and concerts. Bette was beside herself. "It was so difficult to do!" she said. "I was so disappointed I cried every single day. It was the horrors!"

That's when the mishandled Barry Manilow was brought back to perform the synergistic magic that he alone could do with Bette. When the album was finally released in November 1972, it was a great success, selling 100,000 copies the first month and then quickly going to gold (500,000 copies sold). The public had no idea what piercing labor pains were involved in its delivery. Critics analyzing the album said that the special flavor of Bette's work came from the interpretation she gave to each of the songs she did and from the diversity of mood she was able to convey.

In her first successful album, we encounter again the musical multiphase personality of Bette Midler that so confounded niche-oriented critics. She was many different kinds of singers in one, changing her style and the mood at will and without disrupting the attention or appreciation of anybody but the critics. Moreover, the atmosphere she created for each of her renditions made it clear that she was essentially a Method singer in the same sense that Brando was a Method actor.

Critics Dave Marsh and Robbie Cruger, writing in the magazine *Creem*, said, "Bette Midler loves old rock and she knows how to divert some of the energy of the sixties material into a torchy style that is unique. She can also impart torch songs with some rock and roll spunk and that is her biggest plus. She defines herself so acutely that each song has its own veracity."

The same month *The Divine Miss M* was flying out of record stores all over America, Bette returned to the wellspring that had first given her the Divine title. In November of 1972 Bette made her final, never-to-be-repeated, absolutely farewell appearance at the Continental Baths, which erupted into a hassle between Russo and Steve Ostrow—her new and her old mentors. Russo hated Ostrow jamming people into the place to milk this last appearance, and Ostrow hated the Johnny-come-lately Russo.

Both men vented their anger at each other in the pages of *Rolling Stone*. "Bette has outgrown the Continental Baths," Russo said. "I mean she's a star now, she needs the baths like a hole in the head, right? But we agreed to do one last show as a favor. So what does Ostrow do? He decides to make a killing. He throws us to the lions."

Despite the mixed analogy, the point is clear, and we might note in passing Russo's use of the plural personal pronoun because, to him, it wasn't Bette who was the star of the focus anymore, it was "we." Ostrow replied, "Bette came to me and *asked* me for that date. I think she wanted to dispel some of the rumors going around that she was becoming sort of, well, anti-homosexual."

After the friction-filled but successful appearance at the Baths, Russo demonstrated that he knew what was needed to follow up her hit album and mandated a series of hard-driving concert tours— first, a thirty-city, three-month tour in the late summer of 1972 and then a forty-five-city tour throughout the country during the remainder of 1972 and all of 1973. The tours and the album were synergistic, helping each other and hyping the sales of the album and the sales of concert or club admissions. The wisdom of his management was demonstrated at the box office, particularly in the large metropolitan areas such as at the Club Bijou in Philadelphia, the Boarding House in San Francisco, the Troubadour in Los Angeles, and her New Year's Eve double concert—one at eight P.M. and one at eleven P.M.—at New York's Lincoln Center. She sold out everywhere she went. The year 1972 ended with her big New Year's Eve concert at Lincoln Center's Philharmonic Hall, where she was carried in riding in a sedan chair lined with red velvet.

As usual, the music was interspersed with some more of Bette's scandalous banter, such as, "I loved Tricia Nixon's wedding, didn't you? I was very put out that they did not send the Divine an invitation. But I sent a present anyway—I sent her a man-eating plant. I thought maybe she'd get the message. After all, she did marry a man named Cox."

Intermission ended just in time to ring in 1973, and Bette was standing on a platform that rose up from the orchestra pit wearing nothing but a giant diaper with the numerals "1973" on a sash across her chest and began leading the audience in "Auld Lang Syne" to everyone's delight. Other treats she rendered for the ecstatic gathering included "Higher and Higher," "Do You Wanna Dance?" and finally ended with "Chapel of Love." After her usual standing ovation, she finished the evening with her galvanizing version of "I Shall Be Released" and brought down the final curtain with "Friends." The *New York Times* review of the concert was summarized in its headline, "Good, Better, Best, Bette!" it was a fantastic way for Bette to start the new year.

The raves from the live audiences were matched in the press and one probably affected the other. It is hard for a reviewer to sit in a sea of cheering, adoring fans and then go back to his word processor and write what a bomb the artist was. Even the *New York Times* lost control of itself, forgot its earlier iffy review, and popped the studs off its stuffed shirt with "A bona-fide original! An enormously theatrical young woman who possesses an uncanny singing talent. The first white show woman of the current pop era!"

The *New York Daily News* waxed ecstatic through its rock music critic Lillian Roxon: "It was heaven. I can't remember when I last saw a performer work so hard and give off and get so much love. She does all the things no one does anymore and I wish the rock-and-roll brigade would learn from her—stalking and stomping around the stage like a hyena on speed!"

Atlantic Records was so pleased with the sales of *The Divine Miss M* that it asked for an immediate follow-up album, but that proved tougher than expected. Ertegun had learned from past mistakes. He knew that the new album had to be directed by Barry Manilow in order for it to be the kind of Midler hit that would go gold too. Barry didn't have the free time because he was now busy with his own career and, indeed, was about to finish up an album of his own.

And while the principals didn't talk about it publicly, Russo's presence on the scene had a negative effect on the Bette and Barry team that had worked well together before. Aaron had been in her bed, been thrown out, and then determined to get back in that warm and wonderful place. Moreover, his egocentricity and his passionate obsession with Bette joined to make him determined to be the center of her life, to be in control of everything, even if it meant riding roughshod over everyone else. He would, for example, constantly intrude on rehearsals, interrupting with his appearances or endless phone calls, pushing his nose into situations where he wasn't needed or, more important, wasn't wanted. He hurt Bette's preparation for a performance. Barry stuck it out for a time, Melissa left the Harlettes to pursue her own rainbow, and former lover Michael Federal left her bed but stayed in her band.

The first big national tour involving Russo was launched in Rochester, New York, in February 1973. It was scheduled to hit thirty cities at an average rate of one every three days! Tough schedule, but Bette was ready. She said then, "I'm all my fantasies! Every time I get up there it's 'magic time.' I used to want to be Bette Davis in one of those great thirties movies where everyone's wearing furs and drinking martinis. I don't think I'm rabid to be a star. Now that I've met a few, I realize it's all the same, we're all the same. There's no difference. I met Bob Dylan after looking for him for seven years and I was in shock. I had worshiped him, but he lives, he has flesh, he has those shirts, sometimes he plays good, sometimes he plays bad, sometimes he sings good, he writes a good song, he writes a bad song, he's a human being."

In spite of the tight schedule which also included some work on the new album for Atlantic, Bette's crew kept packing the houses everywhere they played. They used one old showtime technique that worked every time. When they hit town, the Harlettes and others would spread out and spend a few hours talking with people and learning the local gossip and jokes and something about the community's hangouts. Then Bette's writer Bruce Vilanch would incorporate that trivia into her patter for the show.

In Passaic she took a dig at the locals and at herself: "Well, I missed my stop on the Seventh Avenue [subway] and wound up here in Passaic. Passaic, darling," Bette continued, "I do not believe. Honey, I never saw so many women in curlers in my life! For those of you who haven't the faintest idea of what this creature is who is standing in front of you, my name is Bette Midler. My friends refer to me as the Divine Miss M—everything you are afraid your little girls—and your little boys too—will grow up to be. Also known as the last of the truly tacky women."

In Buffalo, where gays have long avoided any public display because of the intense prejudice there, those fans were out in force at Bette's concert, prompting Bette to observe, "God forbid anyone in this town needs any emergency comb-out tonight."

And that's how the first tour of 1973 went, ending up in San Francisco, at which point two of her Harlettes, Merle and Gail, decided to leave the troupe to make a name for themselves.

Besides the cross-country tour, Russo had Bette squeeze in TV appearances whenever possible, including one on *Burt Bacharach—Opus No. 3*, which prompted ABC-TV to offer her a special of her own for the 1973–74 season. That, as it turned out, never happened, since ABC executives and Bette could never get together on the format and content. Midler's main television debut would have to wait. When it did happen, it wasn't on ABC; it was performed the way Bette had wanted, and it was a smash.

She said, "I really want to do a sleazy, tacky, shabby show. But the agency and the network [ABC-TV] are a bit conservative. They want Johnny Mann, they want the Ding-A-Lings. I want sleaze. I want sequins."

Well, she didn't get sequins, but she and Barry did create her second album, *Bette Midler*, which Atlantic Records and Ahmet Ertegun were most anxious to get into the radio stations and stores around the country on the heels of *The Divine Miss M*. By that time, her smash album had sold just shy of *three million copies*, making at least $10 million in profit for Atlantic.

This time there was no debate over who was going to produce the album—not with another $10 million profit probably on the line. It would be Barry Manilow, and for this album, Barry did something to make it easier for the bewildered critics who couldn't figure out what and who Bette was musically.

On *Bette Midler*, Barry put the torchy, bluesy, ballad-singing Bette on one side of the album with songs such as "Drinking Again," "Skylark," and her drop-dead heartbreaker "I Shall Be Released" on one side. On the other side, Manilow placed the swinging, rocking, brassy material, like "Don't Say Nothin' Bad About My Baby," "Da Doo Run Run," and "Lullaby of Broadway," one of her best and favorite songs ever since she won a prize for singing it in the sixth grade.

While this talented performer, Barry Manilow, wandered around Atlantic's studios cranking out two blockbuster albums, no one—not even the genius Ahmet Ertegun—whipped out a pen to get Barry's name at the bottom of a contract. Instead, Barry kept plugging along, determined to showcase his own talents somehow and to make the breakout on his own when the chance came.

He was working on winning a recording contract with Bell records about the time Clive Davis was unceremoniously dumped as president of Columbia Records in a scandal involving payola, drugs, and improper expense accounts, to which he pled guilty.

Shortly thereafter, Davis was summoned from his office in Columbia Records on the lower floors of CBS headquarters to the office of company president Arthur Taylor. He walked in, was fired by Taylor before he could sit down, walked out, and took the elevator back down to his office. As he got out of the elevator at his floor, he was greeted by two security guards who accompanied him back to his office, watched him pack his personal belongings, and ushered him out of the building to his limo. The limo driver was instructed to take Mr. Davis home and to return immediately. The whole thing took about ten minutes.

Snapping back from this career disaster, Davis bought up Bell records, with whom Barry Manilow had been negotiating, changed the name to Arista Records, and signed Barry and one of the former Harlettes, Melissa Manchester, to contracts.

Meanwhile, Bette and Barry were getting ready for another tour. For the remaining five months of 1973, Russo laid out another major tour, with the emphasis on big auditoriums and concert halls in thirty-five cities. The plan called for Bette and Barry being on the road for four months starting in August and ending up at the famous Palace Theater in New York.

Early in the tour, in August, Bette would perform in Honolulu. Her mother, sister Susan, and brother Danny sat in the third row for both her performances and heard the standing ovation that greeted her when she came on stage. She cried when the emotion welled up inside her, and when the two-hour performance was over, she told the audience, "I don't mind telling you I was scared shitless tonight. God, if you only knew how happy you've made me!" which brought her Hawaiian fans to their feet for a seven-minute standing ovation.

On the second night, most of her graduating high school class attended and gave her the traditional Hawaiian love offering of a lei. Later, there was a luau in her honor about which she joked, "Well, now I'm going to a reunion of all the people who couldn't stand me."

But flippancy turned to vulnerability, because the luau was the one public appearance she made in Hawaii which her father attended. It meant more than she could say and more than he could know. Her father had not attended either of her concerts, and, hurt as it did, Bette tried to put the best face on it. "I was glad my father didn't come to see me perform," she said. "I would have been afraid to be dirty or gross, afraid that he would walk out or start yelling at me."

She went on, "My father is very, very conservative. He's read some things about me, and he likes Lawrence Welk [the bandleader who once refused to dance or touch Bette on a TV show appearance in Philadelphia because he was sure she would infect his private parts with crabs if he did]. If he saw my act, my father would *die*. He would kill himself, he would jump off the roof. He doesn't like too much cleavage. In fact, every time I went over there to dinner, he made me safety-pin my dress together."

So, as it did whenever she returned to Hawaii, the pain came back. The pain of the past as an ugly-duckling minority in her neighborhood and school and the pain of the present when her father refused to attend her concert because he was ashamed of what he regarded as the tawdry performance she put on in public. In a sense, Chesty Midler viewed his daughter as a bad girl on the stage. "He doesn't want anyone to think that anyone from his family is cheap," she would say. "I don't know why I love to parody all that cheap music and stuff. It's so dumb, but I have so much fun doing it."

Whatever her father thought about her act, Bette did take comfort from the wildly enthusiastic reaction of her adoring mother at every performance she attended. "Oh God, my mother got a charge, though. She kept screaming, 'Faaaabulous! Faaaabulous!'" And Bette reported that after the concerts, her mother said, "We always knew she was witty, but we didn't know she was *that* witty. I'm so proud of her because she makes so many people happy."

Bette was in command when she went on stage, and she was also a sensitive and generous artist, as the tour demonstrated. Sympathetic to Barry's ego and need for recognition and a boost to stardom himself, Bette continued to give Barry a twenty-minute segment at the beginning of the second half of her show for him to showcase himself and his own songs. This was a perfect opportunity for Barry, because he had stage fright when it came to performing alone. By playing his bit at the end of the intermission, it was like an introduction to the second half of Bette's show. It helped Barry gain more self-confidence. As he said, "At the time Bell Records wouldn't give me an album deal unless I promised I would go out and perform. I didn't really want to go out and perform, but I did want to make records because I really loved being in the studio. So we put an act together and it came out real strong, and it gave me a foundation to be able to make mistakes as a performer."

When Bette and Barry weren't performing, Barry was finishing work on his own album and working on Bette's second one. Often they split the day in the recording studio, with both working on Bette's second album from noon until six and then Barry coming back to work on his own from seven until the early morning. This multiproject effort of concert tour and two record albums at the same time was completed in only three months, and Barry almost wore himself out.

In the course of this tour, Bette arrived in Los Angeles in mid-March 1973 and played to a sold-out Dorothy Chandler Pavilion with its 3,200 seats, something she would do again at the Pavilion a few months later in September.

And she made another appearance on *The Tonight Show* with Johnny Carson, who said, "One of the great kicks of doing this show is seeing people who come on and make their initial television appearance and then seeing what happens in their career. This young woman was appearing in a men's Turkish bath in New York—very strange—but as soon as you heard her sing, you knew there was a very unique talent there, and this year she's been hailed as the first star of the seventies."

That stop on the tour also included a pilgrimage by Bette and the Harlettes to the Shrine of Tacky, Mr. Frederick's of Hollywood, located on the south side of Hollywood Boulevard between Vine and Highland avenues. It is also the home of Mr. Frederick's Museum of Lingerie, containing famous undergarments of stars and notables, including Madonna's bustier, which was the only item stolen from the museum during the Rodney King riots of 1992.

Another tribute to Bette and a rare moment in the history of show business came when Bette appeared in the Universal Studios Amphitheater to a sellout crowd. To the surprise of everyone, Patty and Maxene Andrews, the two remaining Andrews Sisters from World War II fame, were in the audience. At Bette's urging, Patty and Maxene came on stage and joined Bette in their classic from the 1940s, "Boogie Woogie Bugle Boy." They received a tidal wave of applause as these two legendary figures sang with a contemporary superstar.

During the 1973 tours, Bette and Barry played audiences in the thousands at concert venues and state fairs, and they ended up at the Palace Theater in New York that December. The Palace, at Broadway and Forty-seventh Street, was the mecca for major performers in the days of vaudeville from the time the theater was opened in 1913. Everyone from Jack Benny, Houdini, W. C. Fields, and Fred Astaire to Will Rogers and Sophie Tucker had the same goal, "to play the Palace." When vaudeville died and was replaced by movies in the 1930s, the Palace stayed with the times and converted to a movie theater, but in 1966 the Nederlander brothers bought the Palace and returned it to a legitimate theater, opening its reincarnation with *Sweet Charity*. Since then, Diana Ross, Josephine Baker, Shirley MacLaine, and Bette have played one-woman shows at the Palace, and Judy Garland did her next to last New York performance there before she died.

Author Ann Morse described how their appearance there enhanced Manilow's stretch for stardom. "Bette would end the first act with Barry's arrangement of "Do You Wanna Dance?" The audience would be screaming and on their feet after Bette completed her number, and then it was Barry's turn. Unannounced, Barry Manilow proceeded to take his spot and do his three songs."

When he had performed his segment weeks earlier at the outdoor theater carved out of a mountain, Red Rocks Amphitheater in Colorado, Barry had chosen to sing one of the numbers from his first album, "Could It Be Magic?" Somehow with the mountain setting, the open air, and the real magic of his singing, the audience was overwhelmed. The song differed completely from Bette's songs because of its classical arrangement around a Chopin prelude. Despite the contrast with Bette's performance, the audience gave Barry his first standing ovation.

This ethereal natural setting also had its effect on Bette. Being quite different from the traditional indoor theater, it made Bette introspective about herself and the Divine Miss M she was portraying on stage. She recalls:

"We were playing out in the middle of God-made country in the Red Rocks Amphitheater, and I felt so helpless against the elements that I thought I had to do this big showbiz thing, you know, shake my tits and be divine. Well, it got to the point where I was giving the people only what they expected of the Divine Miss M, but nothing of myself. During the break I sat there and figured it out and for the next set I took off my makeup, put on my pants and shirt and tried to harmonize with Red Rocks just by being little old me. Miss M is a show—much larger than life. Bette Midler is just a person with a few things to say and a few songs to sing. From now on, I'm going to be Bette Midler."

The worst thing about these tours was the enormous physical endurance required by everyone for moving the entourage to a new place every few days and setting up, rehearsing, performing, tearing down, and moving on to the next place to do it all over again. The second worst thing was the emotional exhaustion resulting from the gossip, double-dealing, backbiting, and interpersonal problems that poisoned such ventures. Many attributed this vicious atmosphere to

Aaron Russo and his obsession with Bette. Charlotte Crossly said, "He was so jealous of anyone getting close to Bette that he would always tell her things about people, tell her that no one cared about her and he was the only one she could count on. It was very tough on all of us."

According to Bruce Vilanch, her longtime writer and colleague since she first performed at Mr. Kelly's in Chicago, this corrosive situation was exacerbated by Bette's private life. "Bette was having an affair with one of the band members, and Aaron didn't like that one bit. So he made things particularly unpleasant."

The emotional pressure finally drove Bill Hennessey to quit the tour. He complained that Russo froze him and Barry Manilow out of meetings with Bette so that they did not know what was happening even though they had integral responsibilities for making the show work.

Bette felt drained because she needed always to be "on," including those times when she just wanted to pull back and catch her breath. The physical requirements, the timing both on- and off-stage, the demands, and the number of people involved all exhausted Bette, even though Russo was always there to help. The atmosphere was reminiscent of Bette's early family life, which consisted of continual confrontations of each family member against the other, with excessive yelling, door slamming, and furniture pounding. Charlotte characterized it this way on the 1973 tours:

> We would scream back and forth—Bette is a very confront [sic] kind of person. That's her way of communicating. And there was so much responsibility on her shoulders. If she raised a lot of hell, things would get done.
>
> The more I got to know her and see the much more temperamental sides of her, [the more] I kind of understood where that came from. She grew up in a family where there was constant fighting, and you couldn't get any results from being nice. It was only when you screamed and yelled and got everything to a crisis point that anything got accomplished. And that, unfortunately, spilled over into her work and what happened was that in her relationships creatively

with people, it was just too much for them. It really pushed
a lot of people over the edge and away from her.

Aaron, in turn, exacerbated the problem. That's because Bette
had a cadre of loyal professionals with whom she worked, including
Barry as music director, the Harlettes as musical backup and women
friends, Bruce Vilanch as writer, and Bill Hennessey for lighting and
staging, and she needed to work and bond with them. Russo, on the
other hand, was so insecure about his position with Bette that he
had to twist and use people. He tried to cause friction between Bette
and her entourage or among the entourage so that by weakening
everyone else—including Bette—he consolidated his own position
and made himself indispensable.

As Charlotte expressed it, "It was heartbreaking to watch him
manipulate her. If Bette was down about something or felt isolated
or that no one cared, Aaron would always be there to reinforce those
feelings in her. It was real weird, he was like this suppressive person
with her, he felt powerful when she was down, because he was then
able to bring her back up. Then he'd have more control over her.
Then, when she was bright and feeling good and could get things
done on her own, he'd sink down and she'd go, 'What's the matter?'
and he'd say, 'You don't need me anymore.' I mean, it was a *very
sick* thing."

Aaron caused additional tension and bad will for Bette by in-
sulting people and making demands—all in her name and behind
her back. So a lot of ill feeling was directed at Bette by people she
didn't know for reasons she didn't understand. Which is not to say
that Bette was entirely innocent, because this was an arrangement
she molded herself and continued to keep in place. She may not
have known what Aaron did in her name, but, more important, she
didn't *want* to know as long as he took care of things.

Charlotte believed that Aaron served a purpose for Bette. "Busi-
nesswise, she needed him. He threw his weight around and made
deals and he was able to pull off a lot of stuff. She stuck with him
for so long because of his obsession with getting the best for her
always."

And Bette herself was ambivalent about Aaron, seeing him alternately as her savior, her warrior, her destroyer, her enemy, her advocate, her champion, and her betrayer. Clearly, she was bewildered in that relationship, and probably Aaron was too, but they stayed together in their business endeavors for those seven-plus years, even though the romance was over after six months. Aaron spoke in his own behalf in a 1983 *20/20* interview: "I guess we fought principally because I was sort of dominating her career in one way, and in another way, in our personal life, I was very insecure."

The year 1973 ended on a positive note with Bette's appearance at the Palace Theater, which produced a Broadway one-day sales record when they sold $148,000 worth of tickets and were sold out three weeks before the opening in December. Russo demanded that the portrait of Judy Garland hanging in the lobby be taken down and replaced with one of Bette. And the Palace management obeyed. The performance Bette gave at her Palace run included many jokes—some political satire, some sexual, particularly about one of Bette's favorite subjects, oral sex.

"Isn't this the most amazing time you've ever been through in your life?" she began. "I'm freaked out. I don't know what's going on. Do you know what's going on? Who's Gerry Ford? I never heard of him. I don't want to be rude before he even gets started, but have you ever had a Ford that didn't break down? And Rose Mary Woods! What do you suppose she's thinking about? You don't suppose Nixon's socking it to her, do you? Couldn't be. He doesn't sock it to anyone. He only socked it to Pat twice and look what a botch he made of that! Did you hear that Dick Nixon bought a copy of *Deep Throat*? He's seen it ten or twelve times. He wanted to get it down Pat."

These jabs were interspersed with fabulous singing and production numbers that got better and better as they were smoothed on the road. The high points included her opening with a sentimental "Friends" in a Hawaiian setting, a hard-driving "Delta Dawn," and concluding the first act with one of the strongest numbers in her repertoire, "I Shall Be Released," which, as usual, brought the audience to its feet cheering.

Following the pattern of most of her concerts, Barry Manilow opened the second act with four songs of his own and moved into the dramatic production number in which Bette reappeared. The curtains parted, revealing a huge silver lamé high-heel pump that took up the whole stage area. Within the pump was a built-in stairway down which Bette began to descend, singing "Lullaby of Broadway" and backed by the Harlettes. Bette and the Harlettes then slid into the thumping, upbeat "Boogie Woogie Bugle Boy." The rest of the second act included "Do You Wanna Dance?" "Surabaya Johnny," and the touching, sensitive "Hello in There." It then moved into "Chapel of Love." All of these numbers were Midler standards to which the audience knew every word and nuance.

For example, as they went into "Chapel of Love," a giant heart was lowered from the top of the stage, and Bette got the audience to join in the singing, accompanied by appropriate swaying. The house lights then brightened and Bette and her fans went into "Friends," with Bette at the footlights clasping hands with people in the front row until the love-in/sing-along climaxed with everyone cheering, yelling, whistling, crying, and laughing. Another memorable night for three thousand people with the Divine Miss M.

By the end of 1973, Bette, then twenty-eight, made the cover of the December 17 *Newsweek* magazine; received the Ruby Award of *After Dark* magazine as the Entertainer of the Year, and the Tony Award for Best Special Performance in a Broadway Musical, presented by her idol, Johnny Carson; walked away with the Grammy for Best New Female Artist—another case of working ten years to become an overnight success; and had produced her next album, *Bette Midler*, for which Barry had arranged and conducted all the numbers. The album once again displayed her incredible range from the gentle, heart-touching "Surabaya Johnny" to the thumping beat of "Lullaby of Broadway" and the runaway "In the Mood."

She found all of this success was wonderful, but it sucked the energy and life out of her. Ellen Willis, reviewing the Palace concert for *New York Magazine*, worried that Bette was paying a high price for stardom, and Bette agreed. "I was tired. I was scared to death," she said. It was perhaps the main reason she needed Aaron Russo.

She had become a hot entertainment property, and booking

agents, concert promoters, movie and legitimate theater producers, and network television were all running up their phone bills trying to reach Aaron Russo to get him to commit Bette. It was a performer's dream. It could also be a perfomer's nightmare if it took more out of you than there was to give.

11

1974—Defusing the Bomb

Nineteen seventy-three had been a wild year for Bette, with a successful second album behind her, two prestigious awards, the Grammy and a Tony, and the presence of Aaron Russo. Whatever their love relationship, he did bring to her life a feeling of safety, that whatever was wrong she was protected and could do as she wished.

During her 1973 tours, Bette transformed from a wannabe performer working small clubs with dingy dressing rooms and low budgets to a star playing huge auditoriums packed with thousands of people, culminating in her appearance at the Palace. She was limoed from place to place, catered to and mobbed by fans and the press, who were often the same.

"I try not to think about it," she said. "It's all very frightening. I just don't know anymore. I just want to wrap it up as a little present and give it to the people. I can't stand it when I have to worry about what they think of it."

The private Midler was a quiet and introspective woman who enjoyed being by herself, reading and thinking. She probably understood the fragility of fame and how her own celebrity had come with the help of people like Steve Ostrow, Bud Friedman, and Barry Manilow, building on the foundation of her natural talent and those two qualities on which she depended so much: her instinct and her guts. She secretly feared that the fame that had come so quickly might disintegrate. "Sometimes I don't know anymore who I am. I used to be Bette Midler and now I'm the Divine Miss M."

She poignantly observed that often when people met her for the first time and didn't know she was the Divine Miss M, they thought she was a rather plain woman. That might have been because the private Bette didn't dress up in flashy, trashy clothes, refused to wear anything with sequins on it in her nonpublic life, and avoided smearing what she called "goo" on her face. She would appear more housewifey plain than show business glamorous. "I am lonely sometimes. I've traded in big friendships for the love of a great, huge number of people, but you can't take ten thousand people home to bed with you."

She could still be wounded by the unflattering references occasionally made about her looks. This was something that carried over from the time her appearance was disparaged when she was growing up in Hawaii and laughed at as an ugly, Jewish haole. In later years, critics have sometimes opened up the wound by marveling at how a plain Jewish girl from Hawaii could make it so big in show business.

She said with bitterness, "I hate it when they call me ugly, when they say I'm homely. I'm the one who's in the body. I'm the one who has the face. I can't have plastic surgery on my heart."

When people compared Bette to Mae West or Judy Garland, she recognized the differences but appreciated that she was considered in the same class. Indeed, she relished the comparisons of herself to other performers, with one exception, Tiny Tim, a geeky kind of man who played the ukulele and sang "Tiptoe Through the Tulips" in falsetto on the Johnny Carson show and who reveled in the ridicule heaped upon him by everyone. He even got married on *The Tonight Show*. She said, "I don't want people to think I'm the object of derision. I don't think of myself as anything like Tiny Tim, even vaguely."

Many observers—friends and industry people alike—continued to think Russo was bad for Bette and that no one should have as much control over an artist as he had over Bette, but these people conveniently ignored one fact: Bette seemed to want it that way.

Bette was comfortable with Russo in charge. And in 1974 Russo would prove the wisdom of her trust in him, because there was a little-known time bomb ticking in Bette's career.

With everything going so well, Bette no longer had to worry about money—she tended to be frugal anyhow—or acceptance as a person or a performer. She had arrived, although exhausted. It was no surprise that, after a tour and an album and special concerts, she desperately needed some time to recharge herself, and that's what she did. She was so rarely seen during most of 1974, her twenty-ninth year, that people began to ask what happened to her.

She said, "When I finally took a step back and a breath, I almost fell down. I almost had a breakdown. I was at my wit's end. I was very, very irritable and desolate, mostly from exhaustion. So I took the year off."

For some weeks, Bette rejoiced in being the other Bette: the shy, quiet woman who needed time to herself for herself. She would hang around her modest one-bedroom apartment in the Village, sleeping late and soaking up the music of other artists she admired. Then she roused herself for a globe-spanning escape, first to the warm, windswept shores of Grenada, a Caribbean island, then to the Pacific island that had been her home for twenty years, Hawaii. After visiting with her family and some friends, she was off to France to soak up the culture and enjoy the men.

"I went to Paris and gained a lot of weight," she said. "I ate like a pig. I spent twelve, fourteen hours a day sleeping. I didn't even see the city. I just slept and called room service."

Part of room service for Bette was Benoit Gautier, who worked in the Paris office of Atlantic Records and had initially been sent by Ahmet Ertegun to check that Bette was all right. Benoit and Bette had a lot of fun together, which was something Bette needed right then.

Bette had learned one of life's secrets as the result of her up-bringing: to stay in the game for the long haul and to pace yourself, sequestering your money so you can last long enough until you ultimately win. Yet a disaster was almost about to happen because of another trait of Bette's that was contrary to her conservative side—her impulsive gene that kept making her want to do strange, self-destructive things. Wanting to put marijuana joints under the seats at Lincoln Center was an example of an impulse that would have been self destructive, while exposing her bare breasts may have been of questionable taste, but she got away with it at that moment.

Now an impulsive moment in Canada that had occurred when she was on tour in 1971 was about to ambush her career. A film-maker who called himself, variously, Peter Alexander McWilliams, Peter Alexander, and Peter McWilliams convinced her to do a twelve-minute appearance in his sixteen-millimeter film satire of religion entitled *A Story Too Often Told* or *The Greatest Story Overtold*, which seemed to ridicule Jesus Christ and Christianity. Alexander/ McWilliams sniffed big profits the minute Bette Midler became fa-mous. It provided him with an opportunity to exploit the star's ap-pearance, as others had when Hedy Lamarr swam nude in an early film or Marilyn Monroe posed nude for a calendar. Midler was vul-nerable and could be accused of being prejudiced, anti-Christian, and blasphemous, all of which would offend record buyers and con-certgoers.

To exploit Midler's new stardom, Alexander/McWilliams needed to show the film commercially, and that meant borrowing forty thousand dollars to transfer the sixteen-millimeter movie onto the thirty-five-millimeter film used in movie house projectors. He did so and cast around for a place to exhibit it. His film suddenly surfaced in New York—the stronghold of Bette's public support—at the Fes-tival Theater under a new title, *The Divine Miss J*, designed to capi-talize on the Midler appearance. The advertisement promoting the film declared that the movie was made "in the tradition of Lenny Bruce and Woody Allen," and that it would open May 24 at the Fes-tival Theater, Fifty-seventh Street and Fifth Avenue. Promoted as the world premiere of Bette Midler's film debut, the movie was hyped as "a religious satire—MORE THAN A MOVIE—*It's a happening.*"

Bette was in France and not immediately aware of what was happening, but Russo was in New York. He instantly counterat-tacked by flooding the media with press releases and public state-ments attacking the exploitative nature of the film and the moral motives of the promoters. He worked behind the scenes to undercut the film's showing and made those connected with it contemplate the cost of taking on an important star like Bette. Russo believed his aggressive and quick action saved Bette's career. For a Jewish woman performer to have offended Christian audiences by blaspheming Jesus Christ may have hurt Bette beyond rescue, but happily, because of Russo, it didn't happen that way.

Russo attacked on every front he could think of: legal, financial, and public relations. Legally he marshaled the lawyers to go into court and get an injunction. Alexander not only advertised in the newspapers, he ran radio ads on stations that played Midler records. Financially, Russo was in touch with Alexander to see if a deal could be made to squash the showing. And when the opening occurred, Russo personally picketed the theater wearing a sandwich board. As Russo recalls the incident:

> Peter McWilliams had made this movie—he's now a famous author. He made this thing, then tried to open it up on Fifty-sixth Street as her [Bette's] first feature film. They had full-page ads claiming it was her first feature. It was lies and she was hardly even in the movie.
>
> She was in France with her boyfriend, Gautier, which made me miserable because I was in love with her. Anyway, I made a sandwich board and went to the theater at eight in the morning because the first show was at noon. I hired a couple of other people to join me. Basically, the sandwich board said, "I'm Aaron Russo, Bette's manager, and this picture was made many years ago. Bette doesn't want you to see it and she's hardly even in it. Don't waste your money." I stood out there for six days in the rain. It was totally out of devotion. I felt it was my duty. She was my artist and I wanted to protect her.
>
> What was really funny was business associates who would pass by—because it was on Fifty-seventh Street, pretty busy street, and they'd look and almost be past me when they'd hear my voice and say, "Aaron, is that you?"

Aaron won a little on several fronts. The legal action resulted in toning down the ads so that they didn't make the film sound like a Midler extravaganza, and the picketing choked off box-office sales. The film slunk out of town with little damage to the Midler reputation.

Four years later Peter McWilliams would write *The Personal Computer Book*, which became a runaway bestseller in the early 1980s, and he founded Prelude Press, a very successful self-publishing operation. Still, he continued to get involved in controversy, with the most notorious being his involvement and dedication to John-Roger, a former Rosemead (California) high school teacher who founded the Church of the Movement of Spiritual Inner Awareness.

In 1978 McWilliams attended a personal growth seminar where he was introduced to John-Roger. Ten years later McWilliams was depressed about a friend who died from a rare form of tuberculosis and was scared he might have the disease. He turned to John-Roger, who promised to keep McWilliams alive and healthy if McWilliams would list John-Roger as coauthor of all the books he wrote and published and give him half of the profits.

"As amazing as it sounds," McWilliams said, "he actually had me believing he had power over life and death, health and illness. Realizing I actually believed all this stuff is humiliating."

It was so humiliating that McWilliams stopped paying the money to John-Roger, who is now suing him for $400,000. John-Roger is more recently noted for his connection with biographer Arianna Stassinopolous Huffington, the wife of California Senate candidate Michael Huffington. McWilliams's most recent book is *Ain't Nobody's Business If You Do: The Absurdity of Consensual Crimes in a Free Society* (1994).

When she returned from France, Bette was appropriately grateful to Russo for protecting her interests while she was gone, and her business relationship with Russo warmed up again. At the beginning of 1975, her thirtieth year, she returned from her self-imposed exile having sorted through many problems and feelings. Besides, her personality would not let her remain an expatriate from show business for too long. She drew strength and energy from the electric synergy she had with her audiences. Both she and Russo shifted focus away from the negatives such as *The Divine Miss J* to planning something positive for the now rested and eager Bette. It was important, Russo said, that Bette reassert herself in the public mind to mark dramatically that she was still the Divine and that she was back in town.

For a long time, ABC-TV had been talking about airing a Midler special without being able to work out anything that Bette liked. Vegas wanted the Divine Miss M back, as did tour promoters, Broadway show producers, and movies in the form of Robert Altman, who wished to sign her up for his movie *Nashville*, and another project for a film on the ill-fated life of Janis Joplin called *The Pearl*. The television and movie deals seemed like so much smoke and mirrors in that no one could actually explain the projects; Vegas audiences were too square; Broadway musicals were too rigidly structured; Russo didn't like the *Nashville* project and Bette didn't think *The Pearl* was right for her; and another tour would be exhausting. It ended up that for 1975 she would do an introductory guest shot on someone else's TV special. For the rest, she and Russo decided it was best to just let Bette be Bette—give her a mike, a spotlight, and a few thousand people and let the good times roll! That's what they did.

The television show they picked and that picked them was Cher's new weekly variety hour on Sunday nights, beginning February 16, 1975. Bette would appear as a guest on that premiere program, since it would have a huge audience, no matter if Cher was able to continue carrying the show from then on. Joining the spotlight with Cher and Bette were Elton John and the then-hot comedian Flip Wilson. The show was broadcast from Hollywood. Bette had to emerge from her cocoon on Barrow Street in the Village and fly to the West Coast for rehearsals and the taping. Upon arriving in L.A. from New York, she had to perform the ritual New Yorkers participate in when they visit Los Angeles—usually done shortly before they move to L.A. from New York—she had to denigrate the city.

"Hollywood!" she exclaimed. "It's a very strange atmosphere. I find it very amusing. It doesn't have the soul New York has. I couldn't live out there. I couldn't deal with that fierce competition of the lifestyle—not just the work, but who you're seen with and what you're wearing. That environment depresses me. Also, it seems that every asshole in the U.S. lives in Los Angeles. They have these little antennae that draw them to the West Coast!"

Bette and Aaron, of course, took advantage of their stay in Los Angeles to pay court to all those "assholes" in the hope that they could get Bette a good movie contract. They couldn't seem to make the right connection, because even though a number of producers and directors wanted her, just as with the television medium, the right vehicle seemed to elude her, or at least that was the view of Aaron Russo.

Russo rejected the famed Mike Nichols when he wanted Bette in his latest Warren Beatty and Jack Nicholson film, *The Fortune*, besides which Mike and Bette had a disastrous meeting at the Beverly Wilshire Hotel in Beverly Hills. Bette arrived late and agitated—she claimed that her masseur had tried to rape her in the shower just before she met with Nichols.

> I would have loved to work with Nicholson, but when I met Mike Nichols, I ended up insulting him because I had just been molested in the steam room at the Beverly Wilshire. I was staying there, and at the time, the masseur was the kind of guy who, if you wanted, would jump on your bones. I did not want that, but I guess he thought I needed to have my bones jumped on, because this guy came on to me and wouldn't let go.
>
> He threw me into the shower and started soaping me up. I was very frightened because I'd never had that happen to me before. I was terrified he was going to whip "it" out and whip it on me any minute. And I couldn't get away. The guy kept me there past my hour, making me late for my meeting with Nichols.

When Bette got back to her suite to meet Nichols, she was bewildered and, for a time, wasn't sure just who he was and what he had done. In fact, for reasons even she can't explain, her mind went blank and she couldn't remember his name at that moment. Nichols stood for her behavior only a few minutes and he left angry. He bad-mouthed Bette to his inner circle of powerful Hollywood friends. As it turned out, *The Fortune* fell on its face and lost a fortune.

Part of Russo's reasoning about a film for Bette was that, since she had never acted in a major film before, it would have been too intimidating for her to appear in tandem with Beatty and Nicholson, who were longtime successful screen veterans. Better for Bette to be in a movie and in a role in which she felt comfortable and that would allow her to make the transition to a new medium with its own special demands. Russo felt it would be ideal for Bette to be in a film where she was the essential core of the story and could put her imprint on the role she played in such a way as to permanently identify herself with that part, just as Basil Rathbone *became* Sherlock Holmes, Raymond Massey *became* Abraham Lincoln, and Vivien Leigh *became* Scarlett O'Hara in the public mind.

This was Russo's genius: he had an excellent sense of many of what he called "the right career moves" for Bette. He turned down roles for Bette in *Rocky, King Kong, Nashville,* and *Foul Play* because they were not the right roles for Bette. What Russo did see on the movie menu that he wanted for Bette was a Ross Hunter movie entitled *Little Me.* However, her appearance was precluded by Bette's self-inflicted wounds again because she had ridiculed Hunter publicly on several occasions and, not surprisingly, the director didn't like being disparaged. He refused to even consider Midler for any of his films. The time for Bette Midler, the movie star, had not yet come.

For now, in 1975, Russo believed Bette should return to Broadway, where she was comfortable, adored, and sensational. He did not think—nor did she—that it should be a scripted show and turned down an offer for her to do *Mack and Mabel,* among others presented to them. Russo already had it settled in his own mind that Bette needed to do another of her one-woman shows where she would be spectacular.

12

The Triumph of *Clams on the Half Shell*

Russo wisely decided on a one-woman show, a sure way to bring Bette back into the public eye. It was her best card and he was determined it would be played well. The genesis of the show title was a flippant remark Bette had made during an interview she gave to *Interview* magazine some months prior to her self-imposed exile. At the time, Bette had no specific plans for the future, so when the interviewer asked her what the future held, she made up the story that she was going to star in a fabulous Broadway show entitled *Dolores Jalapena's Clams on the Half Shell Review*. With that remark she left town and didn't think anything more about it.

However, Russo, planning her return, rented the Minskoff Theater on Broadway and set out a list of rehearsal and performance dates. As he had in the past, he was using one thing to build on another. For example, building on Bette's first public reappearance in almost a year on the Cher show that aired February 16, Russo staged a press conference a week later to announce Bette's triumphant return to the stage in April. The show's title had been altered to *Bette Midler's Clams on the Half Shell Revue*. Russo picked the one place passed by thousands of New Yorkers every working day and indelibly associated with seafood to hold the press conference announcing it: the Oyster Bar of Grand Central Station.

There was Bette chatting everybody up and schmoozing with

the reporters and the chef at the Oyster Bar, followed one week later by a full-page advertisement of the upcoming *Clams on the Half Shell* in the *New York Times*. If there was ever a doubt that Bette was the Queen of Broadway, it was instantly dispelled the very next day, when people were waiting in line all day at the Minskoff box office. Even though that first day in February was icy and rainy, the box-office took in a record-breaking $200,000, and the one-day sales record Bette broke was her own, the previous one-day sales record of $148,000 she had made at the Palace.

As Russo saw it, *Clams on the Half Shell Revue* would be basically Bette with her band, the Harlettes, and one other star, but whom? Midler chose the king of the vibraphone, Lionel Hampton, who had never performed on Broadway before but was famous everywhere else.

She said, "We wanted someone of his strength to work with me. He was willing and he was available. He wanted to open a new door, and here he is seventy years old opening new doors. He has more chops, more interest, more enthusiasm than most guys I know half his age. He just loves to work and so do I. This is a revue, a salute to Lionel and a salute to me. It's not just me anymore standing out there busting my butt. My girls are working: the Harlettes. And we have the Powell gospel group. We have a new dimension."

Russo and Bette started by assembling a first-rate production team under the aegis of director Joe Layton and set designer Tony Walton. Layton was a living concert legend with a shelf filled with awards and, most symbolic, the wildly successful Barbra Streisand TV special, *My Name Is Barbra*. Walton was equally acclaimed for his work with dance master Bob Fosse. Of course, Bette's old stand-bys, Bill Hennessey, Bruce Vilanch, and Jerry Blatt, were all part of the writing and production mix.

While Bette focused on the lyrical material for the show, Russo concentrated on something even more material for the show: money. With the lineup of Midler-Hampton-Layton-Walton, the next lineup for Russo was investors. His approach was tough. If you wanted part of this guaranteed-gold project, you had to be there quickly with checkbook in hand. Russo had hundreds of thousands of investors' dollars in the bank for *Clams on the Half Shell Revue* before he even issued the first news release that there would be a new Bette Midler revue running for ten weeks at the Minskoff Theater starting in April 1975.

He was determined that *Clams* would be a top-of-the-line showcase for Bette's return to Broadway, and Bette herself publicly reassured the awaiting audience. "Suffice it to say there will be lots of tits and ass," she said. "The sets are beautiful. The costumes are gorgeous. The sets are extremely gaudy and real expensive looking in a sleazy sort of way. People want color. They want explosion. It's pretty gray out there, so I give them an evening of color. The show is tight within an inch. There isn't a moment that's not choreographed!"

Russo's finesse and hype almost guaranteed success. *Clams* didn't open until April, but it was sold out by February, and here again Russo showed his skill. He controlled the sale of the tickets so that professional show business types and celebrities *did not* get preference for opening night or the early nights of the two-week run. Professional show business people and celebrities are not a normal audience, and they often come less to see and hear than to be seen and to be heard. They are putting on their own miniperformances while attending the show. Russo wanted to hype the opening nights of the show with Bette's regular, off-the-wall, knocked-out, always-in-love-with-Bette fans who would applaud and yell and scream and swoon at the sight of the Divine so that the press would pick that up and inflame every New Yorker with the uncontrollable need to see the show.

When *Clams* opened, it surpassed the expectation of Bette, Russo, the cast, the audience, and the critics. It was impossible to find anyone who did not love the show and adore Bette for her versatile talent. Bette was caught up in her own excitement of a production that she relished, "the most mind-boggling, stupendous production ever conceived and built around one poor small five-foot-one-and-a-half-inch Jewish girl from Honolulu. All of a sudden I'm a whole industry. People run, they fetch, they carry, they nail, they paint, they sew. I had always dressed my girls [the Harlettes] from stock and now here they are with real costumes. They're pinning here and tucking here and pushing tits up to the neck and showing calves. Do you know what this is? It's a celebration of the sexual rites of a New Yorker!"

The concept of the production as it evolved focused on Bette as a dramatically versatile performer. It also showed her off as spontaneous and reacting to the changing moods of different audiences night after night. So, while the show had to be structured to avoid chaos, it also allowed her flexibility to show her performing rock, pop, and nostalgia music with equal facility.

During the rehearsals, it quickly became apparent that there were literally good vibes between Lionel Hampton and Midler. Bette marveled at him practicing during rehearsals. "Look at Lionel out there. He says doing this show is a learning experience for him. I say it is for me. I have never dared to sing Hoagy Carmichael's 'Stardust.' Really it's a dream of mine, but now with Lionel playing 'Stardust' behind me, I'm doing it. We sound real good together. Wherever I go, he goes right along. You're really singing and it's a big challenge for me to keep up with him because he knows a helluva lot more about music than I do. My ears are opening up!"

On the night of April 14, 1975, the curtain ascended to the overture from *Oklahoma!* and moved to the cast on stage singing a rock rendition of "Old Man River" as Bette was pulled on the set riding in a huge clamshell and featuring her new, slimmed-down figure. She alit and yelled out, "I hope you enjoy this, because we have busted our buns for y'all."

Enjoy it they did, with uproarious laughter and bursts of applause throughout the show as Bette and the Harlettes sang gospel, rock, blues, forties pop numbers; made dirty jabs and puns; and poked fun at every icon, institution, and show business star you could think of. "Oh, listen, you must all rush out to McDonald's—they're featuring a new item on the menu. It's called the Hearst Burger—there's no patty!"

The first act featured Bette's trademark songs that she had been singing to the delight of her audiences from the Baths as well as new numbers she performed for the first time in this revue, including "The Bitch Is Back" by Elton John; Paul Simon's newest, "Gone at Last," and some of Billie Holiday's most notable, "We'll Be Together Again," "If Love Were All," and "Sentimental Journey."

The first act ended with a dramatic illusion created by bringing down one of the far-upstage curtains to reveal the New York skyline with the Empire State Building prominently displayed in the foreground, as seen in the classic picture showing King Kong clinging to the tower. The Harlettes were downstage singing "Optimistic Voices" from *The Wizard of Oz* and slipping in lines from "Lullaby of Broadway." In front of this eclectic extravaganza, a huge mechanical device made to look like King Kong's giant hand swung forward with the prostrate Bette sprawled in a nightgown and high-heeled slippers dangling over the edge. It appeared that Bette was asleep, but then, suddenly waking, she exclaimed, "Nicky Arnstein, Nicky Arnstein!" (he was Fanny Brice's boyfriend in *Funny Girl*) and immediately swung into a pounding rendition of "Lullaby of Broadway" with the full support of the Harlettes. It left the audience weak with laughter and an emotional high.

The second act opened in a way that had become traditional with Bette's show. It spotlighted the other key performer on a solo set of his own. She had done so with Barry Manilow and now she did it with Lionel, who was put in the setting of a giant jukebox with his vibraphone popping out several jazz numbers before Bette came on to join him for a medley of forties hits, "In the Mood," "How High the Moon," "Boogie Woogie Bugle Boy," and ending with Lionel's own "Flying Home."

In the show, Bette was not only the nutty Fay Wray dealing with King Kong, a swinging Joan of Arc, a satire of Barbra, Liza, Tiny Tim, Mae West, Tina Turner, Sophie Tucker, Janis Joplin, and Don Rickles, but she turned into a takeoff on Bette herself. One of her choice pieces was the sketch about her upcoming porno movie, which was a spoof of *Emmanuelle*, a real semiporno production in the art theaters during that era. Bette called hers *Temple Emmanuelle* and told the audience it was about a Jewish girl who was always on the make. All of this offbeat humorous material was accompanied with renditions of Billie Holiday's poignant blues. The revue ended with a full-voiced production of Bette and a gospel choir, the Michael Powell Ensemble, singing "Gone at Last."

It was an emotional ride that had the audience laughing, crying, joyous, and energized for three hours. When it was over, Bette, the Harlettes, the band, and the cast were exhausted, and so was the delighted audience. The critics, however, were not too exhausted to write rave reviews. "At long last a truly exciting musical," reported *Newsweek*. Rex Reed, Richard Goldstein, and Emory Lewis praised the show to the top of the proscenium arch and regretted that everyone in America wouldn't see *Clams*. Even the purist Clive Barnes, who objected to the gimmicks and would have preferred simple, straightforward musical performances, was forced to admit, "New York is still her town and she is still its best Bette."

Clams was an achievement of importance for Bette in many ways, some of them not apparent to the outside world. The show proved a financial success, grossing nearly $2 million, and what had originally been set as a four-week run was extended to ten weeks and sold out. It was a professional, popular, and critical triumph. All of that was clear to everyone.

What was not so clear, but was more important to Bette, was that this was *her* show. She had planned and executed it on her own and she had done it without Barry Manilow. That was really important to her in terms of certifying herself as a genuine talent. And, to ice the cake, her mother, Ruth, flew in from Hawaii so that she could see the way the crowds loved her daughter. It was a high point for both of them to share.

After the adrenaline rush of the show's opening was over, Aaron took the moment as the defining symbol of how important he was to her life. He had rescued her from the squalid Jesus film disaster and brought her back as the toast of Broadway, and now he presented her with an enormous engagement ring and his proposal of marriage. She rejected his proposal immediately, and that triggered another monumental Russo-Midler fight. The ugliness of this fracas underscored what had poisoned their personal relationship for too long. When it was over, Bette and her mother retreated to the famous Sardi's show business restaurant to await the early morning editions and read the reviews. The audience, the reviewers, and Bette all knew one thing for sure in the spring of 1975: The Divine Miss M was back in town!

13

1975–76—Depression
Over *Depression*

ater, when the personal hurt between the two was over toward
the end of 1975, Russo and Bette wanted to build on the excitement the New York media had generated with the glowing
reviews of *Clams on the Half Shell*. They decided Bette would spend
four months in 1976 touring a slimmed-down version of the show.

One important cast change came about when Robin Grean of
the Harlettes decided she had had enough of the road and left the
trio. As the word spread about the opening, scores of singers tried
out because it was a fabulous chance to join one of the most popular
concert production teams in the country. Bette finally chose Ula
Hedwig to join the backup trio. She had flown in from *Godspell* in
Chicago all taped up with a cracked rib. She was also a friend of
Charlotte Crossly, with whom she had worked in *Hair*.

Depression Tour was the name given to the twenty-city road show
and was similar to the name of the album Bette was also working
on for release in 1976, *Songs for the New Depression*. Its premise was
that people were depressed because things weren't going well in the
country. Nixon had become the first president in history to resign.
So Bette wanted to cheer them up and say everything would be okay.
Bette had been recording while she performed at night in *Clams*,
and some of those numbers have yet to be released because, for a
time, she was considering a Motown-focused album with the work-

ing title of *Miss M Goes Motown*. She worked with Motown producer Hal Davis on some of her songs, but the album never materialized. With nightly performances of *Clams*, record sessions during the day, and preparations for the road tour in process, the pressure and tension on Bette mounted.

The rehearsals for this show during the fall of 1975 were the most taxing of any Bette had undertaken so far. Some of the people who worked on the show said Bette wasn't certain she knew what she wanted or how to get it except through yelling a lot and rehearsing long hours. Such a regimen for some artists can be counterproductive, because the longer you rehearse, the harder it is to correct the mistakes you make. Aaron Russo didn't make it easier with his constant interruptions, and Bette kept losing her temper and ordering him out of the rehearsal hall.

Bette avoided interviews because she was tired of the stale questions reporters asked and she was getting a reputation for being a bitch. She finally did give an interview to *Playgirl* magazine and spoke about the bitch business:

"I'm a bitch in the sense that I like the wonderful things about being a bitch, but not the negative things. When I say 'bitch' I mean being on top of it, being aware and knowing the answers. I like that part. But I don't like doing it at the expense of other women. I don't like to sit around and dish the dirt with the girls. I think of it in terms of 'Do I know what I'm talking about?' or 'Do I not know what I'm talking about?' If I do know, then it doesn't matter if I'm a man or a woman. I have to know what I'm doing. If I don't, I'm going to get shit upon no matter what!"

The tension mounted and Bette's publicist, Candy Leigh, decided to leave because working conditions had become too unpleasant. She suggested to Russo that he run an advertisement for her replacement in the newspaper classifieds under the category of "masochist."

Bette also had mixed feelings about meeting and working with other superstars whom she had previously admired from afar and who now accepted her as a contemporary. She met and worked with Bob Dylan and Paul Simon with varied results. She thought Dylan was a kick because he tooled around in a huge red Cadillac. He was such a slight man that his size and the Cadillac's seemed hysterically incongruous.

She recorded the song "Gone at Last" with Paul Simon and was happy it was to be included in his upcoming album. However, when representatives of the two artists couldn't agree on how the song should be handled on the album, Simon solved the dispute by substituting a track by Phoebe Snow and dropping the track he did with Bette. Bette felt betrayed and the friendship between the two was ruined.

Then there was the hassle over "The Vickie Eydie Show," a new satire segment that Bette added to her road show and which caused hard feelings. The concept was created by Toby Stone and a group called Gotham, which one of Bette's writers, Bill Hennessey, managed. Bette met the group and learned about the parody Stone and the others did of a sleazy Vegas lounge singer. Bill Murray of *Saturday Night Live* also had a famous routine where he satirized a Vegas lounge singer.

Bette was entranced with the concept and asked Gotham's three male singers if she could use the routine. They gave her permission but no one mentioned it to Toby Stone, and Toby was angry when she found out Bette planned to copy it. It became part of Midler's new tour show and would remain in her repertoire from then on as "Vickie Eydie's Global Revue: Around the World in Eighty Ways," with the Harlettes renamed the Dazzling Eat-ettes.

All this and the pressure of putting the four-month, twenty-city tour show together in time for an opening just before Christmas got so bad that, when Bette was suddenly hospitalized with an appendicitis attack—on her thirtieth birthday—everyone was secretly relieved, because it gave the cast a break for a week or two.

The show's tour began December 21, 1975, in Berkeley, California, and stunned the newcomer to the cast, Ula Hedwig. "It was my first show with her. The curtain went up and I'll never forget that incredible cheering. I'd never heard anything like it before. I had tears in my eyes and I got the chills."

From Berkeley, they went to Los Angeles, and the rest of the tour became a triumph for the revitalized Midler, with audiences and critics thumbing through their thesauri to find synonyms for "fabulous." In Los Angeles she was feted with a massive celebrity turnout, including one night when Jane Fonda, then married to former Chicago Seven radical and now California state senator Tom Hayden, bought one thousand tickets for the purpose of hyping Hayden's political campaign for reelection.

Robert Hilburn, the respected music critic for the *Los Angeles Times*, praised the show and also went beyond the usual lavish adjectives to include an analysis of the artist's professional personage and interior life.

"Bette Midler is *back*," he began. "She has recaptured the spirit, purpose and innocence that made her such a captivating force in pop music when she arrived on the club scene in 1972." Referring to the *Depression* concert, he went on, "It was simply a stunning tour de force that left little doubt about who is the new queen of the concert-cabaret field in America."

That's the kind of review an artist wants to bronze and take home to keep. Hilburn went on to his analysis of what was going on inside the Divine. "The problem that surfaced as Midler's career progressed was that the Divine character began to smother Midler's own stage personality. Perhaps, it seemed for a while, Midler's main contribution would simply be the creation of the Divine. The triumph of Friday's show was that Midler has reestablished her own identity. She has once again become the star of her own show. And, she is more confident and daring a performer."

Nevertheless, with all her talent, Bette refused to learn from experience and continued to lapse into self-destructive adventures. The foolishness of her Lincoln Center New Year's Eve stunt of contemplating taping marijuana under each seat should have been etched into her memory. It wasn't, and during her Los Angeles appearance on another New Year's Eve in the staid Dorothy Chandler Pavilion, Bette almost blundered into the reefers-under-the-seat ploy again. Her rationale was that you had to do something special for the crowd on New Year's Eve and the California state legislature had reduced the severity of marijuana possession from a felony to a misdemeanor effective at one minute past midnight New Year's Day.

Still, anybody with more brains than the scarecrow in *The Wizard of Oz* would realize a terrific backlash might occur if 3,600 people lit up joints in the Dorothy Chandler Pavilion, where most of the audience's identity would be easy to trace because they charged their tickets with credit cards or paid by check. It was only after Russo and others around her got somebody from the district attorney's office to lecture her again that she relented.

So to captivate her fans that New Year's Eve, she again bared her impressive breasts. She appeared at the close of the show sitting topless in the hand of the giant King Kong prop. Bette later explained:

> At a New Year's Eve show, you have to do something. You have to have balloons or confetti—you have to have a surprise. And we had one, we were going to have joints, but somebody leaked the plan to the press, and the cops said, "No, that's not going to be your surprise." So at the last minute we couldn't do it. Oh, I was desperate. I kept hoping until the last minute that somebody would come up with another idea as marvelous as that, but when push came to shove, I realized it was up to me and what did this poor woman have to barter but her own body, the flesh of herself? So at the stroke of midnight, I duh-ropped my dress and exposed myself to 3,600 people. I don't think they even saw it, you know. It was just my little chest: nipples to the wind. When in doubt, go for the jugs!

After the show, Aaron Russo became angry and had a big fight with her over the breast baring. "Aaron *freaked* out, called me every name in the book," Bette said. Then Russo brought in several broadcast station executives, including Paul Drew, the main programming director from the RKO radio station chain, to meet the star. She was there with her new boyfriend, Hamish Stuart, from the Average White Band, who also recorded for Atlantic Records. Russo understood the RKO people had to be catered to because of the important role radio plays in selling record albums.

So, Bette asked, what did they think of her breasts? Well, they were sure they were nice, but they didn't think it was a great idea for a star to go topless like some desperate, struggling newcomer. Oh? Well, what did they think about her latest album, *Songs for the New Depression?* she asked. Paul Drew told Bette several times that he did not like her new album, until she finally lost it. "My heart was pounding," she later explained, "and I was so livid! The whole evening was just so *uggggh!* So I grabbed the record from his hand, broke it across my knee and smacked him in the face. What can I say? I'm sorry it happened, but that's showbiz."

It was not a pretty moment. Nor was the immediate boycott of Midler recordings on all RKO stations.

Her 1975–76 New Year's appearance at the Dorothy Chandler had not been a happy one, in spite of a smashing performance. She had been thwarted again with her reefer-under-the-seat gimmick, had felt the need to bare her breasts, had outraged Russo with that ploy and with her new boyfriend, and had assaulted an important radio station executive. Then, when she finally returned to her hotel, she discovered Russo had attempted suicide!

She described the painful scene. "When I got back to the hotel, I ran up to his room and banged on the door. 'Aaron, Aaron open up!' and from inside I heard 'Aaaahhhhhh.' He wouldn't let me in, so I had to run downstairs and get the concierge. I mean, my dear, this was drama. When we opened the door, there Aaron was, all two hundred pounds of him in his bathrobe, flat on the floor, with just me and this pissant concierge to drag him onto the bed. Lord, what a night that was!"

That's how 1976 began, and it didn't seem to get a whole lot better as it went along.

While her audience always seemed to love her live performances, they weren't always infatuated with her records. Her first two albums, produced by Barry Manilow, were successes. Her third album, released in February 1976, bombed, which was the source of a new depression for both Bette and Aaron Russo, even though a TV special for HBO and her latest tour did well.

Some thought the flop of *Songs for the New Depression* happened because radio station program directors didn't want to play Bette, thinking she was too campy and out of synch with mainline music.

Bette liked the album. "I thought 1974 and 1975 were a Depression. I thought it was the end of the world, so I was making a very whimsical, reactionary album."

Aaron would later say that he never liked the *Depression* album either. "I didn't care for it, didn't think it was something the public wanted to hear, and I didn't think they got the essence of Bette Midler on it."

Radio station programmers around the country agreed and decided they would not play it, and, of course, there was the boycott by the RKO stations. Obviously, radio play of the album would be critical because of the life-and-death relationship between recording companies and radio stations. If stations do not air your recorded songs, it is as if the songs don't exist, because no one hears them and, consequently, no one goes into stores to buy the album. Still, the alibi that it was the fault of mean or stubborn radio station programmers is too facile an explanation. The popularity of their radio stations depends on what they put on the air, and they happily broadcast Bette's previous two albums and turned them into profitable hits.

Why did the album fail? A simple explanation is that the winning albums were produced by Barry Manilow and the loser was not. Bette's new album failed to give listeners that same taste of Bette that they experienced hearing her live in concert. It was that authenticity Manilow brought to the albums he produced. Apparently, it was a genuineness that only he could capture on disk. It was Bette's first major failure in her career.

On February 15, seven of the Bette cast got arrested in Buffalo for cocaine and marijuana abuse in their Holiday Inn rooms. Russo said it was a Buffalo police scam, and Charlotte Crossly figured it was because Russo had failed to make the necessary payoffs. The charges were later reduced and the matter was quietly settled.

What wasn't quiet was the uproarious time Bette had several days later at Harvard when she was feted by the Hasty Pudding Club as Woman of the Year and given a gold Boston bean pot. Her acceptance speech was as tacky as desired by all the Harvard students in attendance. "I showered, shaved, and FDS'd myself into a stupor, just to get a crock? This award characterizes what the American male wants in a woman: brains, talent, and gorgeous tits."

Harold Banks of the *Boston Herald American* complained to his readers that he couldn't report accurately all that was said and done because it would never have gotten by his editors. Not the least of these activities included Bette mooning the members of the Hasty Pudding.

Early in 1976, Bette finally came to terms about a television special, but it wasn't with ABC, with whom she had been negotiating. She had been talking about a special, *Bette Midler—You Gotta Have Friends*, since 1973. She had originally planned to include Barry, Melissa Manchester, the Andrews Sisters, and the Pointer Sisters along with Manhattan Transfer in a show about friendships. But ABC never could make a deal, because the network wanted tight control over everything Bette said and did, and that wasn't her style. So she made arrangements with the Home Box Office, which was an operation more to her liking and more in step with her personality than the executives at the conventional TV networks.

Home Box Office was the accidental cable operation that Time, Inc., stumbled into through its ownership of Sterling Manhattan Cable system in New York City. In that era, Time, Inc., was dominated by men who took the train in from Connecticut each morning to Fifty-first Street and Sixth Avenue in Manhattan to pontificate about the ways of the world, primarily through *Time, Life,* and *Fortune* magazines. They neither understood nor cared about television, much less cable television, and at one point decided to sell Sterling Manhattan Cable and get out of TV entirely. However, they found they were legally unable to sell Sterling Manhattan under the terms of their franchise from the City of New York. So they turned the operation over to some people in the organization with the admonition that they should try to do something in hopes that it would someday break even.

The HBO idea for Sterling Manhattan Cable was born in 1972 from a proposal created by Charles Dolan on an ocean voyage to Europe with his wife, and it set forth the concepts that are still the foundations of cable TV networks today. Naturally, as with most visionaries, he was fired and his vision was turned over to other men who developed it. The key man in charge of the HBO effort, Gerry Levin, had spent much of his previous time building irrigation systems in Iran.

Dolan eventually became a cable TV multimillionaire after he founded Cablevisions Systems, now the fifth-largest cable company in the United States, with 2,582,600 subscribers and over $1 billion in annual revenue. Dolan pioneered the idea of regional sports networks and launched such cable channels as American Movie Classics, Bravo, and the SportsChannel. Outwardly congenial, he is a tough-as-nails negotiator whom one cable television executive has characterized as "Darth Vader dressed up in a Howdy Doody outfit." In the summer of 1994, Dolan's company achieved another business triumph when it took control of Madison Square Garden. Dolan's and Levin's different efforts evolved into Home Box Office, an operation staffed with a lot of young people who were willing to work cheaply and who were courageous enough to experiment with ideas the traditional TV executives avoided.

Before too long Home Box Office became the prime profit center for Time, Inc., accounting for almost 40 percent of the net income of the company, while the magazine division, *Time, Life, Money, Sports Illustrated,* and *Fortune* magazines et al., slipped to third place. In the early 1990s, Time merged with Warner Communications to become the biggest and most powerful communications and entertainment conglomerate in the world, under the leadership of the man who was largely responsible for the growth and success of Home Box Office, Gerry Levin.

Back in 1976, HBO was producing all kinds of innovative and marginal programs in search of what would attract customers willing to pay for a premium cable TV service. One of the programs HBO wanted to launch was Standing Room Only (SRO) in which they would duplicate the excitement of a live concert. HBO programmers intended to debut the series with a Bette Midler concert because her off-the-wall humor and singing talent appealed to the young staff at HBO. The writers, including Bruce Vilanch, toned down the sleaze but still filled the script with material that may not have been deep blue, but was at least powder blue. Bette decided she would be most comfortable singing the same material that made her the Divine Miss M at the Continental Baths. Bette and the cast taped the SRO show for HBO while on tour at the Cleveland Music Hall for three performances before a wildly enthusiastic live audience. This was followed by days of editing to achieve the "live" quality they wanted for the airing in June of 1976.

The show was a classic performance of what Bette did in most of her stage appearances produced by Aaron Russo. She opened in a setting showing her in a hospital bed and then moved into an upbeat version of one her signature songs, "Friends," backed by the driving Harlettes and Bette's band. Then she segued into her opening monologue for her enthusiastic audience.

"Now, this hospital motif was suggested to me by my recent stay in a very plush Beverly Hills medical center. Now, many of you may have heard that I was stricken with appendicitis, but I am here to tell you the truth, Cleveland, and that is that, in a spasm of sisterly generosity, I donated my tits to Cher."

In her tag line she said Cher was elated to get them, and then she explained the effort she and Harlettes had made for this Cleveland and HBO audience. She explained how they had washed and groomed themselves by spraying themselves with Feminine Deodorant Spray (FDS), a popular product at the time, all to cheer everybody up. Then she swung into a strong, up-tempo production of "Bang You're Dead," followed by her interpretation of the Neil Young song "Birds." This was followed by another comedy routine, in which she said she was going to do a sequel to the erotic movie *Emmanuelle*, called *Temple Emmanuelle*, in which there was a lot of kissing of mezuzahs (a tube containing a household blessing that many Jews attach to the front door of their home). She also noted that, in her film, a woman had an unspeakable liaison with a kreplach (a turnover or dough pocket with chopped chicken liver or other filling served in soup).

She next went into a play on the word *kreplach*, saying it was a person who lived in a small Baltic country and that, occasionally, a kreplach escapes to the West. She poked fun at the girls who backed her up as the Harlettes. Then, Bette and the Harlettes moved into the old Glenn Miller standard, "In the Mood," with the audience clapping to the beat, followed by the classic "Hurry on Down to My House, Baby" and "Shiver Me Timbers."

Coming out of that medley she talked about a dream she had of what she might have become had she not "been blessed with brains, talent, and gorgeous tits." Then Bette and the Harlettes reverted to themselves and wrapped up the first half of the performance with that Bette standard, "Lullaby of Broadway."

Bette opened the second half of the show with her rollicking rhythm-and-blues version of "Delta Dawn," about a woman who lost her mind because her man deserted her after promising to marry her and take her to his mansion in the sky. From there she took the audience with her to a breathy visit with her favorite dentist, Dr. Long John, who thrilled her when he drilled her in a double entendre lyric that titillated the audience.

She switched from storytelling mode to some of Sophie Tucker's best anecdotes, with Sophie saying, "I will never forget it. It was on the occasion of Ernie's eightieth birthday. And, in honor of the occasion, he married a twenty-year-old girl, and he rang me up the very next day and he said, 'Soph, Soph, I have just married myself a twenty-year-old girl. What do you think of that?'

"And I said to him, 'Ernie, when I am eighty years old, I shall marry myself a twenty-year-old boy. And, let me tell you something, Ernie, twenty goes into eighty a helluva lot more than eighty goes into twenty. So, kiss my tuckus and plant a tree for Israel.' "

And another Sophie Tucker story:

"I was in bed last night with my boyfriend, Ernie. And, he said to me, 'Soph, you got no tits and a tight box.' I said to him, 'Ernie, get off my back.' "

Then, from the outrageously boisterous, she went into her parody of a lighthearted French air, "The Story of Nanette," and "Alabama Song" and the sad ballad, "Drinking Again," that had the audience rapt, silent, and filled with its collective memory of a broken love affair.

This was followed with a funny story about seeing a lady on Forty-second Street with a fried egg on her head that led into a poignant song about aging and growing lonely and isolated from each other and how each of us has something inside—each of us has our own fried egg—and we need to say "Hello in there" to each other.

Next, the driving beat by Mr. Don York and the New York Tones in the joyous, toe-tapping "Up the Ladder to the Roof (Where We Can See Heaven Much Better)" melded into a rollicking Midler signature song, "Boogie Woogie Bugle Boy." The emotional, blood-racing evening ended with the Divine Miss M singing her traditional "Friends" to a standing ovation from her adoring fans.

The HBO show aired June 19, 1976, and attracted a lot of viewers and new subscribers, which is what HBO wanted. It may have surprised some who had only heard about Bette, listened to her albums, or seen her on *The Tonight Show*. They probably tuned in for the music and got something they hadn't counted on. The show went over well and inspired George Maskian of the New York *Daily News* to urge his readers to "rush on down to the nearest bar, or a friend's house, anyone who has Home Box Office, and see the sensation of the seventies. Miss M really doesn't have to rely on the risqué. Her other talents are too vast and great. She's Martha Raye, Carmen Miranda, Fanny Brice, and Judy Garland all rolled into one. To sum up, Bette is a wow!"

Ironically, the *Depression* tour ended in Bette's least favorite show town, Las Vegas, where Aaron had booked it because playing there meant a lot of money. If Bette didn't like Las Vegas audiences, the audiences returned the favor, and the show was uninspired except for one segment that the audience loved. It was Vickie Eydie's Global Revue: Around the World in Eighty Ways. The joke about Vickie Eydie's Global Revue is that Bette and her cast were performing it as satire, but the audience took it seriously because that was the kind of entertainment they came to Vegas to experience!

It had been a roller-coaster three years: 1974 was the year of the Big Bette Exile; 1975, the year of the Reincarnation of Broadway Bette; and 1976, the year of the Bummed-Out Bette, with the reefer flap, the RKO radio boycott, the band getting busted for dope, the uneven road tour, the successful HBO TV show, and the album that bombed. And she had lost an appendix too.

Meanwhile, Bette continued to believe in and be grateful for Russo's dedication to her. "I consider myself lucky because he pays a lot of attention to me," she said. "He doesn't have any other clients, and he thinks I'm the greatest thing on God's green earth. I could go on forever with what he's built for me. That's what Aaron has given me, so I consider myself not only lucky but blessed."

Bette Midler with Benoit, her live-in boyfriend at the time, as they leave the off-Broadway hit, *Little Shop of Horrors*. When this picture was taken, Benoit, at first, was angry and cursed the photographer and chased him up the street threatening to break his leg. This was at the time Bette was appearing in five standing-room-only concerts of "De Tour Tour" at Radio City Music Hall in March 1983. (*David McGough/DMI*)

Bette attending the premiere of her film *Down and Out in Beverly Hills* at the Museum of Modern Art in Manhattan on January 22, 1986, accompanied by teen idol Matt Dillon. (*David McGough/DMI*)

Bette and husband Martin von Haselberg at the Live Aid concert held at Philadelphia's John F. Kennedy Stadium. Bette served as a host for the concert, announcing many of the groups. July 13, 1985. (*David McGough/DMI*)

Bette Midler after receiving her own star on Hollywood Boulevard,
February 6, 1986. (*Kevin Winter/DMI*)

Bette Midler, in a scene from her movie
Ruthless People, riding a stationary
bicycle to lose weight. She costarred
with Danny DeVito in this 1986 film.
(*Sygma*)

Bette with baby. Rare photo
of Bette pregnant with her
daughter Sophie, attending a
Democratic Party fund-raiser
at the home of Barbra
Streisand. Sophie was born
November 14, 1986. (*AP/Wide
World Photos*)

After a classic luncheon meeting of three ladies of comedy, Bette
Midler (*left*), Lucille Ball (*center*), and Lily Tomlin (*right*) leave Chasen's
Restaurant in Beverly Hills, May 29, 1987. (*Kevin Winter/DMI*)

Bette Midler and her husband Martin von Haselberg attending the opening night of Le Cirque du Soleil. Martin sports one of his favorite haircuts, which Bette hates. (*Kevin Winter/DMI*)

Bette with Iris Rainier Dart, author of *Beaches*, celebrating the screening of the film based on Ms. Dart's book. (*Peter C. Borsari*)

Bette Midler with her husband and their daughter, attending an
Elizabeth Taylor party in honor of Roddy McDowall, October 23,
1989. (*Kevin Winter/DMI*)

Bette laughs at some material she has read in the courtroom from the script of *For the Boys* in a lawsuit brought by Martha Raye, charging Bette and others with stealing Raye's life story. Bette won the suit and Raye died soon after—a bitter and broken woman. (*AP/Wide World Photos*)

14

1977—The Year of Television

The year 1977 would prove as bewildering as 1976 had been, but it certainly had some interesting high points: a hot new love affair for Bette; a fight with her longtime backup singers, the Harlettes; a giant disaster at the Hollywood Bowl; a great new tour playing to an old audience—intimate clubs; a new record album; and Bette's initiation into another medium, general network television.

It would also be the year that Bette would say something out loud that she had been thinking about for a time. She wanted to do movies. "I'd like to become a great actress," she said while she was touring with her *Depression* road show. "I'd like to do a comedy full of whimsy. I'd like to make the perfect comedy, the perfect musical, and the perfect melodrama." That time would come later. Nineteen seventy-seven would be her television year instead.

With no new record albums or offers to make films, Russo shifted his attention to television again, since the HBO SRO premiere had done so well. He was still enamored of Bette, but she limited his control of her life to outside the bedroom. For inside the bedroom, Bette had found actor Peter Riegert, and it was a dream discovery even if the details of their first meeting are garbled. One version says Bette met Peter in Chicago during a visit to her friend F. Murray Abraham in October 1976. Murray brought her together with Peter, and she was immediately drawn to his mind and the work he had done as a teacher, social worker, and political operative for the brash New York congresswoman Bella Abzug.

Some of the less charitable claimed that what drew Bette to Peter was not his mind but, rather, the male physical asset he displayed in a nude poster he made to publicize the show *Sexual Perversity in Chicago*, an Off-Broadway hit in the Cherry Lane Theater in New York in early 1977. After witnessing his performance from the audience, she went backstage to say hello to him, they had drinks together, and next they were living together.

This time Bette was really smitten, with a man she described as having "this beautiful face and this great body and these gorgeous eyes and this wonderful manner. I'm having a ball right now. I wake up and have to pinch myself all the time. I can't believe it."

Neither could her friends and colleagues, who discovered a new, serene, laid-back Bette who didn't fly off the handle or yell at people—she was a woman in love. It was one of those seamless relationships where two people who haven't ever known each other before come together to make a perfect fit. It was as if they had grown up together in the same family and had the same tastes, the same interests, and the same idiosyncrasies. Bette was now over thirty, Peter was a wonderful man, unlike any she had experienced before, and it was quite natural that marriage crossed her mind— more than once.

She tried to keep the affair secret for fear that too much public attention would frighten Peter away, but that was like trying to ignore a giraffe in the living room—it was there and it had to be acknowledged, as Bette finally did.

"Peter is the first man I've really felt this way about, been able to be myself with," she confessed. "I've got all these crazy characters living inside of me and I always have to act them out. Most people think I'm nuts. Not Peter. He has his own set of characters. We give each other a show every night till we collapse about four in the morning. It's great!"

While Peter kept Bette occupied behind closed doors, Aaron worked on getting Bette before the cameras in two television appearances by booking her on a Bing Crosby special and a *Rolling*

Stone tenth anniversary special. The objective was to convince the broadcast networks that Bette was a mainstream star, appealing to average Americans, so that they would give her a special of her own. No one would quarrel that Bing Crosby was as Middle American as one could get, and it was a perfect match because Bette was a living version of one of Bing's most popular World War II contemporaries, the Andrews Sisters—Patty, Maxene, and Laverne. And the *Rolling Stone* show was contemporary enough to show Bette's range. To do the show, Bette moved to Southern California in February 1977, where she had to live if she was serious about appearing in movies.

Her appearance on the Crosby show displayed a very toned-down Bette melding right in with the crooner and trading little quips as America expected. The two sang "Accentuate the Positive" and "Glow Worm" together, causing Bing to ask how she knew the words of those old songs, to which Bette replied she knew the words to a lot of old songs. In fact, she said, she knew songs that were written at the turn of the century, and Bing replied he knew people who were born at the turn of the century.

All in all, it was a pleasant program in the Crosby mold. A little while later, Bette learned that she had unconsciously made a family breakthrough: Her father had watched the show along with her mother in Hawaii. Her father figured if she was on the Crosby show, it couldn't be too bad, and it wasn't. This was the only time in his entire life that Fred Midler ever saw his daughter perform.

Just before the airing of the Crosby special, Atlantic Records announced it would soon release another Bette album, the fourth one, based on what had been taped at the Cleveland Music Hall performance for the HBO special the year before and entitled *Live at Last*. The announcement told the world that this would be "the necessary step in her recording career—bridging the gap between studio and stage." The bridging of that gap wasn't quite made in this album, because the quality of the recordings at the Cleveland Music Hall appearance was not good enough. So Bette had to re-record some of her numbers in the Atlantic studios.

They also added a song that had not been performed in Cleveland, "Bang, You're Dead," and dropped "I Sold My Heart to the Junkman." The reason for the substitution was political and personal, not musical. Bette liked "Bang, You're Dead" but hadn't been able to do a recording of it, and the authors, Nick Ashford and Valerie Simpson, laid down an ultimatum that she immediately release it on a recording or they would give it to another singer to do, so it was squeezed into *Live at Last*.

The album was finally released in June 1977, and, while it wouldn't do as well as either of her first two blockbuster albums, *Live at Last* performed a lot better than the ill-fated *Depression* release. Critics gave her good reviews for her style, delivery, and humor.

Robert Hilburn said, "*Live at Last* finally documents on record the captivating spirit and enormous talent that Midler has long exhibited on stage." That view was echoed by Frank Rose of the *Village Voice*, who talked about her style and humor and concluded that the set was a sensational performance. He declared, "This double album catches Bette at the best when she is working a crowd, milking it for laughter, delight and applause. Her singing here has a limpid, liquid quality that never made it onto her previous recordings. She sounds spontaneous, eager and breathless."

Beyond the *Village Voice* praise, the *Los Angeles Times* pronounced Midler as being even superior to Barbra Streisand or Liza Minnelli in her range and vision, and *People* magazine said, "She is a showplace of exhausting versatility, singing, dancing; she brings [the] Standing Room Only house to their feet night after night."

These opinions recognized what was true of Bette Midler all along, namely that she was not a niche performer, but a multitalented woman with an expansive and versatile range rare in the entertainment business. She was on her way to do another album, a TV special of her own, and another club tour, but a fiasco intervened first on September 18 when she did a disastrous appearance at the Hollywood Bowl. It was a benefit that drew an audience of seventeen thousand. The program collapsed after comedian Richard Pryor decided to lecture the audience about racism. It was a show that Aaron Russo worked hard to produce and one that he would rather forget ever happened now.

The show also depressed Bette. "That sorry business brought me so far down. I've thought and thought about it, and I'm still not sure what happened that night." It was a valiant try by Aaron to do something worthwhile, but circumstances turned it and him sour on these kinds of projects. So he pushed forward with what he did well: promoting and managing Bette.

Broad mass media and smaller, more intimate appearances worked best for Bette in 1977. She had appeared as a guest on the Crosby show, which pulled her closer to mainstream America in the public mind. She had also done the HBO special, *Ol' Red Head Is Back* for NBC, and a piece on the *Rolling Stone: The Tenth Anniversary* TV special. She was getting good acceptance on the mass medium of television.

In the fall of 1977, she did something she really loved—she toured, and Russo felt it was good for her publicly and personally. She appeared in intimate clubs around the country, including many in which she had performed during her earlier days, even though playing small clubs did not make her as much money. Their environment was an ideal one for Bette because she had an instinctive feel for audience reaction. She demonstrated that awareness from the beginning of her professional career in New York at the Baths, the Downstairs, and the Bitter End.

As Russo assessed it, "The clubs were a natural. That's really her milieu. She really comes alive on stage. Other things add to the excitement." They included the repeat customers and the word of mouth that permeated a community when Bette was known to be appearing at a particular club for a week or more. People returned with their friends to become solid fans who then bought her record albums. About this time, she was also working on her next album, called *Broken Blossom*. So from the end of 1977 to the beginning of 1978—November to January—Bette had three things going: a new album, a TV special, and the small club tour.

The work on *Broken Blossom* was uneven under producer Brooks Arthur, and the mixture of songs was, as usual, eclectic, including those of Edith Piaf, Billy Joel, and Bessie Smith. The uneven work produced an uneven album that did not do well on radio station play or in record store sales, but that failure was offset by the success of Midler's December 7 TV special, *Ol' Red Head Is Back*. The strong rating from the Bing Crosby show in March produced the magic numbers that the network executives loved and convinced NBC to give Bette the special Russo had been lobbying them for over those many months.

Bette planned and rehearsed for the show very carefully, and Russo saw that everything was as perfect as he could make it, because this first Bette special on a major network could make money at many levels. They would earn money from the NBC special itself, but, more important, it would broaden Bette's appeal all over the country and produce bigger album sales and larger audiences when she went on tour. In sum, the NBC special was a gigantic commercial for Bette that would pay off over and over again.

Ol' Red Head Is Back was a steal from Sinatra's specials, *Old Blue Eyes Is Back*. Bette toned down the brassy raucousness of her act and shifted to a more casual and intimate approach, like Sinatra's. She had to overcome the sleazy, trashy image in order to connect with Middle America. The executives at NBC watching from the control booth were terrified she would say "fuck" on air. She did—in a very deft way. She cleaned up the act, toning down the language, with "the girls FDSing themselves into a stupor" becoming "the girls gargled themselves into a stupor," and "We're going to shake our tits for you tonight" becoming "We're going to shake everything we own for you tonight."

Still, the sexual overtones were there, thus maintaining the Midler flavor. She urged the Harlettes to try staying vertical at least until the first commerical, and when she ended up her rendition of "In the Mood" lying on her back on the floor, she slyly commented to the camera, "My favorite position. How does Marie Osmond do it?" Her special had a Sophie Tucker–Mae West quality, as, for example, when she told the audience that this was going to be a serious, cultural show exploring the nature of truth (pointing to one of her ample breasts) and the nature of beauty (pointing to her other ample breast).

Instead of coming on stage and *being* sleazy and trashy, Bette came on stage and conveyed the impression that she was *acting* sleazy and trashy—that she was really just a nice, talented singer who had to play a role. Helping her along was guest star Dustin Hoffman, who displayed a musical talent that most of the public never knew he possessed as he and Bette sang a duet of songs they had composed together and he played Rachmaninoff's *Prelude in C-Sharp Minor* on the concert piano. It worked and the show was a big success, which made Bette feel good about herself because she was being accepted by the ordinary people whom she wanted to win over.

Television, record albums, movies, tours—all that was wonderful, but what Bette really loved was the noisy, hot, sweaty intimacy of clubs, and that was the kind of tour Aaron arranged for her in the fall of 1977. The club tour of 1977–78, *An Intimate Evening With Bette*, began with an out-of-town warm-up at the Cave in Vancouver, moved from there through Bimbo's in San Francisco, the Roxy in Los Angeles, the Park West in Chicago, and the Paradise in Boston, and ended in New York at the Copacabana.

In order to get the Harlettes—Sharon Reed, Ula Hedwig, and Charlotte Crossly—to make the tour, a compromise was worked out because Russo had previously threatened them with massive lawsuits when they went off on their own between Midler projects using the name the Harlettes. Since the name had never been protected legally, Russo was leaning on a weak reed with his threat of legal action. But he had made life unpleasant for the three women, and they were reluctant to come back into the Midler-Russo camp. They finally put Russo's fury behind them, and the tour went on as planned.

The enthusiastic and loving rapport between Bette and her aficionados was evident at every stop with performances making a respectable amount of money, with almost a third of a million dollars coming in from the San Francisco and Los Angeles appearances alone. Beyond that, scalpers, who are good judges of the popularity of a performance or football game, were raking in the money, charging six to seven times the face price of a fifteen-dollar ticket to one of Bette's appearances.

At the Roxy in Hollywood, Bette chatted up her audience as usual. "I just love El Lay. You can always tell when you're approaching it, because of the sound of a hundred thousand blow-dryers wafting across the Hollywood Freeway. I moved here not too long back. I keep going over to Tower Records to move all my albums from the Pop bin—where they rest next to Liza Minnelli—and put them in the rock bin, next to Joni Mitchell. I moved here because I wanted to break into the movies."

A flip remark that would carry more and more truth with it in the years ahead, because Bette had proved her talent was transportable—she could do small clubs, stage plays, musicals, concerts, record albums, and television. The only major medium left for her to conquer was films, and she had had only two experiences in that medium, the bit part in *Hawaii* that indirectly launched her career in New York and the disastrous cheapo satire of Jesus Christ that almost torpedoed her career in New York.

The ever present critic Robert Hilburn had become totally captivated by Bette over the years, and after seeing and hearing her at the Roxy on this tour, he surrendered completely:

"I know the critic's handbook says avoid absolutes, but there's no way around it this time. Bette Midler is the *best*. No other female performer has the range, vitality or ultimately the emotional impact. The only reason 'female' is used is that I haven't seen all the male contenders. But my suspicion is that it's an unnecessary qualification. As with all good performers, Midler responds to her audiences. At the Roxy, the audience kept up with her. Rather than working to keep the audience alert, she was free to explore and maneuver. From the music to the jokes, the 90-minute set was crisply paced and strikingly executed."

While she was on tour, NBC aired her special, *Ol' Red Head is Back*. It scored big in the Nielsen ratings, which made the network very happy. A few months later she would garner the Emmy for Outstanding Variety Special of the 1977–78 season. The special also paved the way for her to do more television and, as she became more mainstream, national exposure would ultimately turn her into a good movie property, since movies today are promoted less on the intelligence and meaning of a great story or concept and more on who stars in them. That is what the term "bankable" means in Hollywood. (There are exceptions, such as films made by the Disney Studio or directed by Woody Allen or Steven Spielberg.) Building public recognition and acceptance are the first steps to being bankable, and Bette was taking those steps.

15

1978 and Bette's Major Film Debut

ette's tour ended in the city that loved her, New York, with an appearance in January 1978 at the fabled Copacabana. New Yorkers responded with wild enthusiasm, paying the twenty-dollar cover charge and stratospheric prices for liquor to jam the place with almost twice as many people as were ordinarily allowed in the club. Columnist Rex Reed, a great Midler fan, reported:

> It wasn't just crowded, it was miserable. Mobs pushed, shoved and groped their way along the narrow stairs in reckless disregard of the fire regulations. My seats were so lousy that I could hardly see the backside of her left earlobe without a mariner's telescope. Sweat poured down our faces and the smell was indescribable in a morning newspaper.
>
> Was it worth it? Well, it all depends on where you place your Bettes. I thought the girl was stupendous. Few contemporary performers could hold and electrify an audience under such intolerable conditions. For any act of less magic and magnitude, I would have walked out. Instead, Bette didn't get off until almost three A.M. and I stayed to revel in every delicious moment of her irreverence and showmanship.

Her NBC special had pleased Middle American viewers who watched Bette playact the trashy broad. In contrast, New Yorkers came to see a real trashy broad. Bette didn't disappoint them, from the first words she spoke to open the show. Thrusting her torso forward, she announced to the delirious one thousand people in the Copa, "I stand before you nipples to the wind."

It went on rocking and raw from there, every night for two weeks, including the night of January 20, 1978, when the city was almost paralyzed by a huge storm that dropped thirteen inches of snow on Manhattan. Undaunted, both Bette and her fans showed up at the Copa, where Bette philosophized, "They promised us five inches and gave us thirteen. If life were only like that."

But the show's run finally ended, and the cast broke up to go their separate ways. The three Harlettes would never again perform under that name, and left hating Russo just as much as they had before.

"Aaron's not one of my favorite people," Ula said. "I wish Bette would break up with him. I think he's making her untouchable. Whenever he wasn't around, we had a really good time together. We hung out together, we bowled, and we'd stay at the same hotel. But whenever he was there, she'd be whisked away to the best hotel in town and we'd never see her. He'd never let anybody get close to her. He just sort of scares away her friends."

There were two major men in Bette's life at the time: One made her feel happy and the other made her angry. Peter Riegert was her lover in private, and Aaron Russo was her manager in public. The Harlettes and other cast and crew members loved Peter because he made their lives easier by keeping Bette serene, while Russo could drive her nuts. Yet, Russo had good business sense, and he was focusing on club dates at this point. Club dates were Bette's favorites because they were relatively intimate—if you can call one thousand people "intimate"—and more spontaneous and energizing. Concerts and concert tours were exhausting, but needed to be done regularly to help promote record albums. Bette made two albums in 1977, *Broken Blossom* and *Live at Last*, and neither did well in the stores. Bette thought that the albums' lack of success was only a part of a run of bad luck—her apartment was broken into while she and Peter were sleeping, the recording studio owner drowned in his own swimming pool, and one of Bette's best friends, songwriter Carole Bayer Sager, was hurt in a car accident.

Beyond that, there were production problems, and creating *Broken Blossom* was strung out over nine months before it was ready to release. When it was released, reviewer Steven Gaines wrote, "*Broken Blossom* is Bette Midler's clearest, most striking album, with vocals worthy of Streisand backed by the superb production of Brooks Arthur." In contrast, Robert Stephen Spitz declared, "*Broken Blossom* is, as the Divine Miss M would say, the bottomless pits. What she has so shrewdly cultivated in the past—the essential emotion of the vocalist—is missing completely. Instead, we are mistreated to naked songs lacking the substance supplied by the interpreter. That's not Bette's style and the rest of the ingredients are too thin to slide the album by."

Bette needed to do something to improve the sales of her albums and to keep in the public eye. Russo was considering two options in 1978: a big tour or a big movie. Aaron could arrange the tour but not the film, until Bette looked again at the script of a thinly disguised movie about Janis Joplin.

Janis Joplin was a legendary rock and blues singer who stunned the audience at the 1967 Monterey Pop Festival with the fury and fire of her singing as part of the rock group Big Brother and the Holding Company. During the next three years, she went solo and became a cult idol noted for the sexual fervor of her performance. Her recording of "Me and Bobby McGee" became wildly popular and originated a phrase that is now part of the American lexicon, "Freedom means nothing left to lose." She was constantly in abusive, exploitive relationships with her parents, her manager, her lovers, and herself. She abused alcohol and drugs with abandon, and on the night of October 4, 1970, she died on stage in concert from a heroin overdose before her adoring fans.

The story of this tragic figure from American popular music had been passed around Hollywood for at least five years under the title *The Pearl*, and from the start, Bette played a role in the fate of the movie. At the start of the project, in 1973, when it was in the hands of producer Marvin Worth at Twentieth Century Fox, Bette was offered the Joplin role, and she rejected the part because it struck her as insensitive that a movie would be rushed into production so soon after Joplin died.

She said later, "It was first sent to me not long after Janis passed away. I thought it was in very bad taste to send the script to anyone. It was like dancing on someone's grave before the body was cold. To be blunt, I didn't like it very much. By '75 or '76 we [she and Aaron] were at Columbia trying to tailor-make a screenplay and having very little luck, mostly because the writers were unfamiliar with my work or I didn't communicate with them. This script [the one about Janis Joplin] kept coming back like clockwork. Eventually, I sat down and reread it and it wasn't bad. It's not exactly the strongest plot in the whole world, but for a performer like me, it had a big emotional range and I was interested in range."

Bette and Aaron eventually left the Columbia lot and, in reviewing what they were seeking as a movie venue, concluded that *The Pearl*, which by 1978 had been renamed *The Rose*, was looking better and better. Bette said at last, "*The Rose* was the one script we'd been offered in all those years that was a real big part and real big good part." Aaron was also taken by the appropriateness of the script for Bette's talents and continued to urge her to take it. Bette ultimately agreed, but only if there could be some changes in the plot. "I'd like to keep this person a rock-and-roll singer," she told Aaron, "and I would like to keep the sorrow and a certain amount of self-hate, this constant seeking of hers for approbation. Everything else has to go."

Coincidentally, it was also in 1973 that the Joplin project was first offered to director Mark Rydell, who had made several successful movies, including *The Fox*, *The Reivers*, and *The Cowboys*, and now wanted to direct *The Pearl*. Rydell's immediate assessment of the project was that Bette was the only one who could play Joplin in a convincing way and do the creative side of the role as Joplin would have done it. "I wanted to use Bette Midler, but at that time the studio didn't appreciate my suggestion. So I passed." The studio gave it to Ken Russell instead. That meant the movie was in limbo, because Russell did nothing with it.

Finally, in 1977, the Joplin project went back to the only director who had been serious about it all along, Mark Rydell. It was renamed *The Rose*, and Rydell and his script writers, Bo Goldman and Bill Kerby, carefully reworked it so the film would convey the pathos that was Janis Joplin as well as the pain and hunger of her voice, which epitomized the 1960s rock generation. As Rydell himself said, "We wanted to reveal some of the heroism of virtuosity. There's a price that people who are that gifted pay. It's a kind of deep hunger that's hard to satisfy." This time Rydell offered the role to Bette and she took it.

The good publicity from Bette and the picture began on April 24, 1978, the very first day of the twelve-week shooting schedule. Thousands of spectators congregated at location sites around Manhattan to watch one of their favorite live singers play one of their favorite dead singers. The concept of the film was to focus on the last eight days in the life of a talented, insecure female singer with a domineering, manipulative manager. It was a story in film that came close to the story in real life of Bette and Aaron. Many people thought so, including Bette. In an amazingly frank recognition of her relationship with Russo, Midler confessed some time later after she and Russo had separated, "Our relationship was so much sicker than anything in that film. He did things that were much worse. He made my personal life so miserable that I became nonfunctional from 1973 on."

After the New York location scenes were filmed, the crew moved to Los Angeles and Long Beach, where several live concerts became the centerpieces of the movie and the story, because this film was a biography of the music as well as a performer. To ensure that the music scenes succeeded, Rydell brought in Paul Rothchild as musical director. Rothchild had been Janis's record producer. He assembled a group of rock musicians: Robbie Buchanan, Norton Buffalo, Whitey Glan, Steven Hunter, Jerry Joumonville, Mark Leonard, and Mark Underwood, and Danny Weiss for the film concert orchestra.

Then they gave live concerts before paying audiences at the Wiltern Theater in Los Angeles and the Long Beach Veterans Memorial Stadium. The audiences cooperated by dressing up in the

1969 style of fashion. The people who attended the concerts were told, "Since the sequence takes place in 1969, would you please dress as close to that style as possible. If you forget, it was the time of blue jeans and denim jackets, army coats and workshirts, pea jackets and Pendletons and T-shirts. Headbands, fringed jackets, and Indian vests were also a sign of those times."

The audiences were transported to another time and place as they got caught up in the hard-driving rhythms of blues songs even if Bette had to sing them over and over to satisfy the director, the film crew, and herself. Although the audiences spontaneously chanted about sex and drugs, they also chanted "Rose, Rose, Rose" on cue for the director, since he needed that response on film.

Bette sang like Joplin and not Midler, because Rydell insisted that she get into the character's voice and mind. Rydell would later say, "All that applause [in the film] is earned. It took a lot of daring for Bette to walk out there and introduce a whole new style. She actually prepared a new style of singing. Her regular fans are not going to expect what they see. I personally think the change will prove to be one of her more courageous career moves."

In this role, Bette was melding her kind of Method singing into a powerful motion picture performance that had a texture most viewers responded to emotionally without realizing how she managed to produce it. She said:

> I didn't want to concentrate on Janis. I avoided Janis because I didn't feel I could do justice to her. I adore her and I had seen her work live and she really changed my life. She changed a lot of people's lives. I think women were particularly moved by her because she was aggressive and yet she seemed vulnerable. I really adored her and I didn't want to use her to further my own particular aims. I have a certain ethical code that I try to work by. The character in the film has a little bit of everybody in it. Physically there is a lot more of men than there is of women in it. The men tend to strut and tend to get into the gymnastics of rock and roll. I did a lot of dieting and I worked in a gym a lot. I listened to Sam Cooke till my ears were bleeding, did a lot

of reading about the sixties, watched a few videotapes and talked to some people. I did it all. I actually spent a good six months on it."

Sam Cooke was the father of soul music who died tragically and prematurely December 11, 1964, in bizarre circumstances. He was shot to death at age thirty-three by a motel owner in Hollywood in the doorway of the manager's office. Apparently, Cooke had gone to the Hacienda Motel (since renamed the Star Motel) with Lisa Boyer, a woman he picked up in a nearby restaurant, Martino's. She claimed he had tried to rape her and she fought him off and fled with his pants and one of his shoes. He went looking for the woman and broke down the manager's door searching for her. The manager, Bertha Lee Franklin, shot him during a struggle.

It was a terrible loss to the music world. As record producer Jerry Wexler said, "Sam was the best singer who ever lived, no contest." In six years of performing popular music, Cooke recorded or wrote twenty-nine top singles—more than anyone in his era.

Like many black artists, he began as a gospel singer and gained fame in that genre before crossing over to pop music, to which he applied the gospel style in popular songs, blues, and rhythm and blues to create the soul style. He also started the first record album label, SAR, owned by a black artist and became a record producer as well as a singer. As a producer he combined sacred music with secular and rhythmic gospel with the flute in daring combinations that delighted his listeners. The results included the Soul Stirrers' rendition of "Lead Me Jesus" that grew out of a popular song, "Soothe Me."

Singer Bobby Womack of the Valentinos described Cooke's courage in rerecording a spiritual they had performed, "Couldn't Hear Nobody Pray," so that it became a pop song, "Lookin' for Love." Womack said, "We thought that was like a disgrace to God, taking his lyrics off the record and putting the Devil's on it. But we did it. And we had a million seller."

Cooke was one of the major influences on the music of the 1960s and beyond, even though he is not well known to white audiences. But he was well known to Bette, and it was from him she drew some of her inspiration for *The Rose*. For his part, Rothchild screened over one thousand songs before he selected thirty for Bette to review, and from these numbers they chose seven plus three of Bette's personal selections. The three that Bette wanted for the film were "Let Me Call You Sweetheart," "Stay With Me," and "When a Man Loves a Woman"—this last is one of the most dramatic numbers in the film. The trademark song of the film was, of course, "The Rose," which was an unusual number in itself because it was written in forty-five minutes by songwriter Amanda McBroom.

The impact of the music was assessed by film critic Jane Feuer, who observed, "Everyone knows the musical film [is] a mass art produced by a tiny elite for a vast and amorphous consuming public; the self-reflective musical attempts to overcome this division through the myth of integration." That is, the good musical tries to integrate the audience in the theater with the audience in the film so as to create the feeling of the theater audience being there with the audience in the film.

Feuer continued, "It follows that successful performances will be those in which the performer is sensitive to the needs of the audience and which gives the audience a sense of participation in the performance." That is what Bette did with her live performances in concert and in clubs. Bette was sensitive to her audience and brought them with her—embraced them and let them embrace her. A perfect example is her standard closing song in performances for a gay audience at the Continental Baths, "I Shall Be Released," which personifies gay men's feeling of need to be free of antihomosexual prejudice. And, for her heterosexual audiences in the filming of *The Rose*, the showstopper was her rendition of "When a Man Loves a Woman."

For those close to the production, it was not the transformation of the audiences in these concerts, but the transformation of Bette. Surely Bette was that trashy lady. But she had a lot of redeeming qualities as a performer and as a person. Not so Janis Joplin, renamed Rose for the film. Joplin was a drug- and booze-dependent, sex-driven, coarse woman without many endearing traits. It was a challenging role for Midler, who was not that kind of human being. Yet, scared as Bette was when she contemplated going before the cameras—and she was terrified—when Rydell shouted "Action," her absorption in the role changed Midler into Joplin before everyone's eyes.

Director Rydell was astonished at Bette's compulsion with perfection and her performing stamina. "For *The Rose*, we shot two full concerts back-to-back, only stopping to reload the cameras. She was brilliant all the way through and, at three A.M., I had enough film for twelve movies. But when I yelled 'Wrap!' she was outraged because she wanted to do a *third* concert. She's obsessive and compulsive, in an endearing way, making it better. Sometimes Bette just needed to be told *"Enough."* But throughout all of it, she was a sensitive, courageous artist."

Alan Bates, an English actor with many film credits, and Frederic Forrest, an actor from Texas, played Rose's manager and lover respectively. Then came the hard part, the editing of the hours and hours of raw footage to turn the film into a believable and coherent story. To illustrate the complexity of the editing process: It took ten weeks to shoot the footage and eighteen months to edit and assemble the final film. The result was a dramatic and musical triumph. Mark Rydell's judgment of Bette's performance: "She'll just take your breath away."

Bette discovered with her first significant film part that she could act in movies and she loved it.

16

The World Tour

S hooting of the *The Rose* finished July 18, 1978, and Bette began to prepare for her world tour set to start in Seattle on September 11. Mark Rydell would use the beginning of the tour to preview *The Rose* for some foreign audiences and build on Bette's presence in foreign countries. All appeared well until Aaron got too smart for himself and made a major public relations gaffe.

Not only did he announce Bette's first international tour, but he publicly demanded that Bette be paid in gold bullion because the American dollar had become a shady currency in the world. Russo was saying Bette would not take American money because it wasn't good enough for her!

During this same period, Bette learned that her mother, Ruth, was suffering from breast cancer, which had spread into other organs, including her lungs. She required a series of painful operations which did not stop the cancer from growing but only made living more painful for Ruth. Bette and her mother spoke frequently on the phone, and Ruth Midler was her daughter's biggest booster, so this was a stunning blow to Bette.

Ruth's illness increasingly turned Bette and her sister Susan against their father, who they felt wasn't sensitive enough to Ruth's suffering. "Toward the end it got very ugly," Bette said. "There were a lot of accusations flying through the air because he couldn't deal with her illness. He just pretended like she wasn't sick."

Even with her mother's illness hovering over the family, Bette was committed to her world tour. The tour Russo had mapped out was eighteen cities including Seattle (the three-day "out-of-town" tryout) and then London, Brighton, Stockholm, Copenhagen, Hamburg, Frankfurt, Munich, Paris, The Hague, Antwerp, Amsterdam, Sydney, Melbourne, Perth, Adelaide, Brisbane, and back to Sydney for a final appearance on November 14.

She would devote three months to the tour, but the current Harlettes—Charlotte Crossly, Ula Hedwig, and Sharon Reed—didn't want to accompany her. So Bette put an ad in the *Hollywood Reporter* announcing an open audition call, and thus began the hunt for three new Harlettes. Two hundred and fifty female singers, plus a few transvestites, auditioned before Aaron and two colleagues, who screened all the aspirants. When the finalists had been narrowed to six, Bette made the final choices. The new Harlettes were Linda Hart, Katey Sagal, and Frannie Eisenberg.

Then they went through Bette's boot camp for backup singers and rehearsed until they were ready to drop, but they stuck with it because this was the most important gig of their lives and because Bette was there with them during those fourteen-hour stints. Finally, the tour moved on to Seattle, where they opened for the tryout. Bette had begun the previous tour in Vancouver, where it was a smashing success. The new production had many of the elements of previous Bette shows, this time modified for non-American audiences. With the bugs worked out, the tour rolled on its way, and the first European stop, in September 1978, was the fabled London Palladium, where her audience enjoyed her irreverent digs at the royal family and at Britain itself:

"What a thrill it is to be here playing the Palladium right in the heart of the Old UK or the YUK, as we sometimes call it. Well, there'll always be an England, they say. Tonight we put that to the ultimate test. You know what they say, when it's three o'clock in New York, its 1938 in Britain. I'm just crazy about royalty, especially queens. Your queen, for example, she is the whitest woman of them all. She makes us all feel like the Third World. Who do you think makes those hats for her anyway? And, of course, I just adore Charles. I read somewhere that he can marry a commoner. I guess he wouldn't want someone as common as my own self."

Then came one of those unplanned moments followed by one of Bette's unplanned responses. A banner suddenly appeared over the railing of the balcony, proclaiming, "We Love Your Tits," which sent Bette into hysterics, and moments later she called back to those in the balcony, "Okay, here they are!" and bared her breasts to the audience.

Reviewer Derek Jewell, writing in the Sunday *Times,* observed that hardly anyone could have been prepared for Bette's show:

> Between songs, she told bawdy tales, tweaked politicians and peasants, royals and renegades, all at a blistering pace that would have destroyed other artists. She can be highly offensive and crude, but she moves so fast that no barb or vulgarity festers. Then, suddenly, she was sitting on a bench, miming and singing a string of desperately sad-funny songs in a tour de force which suggested a cross between tragic Judy Garland and Charlie Chaplin's universal pathos. The audience was still, enraptured. They recognized the vulnerability behind the flashy sophistication. And that remarkable surprise was her final stroke. She received the kind of tumultuously genuine reception which only a star who is many stars in one can evoke.

The *London Daily Telegram* wrote, "Miss Bette Midler has hit London, and London will never be the same. In a series of dazzling solo performances, she has rediscovered and updated for all the essentials of great music-hall!"

There was surprised delight at the marvelous reception she got from Danish audiences. She was uneasy with the German audiences, who were much more restrained and wary of her. She didn't like being there, and admitted to a reporter later, "I'll tell you the truth, I avoided going to Germany for many, many years. I'm Jewish and I've had that with me ever since I was a kid and I've been unable to lose it. I had a sorrow, a sorrow so deep inside you that you don't even know you have it until you're there in the country."

In France they all had a good time, because the troupe had an eight-day break to relax and enjoy Paris. On the ninth night, they performed and Bette made her usual jibes at the audience. "We are thrilled and delighted to be here in the town where good taste was born and, judging from the front row, died not moments ago."

Still, for all the fun they had in Europe, the high point of the tour was Australia, where Bette and her entourage were greeted with typical Aussie enthusiasm and appreciation, because Australians cherish bawdiness. Bette would later write in her book about the tour, *A View From a Broad*, "Once we hit the vast continent Down Under, we didn't have to think again. Or to eat right, for that matter. There is no food in Australia. Not as we know it. The natives do, of course, on occasion put matter to mouth, but one cannot possibly call what they ingest food . . . but brave and feckless as I am, I refused to allow this information to dampen my enjoyment of either the fauna or anything else in Australia."

The response to Bette's show was so strong that it was extended from two weeks to four weeks and still sold out. Coincidentally, *Ol' Red Head Is Back*, the television special, arrived and was shown on Australian TV during the group's stay—enhancing the Midler mania.

Variety reported, "Sydney has never responded better to a visiting artist. In any country, her performance would be considered a total triumph and, unless she is a consummate actress, the warmth of her reception and its intensity clearly surprised her."

It was now close to Thanksgiving, and everybody was drained from the tour and homesick to be back in the U.S.A. Aaron summed up 1978 by saying, "She's got the best of both worlds now. She's got Peter at home, who cares for her and is dedicated to her, and me at the office, who cares for her and is dedicated to her."

But the best of both worlds for Bette Midler didn't last very long after she came back to the States and 1979 arrived. In January, Ruth Midler died in Hawaii of liver cancer and leukemia. Bette's only comfort came from knowing she had made her mother happy and proud of her by becoming a star just like all those glamorous actresses Ruth had idolized all her life.

Bette said, "She had leukemia for a long time, cancer of the liver and of the breast. She suffered most of her life. She just thought I was 'it'! She thought I was so funny and so adorable. She just loved all the excitement. She used to say I was the only thing that brought her joy."

Along with that sadness about her mother, Bette continued to have bitter feelings about her father and how he had treated them all, how insensitive he had been toward her mother's illness, and how he had never accepted Bette for who she was. It took Bette a long time to forgive her father, and she expressed her bitterness about him frequently.

Later, when Bette's movie *The Rose* was a hit, Fred Midler still refused to see his daughter in performance. He told Dave Hirshey, a writer for the *New York Daily News* Sunday magazine, "I'm just not interested in that kind of entertainment. Now I hear she's in the movies, though. Something about Janis Joplin? I think she was some sort of rock singer. I don't like to spend money and I think charging four or five dollars to see a movie is outrageous. But to see my own daughter, well, I guess I'll splurge."

He never did.

After the death of her mother, Bette reexamined her relationship with Aaron and decided it was too painful to continue:

> Our relationship was so much sicker than anything in that film [*The Rose*]. Aaron was very protective of me, and he made enemies on my behalf. You see, we had a personal [romantic] relationship at the beginning of everything, and when our personal relationship floundered, it tainted our professional relationship. I was so dumb. I didn't think it would happen. He was so overbearing and he kept me very isolated, kept the bad stuff away from me and a lot of the good stuff too.
>
> I used to do shows and no matter how good they were, it didn't matter until he told me it was okay. And he used to withhold this approbation from me all the time. I was pretty messed up there for a long time. I don't know why—emotional retardation, I guess. He was the only one I trusted. I started out with a lot of people around me, and eventually they all left and I was alone with Aaron. I knew

that if I didn't get out at that point, I would never be happy again.

I couldn't take it anymore. I felt that what he was doing for me professionally wasn't worth what he was doing for me personally. I couldn't sleep. I was in a state of anxiety all the time because I never knew what he was going to pull on me next.

Eventually, I outgrew my need for drama. At a certain point, when you're thirty-two or so, you just no longer require the raving. You start enjoying pleasant days where there is no drama, where instead you have a little food and some pleasant conversation about wine and books.

She fired Aaron and hired a Hollywood agent, Arnold Steifed, and focused on her boyfried, Peter Riegert. She said, "Since I met Pete, my life has been kind of quiet. Not too many orgies, and we've been staying out of the hot tub. I've been working on my craft. I would like to have children, before my uterus falls out!"

17

Divine Madness: The 1979 Show

s she traveled around the world, she wrote in between performances. She had convinced Simon and Schuster before she
left that she had an interesting book inside her head, so she
signed a contract to write one. About what, for whom, and why, was
not made clear to the publisher, and, clearly, they didn't care. They
just wanted a book from Bette Midler that her many fans would buy.
The result would be *A View From a Broad*, written partly while
abroad and partly after returning home, and it was a humorous view
of her trip and her life.

For much of 1979 she worked on the book, with time out for
an appearance in May on *Saturday Night Live*, where she performed
a new song in her repertoire written by her colleague Tom Wait,
entitled "Martha." It is about how we too often let the chance to
love slip away from us in life to our later sorrow. She was in genuine
tears by the time she finished, because it reminded Bette of her life
growing up and of her mother. The rest of the spring and summer,
Bette continued to focus on her book and working on a new record
album, *Thighs and Whispers*. The book was due out in 1980, while
the album was set for release in the fall of 1979 and would be her
first album release on her own without help from Barry or Aaron.

There was an interval in the early summer in which Bette and
the Harlettes did a short promotional tour to Europe for some television appearances. While touring overseas, she decided it was time
for her to return to Broadway, and she announced that she would

do a one-woman show in November. The timing seemed good to her because it would be coincident with the American release of *The Rose*.

Fox premiered *The Rose* November 7, 1979, and the movie received generally good reviews, with Rex Reed writing, "Remember this day. It's the one that will go down in history as the day Bette Midler made her movie debut. Now *The Rose*, the movie she makes it in, is not all that much to shout about, but Bette's blazing performance saves it from mediocrity, gives it pulse and glamour and heart. Barbra Streisand, by comparison, seems like a has-been. Bette is so great you don't even care how illogical it is. The dynamic Bette sends it soaring to the stratosphere with her throbbing vitality. You can't call this acting debut 'auspicious.' Hell, she tears the theater apart!"

David Denby wrote in *New York* magazine, "What a storm of acting! Midler loads her own brassy, elbow-swinging, big-mama sluttishness on top of Janis's childlike egocentricity and the results are emotionally kaleidoscopic, draining. The transformation is exciting even after you've seen it three or four times."

Other critics were just as lavish as Reed and Denby. The wild-haired, mustachioed Gene Shalit of the *Today* show proclaimed, "With torrential force, Bette Midler sweeps *The Rose* into a film experience; an extravagant performance and an explosive debut."

In many ways the reception of both the audience and the critics of *The Rose* was generational. Those who had been at Woodstock and Altamont embraced the film as they embraced that era.

Mark Rydell, the director, was delighted with the artistic success of the film. "Everybody's going crazy over it," he said. "You don't get this very often in your life. Something spectacular is happening. The feeling is electrifying. It has to do with the fact that we are delivering a new talent. The kind you see once in ten or twenty years."

More important to the film studio, *The Rose* made money. The first weekend it grossed $793,063, and it ultimately earned $55 million—more than five times as much as the $10 million it cost to make. *The Rose* resulted in a hit record album for the first time in the last four, becoming Bette's biggest seller.

To follow up, she launched a six-city tour, *Bette! Divine Madness*, to hone her latest stage concert so that she would be in perfect performance pitch for the tour's conclusion, her six-week gig beginning December 5, 1979, at the Majestic Theater in Manhattan. The troupe toured through Seattle, Portland, San Francisco, Los Angeles, Phoenix, and Detroit and drew sellout crowds as usual, particularly because there was such an advance buzz about the movie *The Rose*, with the usual Oscar talk surrounding Bette's performance in the film. Martin Kent of the *Hollywood Reporter* told his readers, "A Bette Midler concert is an exquisitely packaged theatrical experience. Midler is larger-than-life—a silo of excess. Armed with a voice that is so powerful, expressive and versatile, her ballads are as devastating as her wildest rockers."

While they were on the road, *The Rose* had its premiere opening at the Ziegfeld Theater in New York on November 6, attended by the newly blond Bette wearing a black lace strapless gown, offering a svelte new figure, and boasting a $350,000 diamond necklace. At the party afterward held at the Roseland Ballroom, which was decorated with three thousand roses, Miss M proclaimed, "It was the most exciting opening I've ever been to, and I've been to a few. Thank God this one was mine!"

Then it was off to Los Angeles for the premiere at the Century Plaza Theater and the party at the Century Plaza Hotel across the street. Attending celebrities included Raquel Welch, Jacqueline Bisset, Milton Berle, Hugh Hefner, and Nick Nolte.

After the road tour, the cast of *Divine Madness* arrived in New York and rested for about a month before bringing the show to the Majestic. By that time, *The Rose* was playing in movie houses all over the country. Excitement over her appearance at the Majestic skyrocketed, and, as *Time* would say, Bette's *Divine Madness* was "the hottest ticket in town."

Divine Madness displayed a new Bette because, just as she responded differently to different audiences when on tour, she responded differently to the changing national mood—it was the beginning of the Reagan-Bush era. Bette opened with pink hair and daring décolleté, singing an unusual first song from the 1930s, "Big

Noise From Winnetka." From there on, Bette gave them two hours of solid entertainment with a good lineup of songs, punctuated by her ever-so-slightly naughty jokes. Even so, the show wasn't up to her usual standard, according to Rex Reed, who wrote, "Unfortunately, there's a lot of trash cluttering the stage at the Majestic between solos that convinces me she needs outside help. This is a show that has been poorly organized and badly put together."

Ironically, she left them cheering in the audience, but the gloom descended when Russo attended the last night of the performance in mid-January and came backstage afterward to tell her she was just awful and that she needed him back if she was going to survive. She said, "He told me it was a terrible show. He said I was ruining all he had done for me and that I looked like an albino on stage. When he told me this, I was sick with bronchitis. I had my head in the toilet, barfing. Aaron always did know my weakest moments, and then he would strike."

Bette's emotional state was brittle, and one of her earlier biographers, James Spada, said of this time, "Riding the crest of an incredible wave of popularity and success, Bette Midler should have been on top of the world. Instead, she was an emotional wreck. She never had been able to handle the pressure of stardom; more success seemed only to make her more insecure."

Apparently, Bette's reaction to the lukewarm critical response to *Divine Madness* was to flail out at everyone around her. She cut herself off from press interviews and decided to dump all of her cast and crew—the three Harlettes and fifteen musicians and associated other people—before returning to California to do the film version of *Divine Madness*. She was successfully sued by the fired members of her cast and crew for $2 million.

At the beginning of 1980, Bette had become one of the biggest names in show business. Certification came with two major interviews on television with Barbara Walters and Phil Donahue and several feature articles in leading magazines. Still there was something not quite right. Had Aaron Russo been *that* important in her life for those seven-plus years, and was she really free of him? Here's what she told Barbara Walters about the firing of Aaron and the death of her mother.

"Well, I'll tell you," Bette said tentatively, "it's been very rough. This is not fun. It's hard work and it's terribly exhausting. To be quite frank, I don't like to think about it. It's been very, very hard for me, this last year. There were a couple of times I really thought I was going to go under. I was ready to call in the men in the white suits. I had no idea until I decided to do it myself what Aaron really did.

"The picture [*The Rose*] did good business, I got fabulous reviews, I was nominated for an Oscar, but the fact is that I *never got another offer*. I died. I was devastated. I really felt I had been shut out."

The anxiety of being snubbed by the movie industry after making *The Rose* would set Bette up for cinematic disaster three years later.

Part IV

1980s: A View From a Broad

18

Divine Madness: The Movie

Peter Riegert was one person who helped Bette make it through and who brought her the happiness that eluded her in her public life. With his good looks, ready smile, and easygoing, patient manner, Peter made people feel good. He was very different from Aaron Russo, and most of Bette's friends thought Peter was a calming influence on Bette, but inexplicably she pushed him away too during this time of turmoil.

Bette said, "Relationships are so hard. It's difficult enough to come to grips with your own self, but to have to deal with another self and you have to worry about them and put them above you. You have to nurse them when they're sick. My father always wanted me to be something steady, like a nurse, and sometimes I think, 'Daddy, I grew up a nurse after all.' "

In February, Bette received two Golden Globes: one for Best Female Newcomer and one for Best Actress in a Musical or Comedy. She accepted with a typically humorous, brassy remark: "I'll show you a pair of Golden Globes!"

She was nominated for an Oscar but lost to Sally Field for *Norma Rae* and went on in March to shoot *Divine Madness* at the Pasadena Civic Auditorium. The song "The Rose" was to be nominated for an Oscar, but the Motion Picture Academy disqualified it because it was not written specifically for the movie. Later, Bette would garner a Grammy for the Best Pop Performance of the year.

Now that Bette was on her own with success coming her way,

the next question was which way Bette should be going. There were now a lot of offers from people who felt that if Bette would only appear in their stage show, their movie, their concert, or their television special, it would be a success. She opted for repeating *Bette! Divine Madness*, but this time as a movie. What had to be done was to integrate the excitement of a live performance into the limitations of film as Bette and Mark Rydell had done in *The Rose*. Since *The Rose* was such a big success for Bette, she wanted to try duplicating it. The question was whether that could be done again with her stage concert, *Divine Madness*.

Alan Ladd Jr. headed Ladd Productions, which was going to try. Ladd said, "My objective is to break down the barrier between the screen and the audience. To capture the energy and spontaneity of a live performance."

Ladd started with the correct understanding that the audience at a Midler concert was as much a part of the show as the performance by Bette, the Harlettes, and the band. The audience consisted mostly of devoted Bette fans who had heard every song, every flip remark, every dirty pun over and over again and still loved reliving the experience.

Writer Craig Karpel, who had written "Notes on Bette" for *Oui* magazine in 1973, commented that Bette's audiences were a show in themselves. People felt empowered to emulate the zany costumes and behavior of their idol on stage. Bette saw it too. "Whenever we'd play some of the smaller cities, the people who came to see me were very far-out people, and when they all get together in one place, they're amazed that there are so many of them." Her writer, Bruce Vilanch, added that her loyal fans would come to the concert in raincoats, fill up the front rows, and, as soon as she came on stage, stand up, doffing their raincoats to reveal themselves dressed only in towels.

Normally directors would have two or three cameras in plain sight of the audience, and their obvious presence would affect how people behaved. In this concert filming at the Pasadena Civic Auditorium, producer-director Michael Ritchie carefully instructed his camera crews that he wanted them everywhere but seen by no one. He didn't want the presence of a camera crew to become part of the equation. He wanted them blended into the audience, shooting everything and everyone. Instead of the usual two or three camera crews, he used ten. The stage crew turned up the sound and lighting systems with the best equipment available, vastly improving what was in place, and then the show began.

For four nights, from February 13 through 16, 1980, the camera crews set to work shooting three concerts on a million and a half feet of film. They would pare the million and a half feet down to less than 2 percent of the total footage used in final film. In spite of the careful advance preparations, the three days of filming were difficult because Southern California had a major rainstorm that flooded low-lying spots, including the basement of the Pasadena Civic Auditorium.

Bette became ill with the flu, which affected her performance. Once she collapsed on stage, which finished the show for that day. Back the next day, Bette was still sick with a temperature of 103. She wanted to postpone the filming, but that would have been very costly and the production company wouldn't do it.

The show went on, but Bette's rendition of certain numbers was below standard and had to be dubbed from a studio recording session after she overcame her illness. The flip humor, however, was intact as she jibed at her new Harlettes trio, "Oh, my girls! They function as a Greek chorus. These girls don't know shit about Euripides, but they knew plenty about Trojans!"

The concert ran three hours and was repeated three nights running, which meant the ten cameras ended up with a total of ninety hours of film. From that, Michael Ritchie crafted a film that ran ninety-four minutes and in which not a single camera is seen. The critics were unanimous in their praise, and the audience reacted favorably when the movie was shown around the country. It gave Bette a second convincing film credit and kept that medium open to her.

Los Angeles Times critic Kevin Thomas wrote, "*Divine Madness* is pure, exhilarating joy, a definitive concert film culled from more than ninety hours of footage shot during three shows. Dynamic, uninhibited, electrifying—all such familiar adjectives seem threadbare to describe the Hawaiian-born superstar. Midler's immense talent is matched by her energy, but she's clearly having such fun she charges rather than drains an audience. *Divine Madness* is definitely, most definitely, not for prudes. But, oh, is it a winner!"

And Janet Maslin of the *New York Times* wrote, "*Divine Madness* presents Miss Midler's act in all its gaudy, irrepressible glory. Miss Midler knows full well what her audience expects of her and what the traffic will bear. Only a thin line separates her from vulgarity, from maudlin excess, from material that shows her off to poor advantage or gives her self-deprecating humor a nasty edge. And her ability to steer clear of such things is remarkable."

Most other critics echoed these laudatory reactions, with two major exceptions, the theatergoing public and Aaron Russo. In spite of the exceptional filming produced by Ritchie and his crew and the critical plaudits, the theatergoing public was not enthusiastic about *Divine Madness* the way it had been about *The Rose*, and the new film did not do well at the box office. Aaron Russo didn't like *Divine Madness* either. He said it was too much rehash of what people had seen in bits and pieces over the years and that Bette's loyal fans were entitled to fresh Midler material and Bette at her best. Comparing it to *The Rose*, Russo said that it was stupid to follow a powerful picture that gained four Academy Award nominations with a weak movie.

"With me," he said, "everything Bette did was eventlike; it had a certain air that the concert film [*Divine Madness*] didn't accomplish. The thing about Bette is her heart; the film missed that essence. From a creative standpoint, it was wrong. It didn't have any importance. It was terrible."

Even so, Bette was initially satisfied with *Divine Madness*, but began to shift her opinion as box-office reactions came in. Then she recalled that director Michael Ritchie hated music but had been foisted on the project by the Ladd Company people and that there had been constant fighting among the various technicians on the film—between costumes and the director; choreographer and the designer; lighting and the director.

Bette said later, "It was an enormous thing to do alone. It was all my fault. I made all the mistakes. The concert picture is a scary form. I felt it should have been peddled as a spectacle rather than as a concert, because there I was, making a spectacle of myself."

It prompted Russo to reflect on his role in their long business relationship:

> When I met Bette, she needed somebody, a manager who would dominate her life, give her everything she had. Eventually she started resenting it. I did dominate her, never allowing enough room for the person inside to come out. But if I hadn't, her career wouldn't have gone anywhere. I don't think she ever understood what I did or what it took to do it. She was incapable of making decisions. She'd get angry when the press or somebody else would give me credit for something. She wanted nobody else to get the credit.
>
> She doesn't come to me for advice anymore. We don't have a relationship. I wish we did. I miss her. I know the pain, the insecurity she lives with all the time. That's who the girl is. I want to put my arm around her and give to her. I want her to understand that. I do have a broken heart and although I've moved on, there's still that piece of my heart she can have whenever she wants.

Bette's reaction was that she might call Aaron up sometime and ask him to come back, but with some different understandings about their relationship. That was fifteen years ago and Aaron's phone hasn't rung yet.

19

1980–81—Bette as Author

One thing Bette definitely could do alone, without Barry or Aaron, was write a book, which she did on her 1978 worldwide tour and after her return home during 1979. The result was *A View From a Broad*, published by Simon and Schuster in April 1980.

The surprise was that Bette Midler—concert singer, movie actress, recording artist, stage actor, club performer, and TV star—could also write a good book. Douglas Cramer, the Hollywood producer, was asked by the *Hollywood Reporter* to review the book. He wrote, "There's good humor and many solid guffaws, in Bette's multitude of bawdy stories. This book is a hot diary; a new-wave yearbook; a collection of Halloween-type drag snapshots."

The book was a perfect illustration of William Goldman's observation that no one is ever sure of what will work. *A View* had pictures of Bette dressed like a hot dog, hugging a kangaroo, and prominently displaying her ample breasts on the cover and it sold well. However, if anyone expected that Bette was going to bare more of her breasts and let America know more about Bette, they were disappointed. As an earlier Midler biographer, Ace Collins, observed about *A View*, "Deep down, Bette, the woman who had conquered the movies her first time out, had earned a Grammy and a certain amount of success in the record business, and the entertainer who owned Broadway each time she stepped on stage, still seemed to lack a degree of self-confidence. Now that everyone knew who Bette was—did she know herself?"

The book is a funny, self-deprecating combination of Bette's observations on herself, her life, and the world. "I knew so little of the world, really. Slander, not geography, had always been my strongest suit."

It covers the four months she was on her world tour—traveling and performing, with the attendant problems and delights. Some of the delights included finding out that the two things she was most terrified of in life—salespeople and Frenchmen—could be combined into one French salesman who seemed belligerent but turned out to be a teddy bear. "As I set foot in the store all I could think about was whether I had brushed my teeth and if I had half as much class as the counter display."

A poignant episode occurred when her limo driver in Copenhagen took her to see his family's boat and talked about the Jews his father had rescued during World War II. He also took her to visit the symbol of Copenhagen, the statue of the Little Mermaid.

She wrote, "For one incredible, breathtaking moment, the Little Mermaid glowed pure gold. I suppose there will be other moments in my life as awesome and mysterious, but none, I think, more moving. For there in that little country of cottage cheese and courage, I became a child again and, for the first time since I was six, I felt something we all should feel at least once a year, but hardly ever do: the thrilling rush of insignificance."

She admits she was reluctant to leave Los Angeles and go on such an extended tour at first. "How could I leave this throbbing center of vitality and delight, this modern Athens, this garbanzo in the salad of human achievement and travel to places where the plumbing was uncertain and where there might not be even one Chinese restaurant?"

Still, she admitted to a strong desire to see foreign lands and unusual people, and besides, the tour would be profitable for her. "Fortunately, good sense and a slap across the face were to prevail. In fact, after several hours of pouting and pacing and just the teeniest nip or two of Courvoisier, going around the world began to have its appeal. . . . Secondly, I felt that my mind, unquenchable in its thirst for cultural enrichment and cheap thrills, might benefit from such a world-girdling juggernaut. . . . But beyond all that, the fact was that I had always had a burning desire to see the world."

While revealing why she was an unhappy teenager in the paradise of Hawaii, she makes a rare kind remark about her father. She is a little off in the timing of her parents' move to Hawaii, since it wasn't in the Great Depression, but she wrote, "My father had moved out to Hawaii during the Depression, not so much to find work as to find a proper setting for my mother, whom he always thought too beautiful and delicate for prosaic Passaic. But growing up in paradise was difficult for me, so colorless. In such exotic company, I was a hopelessly mundane transplant, a common, worthless dandelion lost in a garden of orchids."

A View From a Broad is valuable for anyone who wants to understand Bette Midler as a person as well as a performer, because it is Bette in her own words as contrasted to the filter of a reporter, interviewer, or biographer. She shares with the reader that the two great therapies for her are making lists and talking: "Dizzy with exhilaration and dread, I took my favorite Paper Mate in hand and began to do what I always do in a situation that demands bold and forthright action: I made lists. . . . You see, on stage, as in life, I talk *a lot*. In fact, random, rambling raillery makes up a rather large part of my act. . . . Chatter is respite for me."

Then there are the insights she provides about her views of herself and her fans. She talks about her dresser, Miss Frank, who had the ability to remind Bette that she was human and who deflated her self-assessments of grandeur at appropriate moments, noting that Bette was *not* something the entire world and Canada were panting for. Miss Frank was also a moral guardian concerned about Bette's virtue and immortal soul. "I'm sure the only reason she comes along with me on these monumental shleps is because she considers it her duty to save me from the perils that can befall a young woman of my station and bodily proportions."

As for her fans, Bette said she would be tempted to dismiss their behavior as crazy and warped except for the impact their devotion had on her. She wrote, "There is something so essentially sweet about the whole thing, something so naive, that I find I can't dismiss it, or ignore it or belittle it at all. I embrace it. They give me meaning."

And she recognized that her fans sometimes had to endure less than perfect shows and were patient and forgiving. So she had to be as patient and forgiving of them as they were of her. Bette discovered that to have a great personality, she didn't have to be a wonderful person, but only a wonderful persona that she herself invented.

From 1980 on, Bette was learning about life as her own manager. "I'm doing fine without a manager," she declared. "I have a lawyer and lots of help. If I ever get a new one [personal manager], I'm going to get one that's blind to my sexual charms. Managers have to do with creativity. A good one makes sure that the artist survives, is compensated properly for his services and the moves he makes in career building rather than laying it to waste."

She was a frugal woman by nature, but her career now demanded a bicoastal existence, and she could also afford to upgrade her living arrangements. So when her remaining sister, Susan, decided to move to Manhattan, Bette let her have the Barrow Street apartment in Greenwich Village while Bette got herself another place in the lower Manhattan district of Tribeca. She split her time between that home and a rented place in Los Angeles where she read script after script to find something suitable for her next movie.

She wanted to show off her comedy talents, and she made a deal with United Artists that she could pick a script and a director and have a say about the creative side of the production. She finally settled on a movie called _Hot Streak_, which was immediately rewritten and changed to _It's All in the Game_, which in turn was re-rewritten and changed to _Jackpot_, only to be re-re-rewritten and changed to _Jinxed_, which very quickly stopped being the name of the picture and became a description of the whole production.

The premise of the film was simple, and the crew and the director, Don Siegel, putting it together were experienced, so it should have been an easy movie to produce. In the story a Nevada blackjack dealer, Willie, is harassed by a conceited cardsharp, Harold, who trails him from one casino to another. Willie repeatedly loses his job because Harold keeps beating him at blackjack. According to the mystique of gamblers, the only way Willie can regain his gambler's soul and break Harold's jinx is to make Harold lose—something, anything.

Enter Harold's girlfriend, abused and disenchanted country-and-western singer Bonita, with whom Willie falls in love. Bonita is the solution to Willie's problem. If he can make Harold lose Bonita, Willie will have broken the jinx. Bonita wants to be free of the abusive Harold but is afraid to leave him. So Willie and Bonita try to kill Harold, but he commits suicide first. Unfortunately, Harold's life insurance, of which Bonita is the beneficiary, will not pay off for suicide. So Willie and Bonita try to rig the suicide to appear as an accident. That doesn't help, since the policy has lapsed because Harold stopped paying premiums.

After all this, Willie and Bonita have a fight and split. Then Bonita discovers she has inherited Harold's ability to beat dealers at the blackjack table. Willie and Bonita reunite and, as the movie ends, they are going from casino to casino beating other blackjack dealers.

In retrospect, Bette said, "I liked the *Jinxed* script because of its dialogue, nice and slangy. I didn't know whether it was a comedy or a thriller, but I thought a good director could find the proper tone for it. Don Siegel had directed *The Killers*, *Dirty Harry*, *The Shootist*, and *Invasion of the Body Snatchers*, which were kind of somber, so I thought with Siegel being good at that and me being good at comedy, we'd have a nice marriage. Many, many, many people told me I was crazy, and this is one time in my career I should have listened. I just had never encountered Mr. Siegel's school of directing—the adversary school of directing—where everybody chooses up sides and it's a fight to the death!"

The screenplay writers were either Brian Blessing or Bert Blessing, Jerry Blatt, or David Newman. The Blessing name, Bert in one context and Brian in another, was a pseudonym used by the original screenwriter of *Hot Streak*, Frank Gilroy, who didn't want his name on the final script. Jerry Blatt's name is totally missing from any of the film credits for *Jinxed* because the Writers Guild of America was on strike and Jerry should have been on the picket lines instead of in the studio writing.

Bette picked Ken Wahl, who she thought was a rising actor because of his work in _Fort Apache—The Bronx_. He turned out to be an actor with a bad attitude who seemed to think that rudeness was the mark of a star. Reportedly, the first words out of his mouth when he met Bette Midler were not "Hello" or "Nice to meet you." Instead he spat out, "I hate niggers and faggots." He also didn't like a woman having creative control over the picture as Bette did.

So, from the day filming began in Lake Tahoe on May 5, 1981, there was tension on the set. There were constant confrontations and disputes about lighting, blocking, dialogue, and everything else imaginable. Wahl seemed to love causing trouble and having people try to placate him. Bette would lose her temper, too, cutting people up and storming off the set. "I never knew it got so ugly," Bette said afterward. "I never knew it got down to such mudslinging. It was an enormously painful experience."

Off the set, the battle continued in the gossip columns, which by August had begun reporting about unrest on the set and how Bette would walk off in a huff. Slanderous comments were made by both sides, such as Wahl declaring the only way he could force himself into kissing Midler on camera was to pretend that he was kissing his dog.

When _Jinxed_ was finally finished, both Siegel and Wahl announced that they would never again work with Bette Midler. Siegel put it this way: "I've worked with several tough characters, but she's the toughest. It's been the most unpleasant working experience of my life." To which Wahl added, "She was hard and in control and the vibes were bad from the start. If I'd known what it would be like, I never would have accepted the assignment to begin with. Who needs this aggravation?"

In September, two more stories appeared that did not help the public, or rather the Hollywood, image of Ms. Midler. Army Archerd, longtime gossip columnist for _Daily Variety_, wrote on the fifteenth that Don Siegel said working with Bette "was a miserable, a very unpleasant experience."

Anthea Sylvert, the vice president of production for United Artists, presented another view when she claimed it was gender bashing. "Everybody got into a habit of blaming everything on her [Bette]. Bette Midler is an extremely hard worker and conscientious. The dailies [review of the film shot each day] were consistently wonderful and one of the people responsible for them being wonderful was Bette Midler. She is obsessed with perfection. Some people are troubled by that, but I've always admired it. We're talking about a director who spent most of his career dealing with men. There may have been resentment for a woman having some kind of power."

Bette said, "I was trying to make the best movie I could and I was resented for it. When somebody gives you that much money to make a picture, you can't shortchange them. But these people, there wasn't a single one of them who wasn't out to stiff the studio, they're lazy and uncommitted and they resent you for being so square. They didn't want to work that hard. They didn't want to make the best *Jinxed* they could make. So it was like pulling a caravan up Mount Everest all by myself."

The whole experience pushed Bette into a nervous breakdown. She later said:

> I never thought about being "a woman in the business." A lot of times during the woman's movement, I would think, "What's all the fuss about? If you're smart, you go in and say what you want and that's that." Well, that's *not* that. This picture opened my eyes to the world. I said to myself, "I'm not the only woman who has gone through this." Every day, every morning toward the end, I felt I was holding on for dear life. I would wake up with heart palpitations. And sometimes in the middle of the night, I would wake up, not screaming but not being able to breathe.
>
> I had a terrible nervous breakdown. I was sick for a good three months. I was very, very ill. And I started to see a doctor because it was just too much for me to deal with by myself. I couldn't walk. I couldn't get out of bed. I just cried for weeks on end. I couldn't control myself. I had just been

so attacked and so humiliated. It was as though they wanted to destroy me and I couldn't understand what I had done.

After the long period of withdrawal and communion with herself, Midler assessed what had to be done. She made one public appearance, at the 1982 Academy Awards as an Oscar presenter, wearing a flashy and trashy strapless gold gown. She opened by saying, "I guess you didn't think it was possible to overdress for this affair." That brought laughter and then she said, "So this is what it actually feels like to be up here, this is fantastic. I've been waiting for two years for the Academy to call me up and say they made a mistake [referring to her losing out to Sally Field for an Oscar]. But do I bear a grudge—no, no. I bear no grudges. My heart is as big as the sky and I have a mind that retains absolutely nothing. This is the Oscars. We have to be dignified, as dignified as humanly possible. That is why I have decided to *rise* to the occasion." Then she put her hands under her breasts and pushed them up. The Academy audience loved her. Unfortunately, the same can't be said for *Jinxed* when it finally was released that fall and received bad reviews, although Bette got some good mentions. David Anson told his *Newsweek* readers, "What Bette Midler did for last spring's Academy Awards show she does for *Jinxed.*" In summation, Anson thought that *Jinxed* was a poorly done movie, saved only by Bette's presence.

Oddly, Don Siegel continued to pan his own movie. "I'd let my wife, children, and animals starve before I'd subject them to something like that again." Yet he, too, praised the work of the woman he had labeled "bitch" in ten-foot-high letters to all of Hollywood. "To my great surprise, I like the picture. I like Bette Midler's work in it. She was absolutely awful in *Divine Madness*, but there are moments in this [*Jinxed*] when she's brilliant."

Jinxed did poorly at the box office, ultimately losing $20 million for the studio, and the whole convoluted affair prompted columnist Marilyn Beck to observe, "That has to be a crushing defeat for Bette, because, flawed as the movie might be, it is not bad enough to deserve the whipping that it is receiving."

The Hollywood establishment treated Bette like a pariah and

froze her out in spite of her dreams of acting. "I keep hoping. I keep thinking. Surely something must turn up. But it doesn't. I'd like to do another film, but they aren't exactly beating down my door."

Eight years later Bette would recall this trying period of her life and career:

> My manager [Russo] was beating me and I decided I couldn't take it anymore, so I left him. Then I was on my own and I had to scramble. I didn't get any offers. I was waiting for *The Rose* to open so I could judge where I was going. I made that picture in '78 and it didn't come out until '79. And I was nominated for an Oscar in '80. But then I got mixed up with people who didn't have my best interests at heart. I had a very unscrupulous agent who told me that if I didn't make this picture, I'd have been off the screen for two years and no one would remember my name, so I *had* to make this picture *Jinxed!* So I made it. I suffered terribly for it. I behaved *exactly* on that picture as I've behaved on all my pictures, with complete and utter goodwill. But they were looking for a scapegoat and I was it. I never to this day understood it.
>
> I was so crushed by the whole situation that I had a breakdown over it. I got over it, went back to work, started to sing again. Singing has always had a great revitalizing effect on me. Music is so healing, I just love it. I forget everything when I sing.

20

De Tour Tour

At age thirty-seven, Bette decided late in 1982 to make another tour, which she labeled *De Tour* and for which she created an entirely new show. At the same time, she was starting work on a new record album, purchased a Spanish-Mediterranean-style, high-beamed mansion in the Coldwater Canyon district of Beverly Hills, and was back living with Benoit Gautier.

"Benoit I've been with, on and off, for about a year," Bette said in mid-1982. "We went to Europe together last fall. He's a personal manager. He's in zee show bis-i-ness. He manages John Anderson, who used to be the lead singer in Yes, [and] who's now on his own and is making those wonderful records with Vangelis. Beautiful symphonic pieces, long tone-poem things. But Benoit has a public relations firm in Paris."

She called her new album *No Frills* because it would consist simply of ballads and rock with music synthesizer equipment creating the musical background and no other production sounds. "It's music with no strings," she explained, "and no horns. It's barebones music, as unpretentious as it can be. Just stark. But I'm enjoying this album more than any other I've ever made. The people I'm working with are fabulous, funny, silly, silly people."

Looking back on *No Frills* some time later, Bette saw it differently than she perceived it at the time she was working on the project. "The last record I made [*No Frills*], I was in the studio for over a year, and I don't like that process. There's so much technology, whatever humanity I had was slowly being eroded. And I spent a year making that record and nobody bought it. Nobody cared except me. I considered not singing anymore. I thought I wasn't taking my singing seriously. I wasn't paying attention to it. It wasn't just because I wasn't selling records anymore. It had just fallen by the wayside."

The new *De Tour* was important because she needed to salvage her reputation as a performer after the *Jinxed* disaster, and she worked hard to put it together. She organized a new band and convinced Hattie, Ula Hedwig, and Linda to became the Harlettes once more. By December 1982 *De Tour* was ready to go, and it opened December 6 at the Universal Amphitheater in Los Angeles. It was an entertaining program with a new lineup of songs, including "It Should've Been Me," "Pink Cadillac," "Pretty Legs and Big Knockers," and new oldies that Bette hadn't done before, such as "Rolling on the River," "We Are Family," "Everyone's Gone to the Moon," "That May Be All I Need to Know," "Got My Eye on You," and "My Mother's Eyes."

For Bette personally and privately, this tour was different, and she told her audience why: "This show is so new, so artsy-fartsy, even I can't keep up with it. But do I give a shit? Nooo-oo-o." Then she went into her new material such as the then-current practice of blaming everything that went wrong on cocaine. "Have you noticed that whenever anyone has a problem these days, they blame it on cocaine? Your marriage is collapsing—it's the blow. Can't keep a job—it's the blow. Liberace is accused of being a homosexual—now that *was* the blow! And then there's herpes. Oh God, 'You always herpes the one you love.' "

What amazed and amused her sellout audiences was her self-satire which focused on her breasts and on the film that had been the bane of her life for the previous year, *Jinxed*. She did several minutes in which she talked entirely about her breasts.

"I've been wearing my bra for years and years," she told her *De Tour* audiences. "That is my field of expertise, you know: brassierres. I know all about them. . . . I got my first one when I was eleven years old: I was a D cup."

Then she would launch into her breast routine with the Harlettes, "Pretty Legs and Great Big Knockers," and conclude by sharing with the audience the intimate experience she once had in a U.S. Post Office where she weighed her breasts on the postal scale. "I won't tell you how much they weighed, but it costs eighty-seven dollars and fifty cents to send them to Brazil!"

For her parody on *Jinxed*, a big screen was lowered for the audience and Bette introduced it as a film suffering from "projectus interruptus—it went before it even came." Then, as the selected clips rolled on the screen, the audience saw it had Italian subtitles. As her character, Bonita, enters a desert ghost town, the subtitle flashed, "Oh, the MGM lot! I can't believe it. Louis B. Mayer must be turning over in Joan Crawford's grave." And as a tumbleweed comes rolling onto the scene and hits Bonita, "Ah, flowers from the director." Then she has this exchange with the old prospector in the ghost town about a package her movie lover, Harold, has left for her:

"That's the script," says the prospector, "but your skin is the wrong color."

"Wrong color? What are you talking about?"

"Aren't you the girl who played that rock singer who did drugs and died?"

"Yes."

"Well, isn't Diana Rose black?"

A few moments later, the prospector pretending to be a movie producer says to her, "You may be a good actress. Show me your tits."

The new songs and the new comedy material brought out the admiration of the critics. Early in *De Tour*, John Karr in San Francisco reported, "Bette Midler peaked with this concert. I've always loved her, laughed and cried with her, but I was caught unprepared for this sort of unity of conception, assimilation of styles and increased singing prowess. Here is the Bette we've always predicted. It's as if the struggles of Hollywood were a cocoon from which Bette has emerged transfigured."

And at the end of the tour in New York, Stephen Holden told

his *New York Times* readers that previous performances by Bette had
left him a bit uncertain about the range of her talent and the strength
of her voice. However, this time, Holden said, "It was a happy surprise when [there was] unveiled a newly-fortified rock singing voice
and not only did Miss Midler stay consistently on pitch, she inter-
preted demanding rock ballads like 'Stay With Me' with an impressive dynamic control."

De Tour had opened December 6, 1982, in Los Angeles and
played there through New Year's Eve, when the audience was
treated to a special surprise. Bette appeared on stage as the New
Year baby, swaddled in a giant diaper as usual with the number 1983
on it, accompanied by an old man representing the year 1982 just
gone by. They led the audience in "Auld Lang Syne." It took the
audience a moment before it realized that the "old man" was Barry
Manilow.

De Tour, which would take in gross box-office receipts of $8
million, covered nineteen cities through to mid-March, when it
ended in the Radio City Music Hall. And most important, it restored
Bette's confidence in herself.

De Tour went so well the first time out that Bette decided to
take it back out again in modified form in the summer. This time
she had a new set of Harlettes with her, Jennifer Lewis, Siobhan
O'Carroll, and Helena Spriness. Bette began telling reporters in the
various cities of *De Tour* she wanted to make funny movies. She
thought comedy was natural to her and she wanted to make people
in movie theaters laugh. At her Minneapolis performance she had
HBO taping the show again for a special, and all of this was pushing
her pretty hard. So it wasn't a surprise that a few nights later at a
concert in Clarkston, Michigan, near Detroit, Bette collapsed.

She said later, "It was 104 degrees. I hadn't been sleeping, and
I felt sick as a dog before the show. During the number "Pretty
Legs and Big Knockers" I felt ready to faint. I ran off stage for the
balloons I needed for the number and I blacked out. One lonely
little balloon came bouncing back on stage with no Bette behind
it."

A podiatrist was in the audience and immediately came backstage to help until the paramedics arrived and took Bette to the hospital. It was a sobering experience for her. "I was sure I wouldn't get better. I felt panic-stricken and I couldn't stop crying. Then I started to take stock. I thought of all the people I hadn't seen. And I really wanted to see my mother but I couldn't [her mother had died of cancer in 1979, four years earlier].

She got well soon and her spirits revived with her health. The doctors concluded she had suffered from a combination of the hot weather, physical burnout, and a gastrointestinal problem.

De Tour continued a few days later, and she was giving interviews to reporters. "I was beat to a pulp. I was working too hard and I couldn't stop thinking about my mother. I was racked with guilt and really terrified. When you're in a weakened condition all the guilt of your life floods back to you."

In spite of her momentary setback, she received good reviews for *De Tour* and her book *A View From a Broad*, which prompted her to write another book, *The Saga of Baby Divine*, with illustrations by Todd Schoor. Crown Books gave her a $50,000 advance and she wrote a fairy tale in verse for children. Baby Divine wore purple heels, a feather boa, and constantly repeated the word "More!"

Baby Divine arrived in the world to the shock and astonishment of her conservative parents, as Lillie, Tillie, and Joyce, three dizzy ladies living in a boardinghouse in another part of town, witnessed the sky over Baby Divine's house light up and journeyed to Baby's house bearing gifts.

Baby Divine's parents ordered Lillie, Tillie, and Joyce to leave, which they did. Her parents wondered if Baby Divine was really their child, and when she heard that, Baby Divine ran away from home and encountered a bird who offered to take her on a tour. Flying high in the sky, Baby Divine learned that the world varied depending upon one's perspective. When the parents found Baby Divine gone, they were worried and started to search for her, and the three dizzy ladies offered to help.

Meanwhile, Baby Divine fell from the bird and, alone and lost, looked for a way back home, only to encounter the monster that lurks in all our nightmares.

I am Anxiety, friend to Despair!
I appear when your Courage departs.
I find you whenever your Confidence fails you
And Fear makes a Home in your Heart.

Fortunately for Baby Divine, the three ladies rescued her from the monster, and Baby Divine realized that she created the monster in her own mind. The three ladies taught her how to keep the monster from ever coming back by her being cheerful. Soon Baby Divine and her parents were back in their home, and Baby snuggled safely in her bed thinking about her wonderful adventure and the joy of being accepted and loved by her parents. As she drifted off to a happy and peaceful sleep, what danced in her head was

And Baby Divine felt the Call and the Challenge,
Of Life and the Urge to Explore,
And she vowed as she started to dream of Tomorrow,
To never stop calling for "MORE!"

Bette described the book this way: "This isn't a baby children's book, it has something for everyone. It's a book about being different. I always felt very different when I was a kid. We all want to be king of the playground when we're kids and we spend our adult lives still wanting to be king of the playground. This book says you don't have to be that. You can be happy just being yourself."

Part V

The Kipper Phase

21

The Man Arrives

Until 1984, Bette's view on marriage was, "Oh, nevair, *nev-air!* There's community property in this state! I'm not giving away a nickel, honey! I think marriage is great—if two people are equals, but not if it's a master/slave thing—not unless that's what they're into."

On the subject of babies, she believed children required two parents and she wasn't sure who the father would be. Then something happened that cleared away all the uncertainty. Her affair with Benoit Gautier ended, and the questions about marriage, babies, and all that were settled because, within days of her fortieth birthday, she got married. The groom was an unusual commodity broker of German heritage by the name of Martin von Haselberg. However, he had a second personality as a performance artist working as Harry Kipper.

In reality he was one of two performance artists working under the name of Harry Kipper. The other one was Brian Routh. Von Haselberg and Routh worked together in an eccentric performance art comedy act where they each played Harry Kipper and did everything in tandem.

"Most of his friends call him Kipper," Bette explained. "He actually sells commodities under the name of Harry Kipper as well. And he performs with Brian Kipper, which is not his real name either. I met some performance artists and I wanted to meet others. A girlfriend of mine, Toni Basil, introduced me to him as one of

the Kipper Kids. I always remembered him as that. I thought it was
his real name. I ran into him a couple of years later, and he reminded
me that we had met, and I put his name in my book. Two years later
he called me out of the clear blue."

That call led to a date. Bette described how it started: "He's
quite eccentric. He showed up for our first date wearing a great big
yellow plaid suit that seemed to have a life of its own. He looked
like a used-car salesman, and I said to myself, 'I have to go out with
this suit?' " She did and found von Haselberg appealing, and, as she
said, "After two months of *intensive* dating, we were married."

The Kipper Kids were jointly created by von Haselberg and
Routh, taking the Kipper name from a classmate of theirs in England whose face looked remarkably like that of a fish. When they
began, one played Harry Kipper and the other played Alf Kipper,
but they could never remember who was who, so they both adopted
the stage name Harry Kipper. The Kipper Kids were into performance art, which is avant-garde art that features a performance by the
artist and is little known by mainstream audiences. Performance art,
for example, was among the most controversial of the National En-
dowment for the Arts grants made during the Reagan and Bush
administrations. Particularly when some grants were made to Karen
Finley, a performance artist who comes on stage and smears her
naked body with chocolate and launches into a scatological
monologue about the suppressed sexual fantasies of America's middle class. She concludes her act by allowing the audience members
to peer though a tube inserted in her vagina. The Kipper Kids performed wearing jockstraps and phony noses and smeared each other
with food.

Bette and Harry Kipper first met in 1982, but neither was attracted to the other. In fact, at the time, he had no idea who Bette
Midler was. When they met again while going to clubs in Los Angeles in 1984, it was instant chemistry and they saw each other full-
time for two months. He proposed to her on Saturday night, she
said yes, and soon after they were driving from her Los Angeles
home to Las Vegas. It was Sunday morning at two A. M. when they
got there, but the marriage license bureau in Vegas is open twenty-
four hours a day, and they soon had the license and drove to Caesars

Palace. After they checked in, they changed clothes and went out in search of an all-night wedding chapel. They selected the Candlelight Wedding Chapel, where, to a tape of *Juliet of the Spirits*, a minister who moonlighted as an Elvis impersonator joined the two lovers as man and wife, Mr. and Mrs. Martin von Haselberg, on December 16, 1984.

"The Elvis impersonator was an accident," Bette later told her friends. "We wanted to get married quickly, and Vegas sounded like a good place to do it. We didn't know he was an Elvis impersonator till the end of the ceremony when he handed us his single. It was the Chapel of the Twilight or something. We had fun. We got all dressed up. I had my dress that I wore to the premiere of *The River* and Harry had two used-car-salesman suits. The first one was a houndstooth check suit that he had made a couple of years ago. He looked like something out of *The Music Man*. I said, 'No, Harry, I really can't marry you in that suit.' So he changed into a nice black suit. The long drive to Vegas had been a lot of laughs. But the long drive back from Vegas was kind of quiet. We were fairly shaken. We went there on a lark, but now it was going to be real."

The Midler career, idling in neutral in 1984 after the disaster of her 1982 movie *Jinxed*, was essentially shut down for the next several months while the newlyweds got to know each other and consummated their marriage. Harry, for example, didn't know Bette had been born in Hawaii and had never seen any of her movies or stage productions and was only barely acquainted with her albums.

Bette said, "For the first couple of weeks after we got married, it was 'Uh-oh, what did we do?' There were some rough spots, but we did our talking, we did our compromising. Fortunately, we liked what we got to know."

When one reporter asked Bette why she was rarely seen in public during this time, she responded, "Why go out? The only reason you go out is to find someone to bring home."

One of the most sensitive issues the two had to face was their respective ethnic origins, since Harry was German and Bette Jewish and very uncomfortable with the whole Nazi experience. She had even been nervous about touring in Germany.

"I have to say it was a trouble spot," Bette said after the wedding.

"Harry has shown great restraint and patience when I've talked to him about it. He says all Germans don't hate Jews and he does insist upon it. I'm still not comfortable being in Germany. . . . The truth is that even if we were married forever, I don't think he could change my mind about it. But I don't resent him because of his nationality. He is an individual first and the citizen of a country last."

For Bette, Harry's strength and stability as a man was also important, and even early in the marriage, he gave the support that she has always needed and never had before. "He's secure. He's stable," she said admiringly. "He's not wrapped up in the business. He's an adult."

The two of them seemed comfortable in their Los Angeles home, with Bette not missing New York as much as she yearned for a new movie. Meanwhile, Harry and Bette put together a comedy record album, *Mud Will Be Flung Tonight*, featuring Bette telling funny stories and her comedy routines in which she satirized everybody. Referring to her marriage to a German husband, she commented, "He's a German. Every night I dress up like Poland and he invades me." Or, casting a cutting remark at the French, "The nation that gave us Renoir thinks Jerry Lewis is a genius."

Mud Will Be Flung Tonight was taped April 30 and May 1, 1985, at Bud Friedman's Improvisation club in Los Angeles, where Bette sang and returned to one of her favorite subjects, breasts, with a routine about the inventor of the bra, Otto Titzling. It was Bette's tenth album and her first comedy offering.

"I haven't had much luck with music," was her simple explanation for *Mud Will Be Flung Tonight*. "I wasn't camp for a long time and I really miss it. Life is a drag and people need to be tickled by someone as twitty as my own self. What I've got is a really good take on tits. Because I've had mine for so long and thus they're a big part of me. I weigh more now than I've ever weighed, more than I could ever conceive someone my size weighing. But you know what? I was zooming toward forty and I suddenly realized I didn't mind anymore how I looked. It's a great weight off my mind!"

There were a lot of things that changed about Bette's life by

1986. She had a new life with a husband, a new album, and a new movie, *Down and Out in Beverly Hills*—the first in four years.

"Since I got married [in 1984], I say every night, 'Thank you' to God or whoever it is who's listening up there. The word blessing: I never paid much attention to it, but I've been so happy the last year, in a way I didn't think was humanly possible."

The home she shared with her new husband was a four-bedroom Spanish-Mediterranean-style residence in Beverly Hills and was once featured in *Architectural Digest*. "This house is like a canvas to me," Bette said, referring to her penchant for remodeling and redecorating. "I have a nesting instinct that didn't come out until I bought [the house] and now seems to be overwhelming me."

22

Who Is Harry Kipper?

Bette and Harry made a charming, if unusual, couple. One of the unit production managers on her film *Outrageous Fortune* said the two of them acted like love-smitten teenagers: "When he came to the set, they would sit at the edge of the stage together holding hands. Very cute. Her relationship with her husband was almost teenagerish. It's lovely to see people who are that much engrossed in each other."

Yet, it seemed an odd combination. "They make an unusual couple," the manager said. "I understand he's very nice. They were very much in love. It was quite obvious. Strange combination: a Jewish lady and a German guy. Not an everyday sort of thing, but they seemed very happy."

So, who is Harry Kipper, a. k. a. Martin von Haselberg? And why has he been so immersed in shock art and performance art? Moreover, what is shock art and performance art? Let's try to get some insight into Bette and Harry's relationship by understanding the endeavor to which Harry has devoted so much of his life.

In California, where Harry and Bette live, the school of radical artistic expression—performance art—was centered around the Irvine campus of the University of California, ironically in the heart of traditionally straitlaced and conservative Orange County, south of Los Angeles. In the 1960s and 1970s, graduate students at the school formed the core of the performance art movement, led by Chris Burden, Barbara Smith, and Nancy Buchanan. In 1971, in a dramatic high point of performance art, Burden had a friend shoot him through the upper arm with a .22-caliber pistol on the stage of F-Space art gallery in Santa Ana. This art was meant to represent personal involvement in America's tumult over the Vietnam War. Another bizarre act took place in Austria when artist Hermann Nitsch poured the blood of a slaughtered lamb over a naked man and woman together.

According to Barbara Smith, "Starting around 1969, UCI [University of California at Irvine] became the hot place for performance [art] in Southern California. It was a place that was just sort of pregnant with ideas. It was a dialogue among some very intense people."

One of those very intense people was Martin von Haselberg. He and others believed they were scrutinizing society's mores and norms through various art forms with the objective of transforming society into what the artists thought would be a better form. For several years the Kipper Kids were an integral part of the performance art movement and widely acclaimed as avant-garde clowns. The Kipper Kids—Martin von Haselberg and Brian Routh—became famous among the movement for their bizarre boxing matches which also involved smearing food all over each other and making strange noises through grunts, snorts, and flatulence that they claimed were musical. They also assisted Hermann Nitsch with his lamb's-blood cascades.

Von Haselberg and Routh met in the East Fifteenth Street Acting School, where Routh was part of a theatrical family. Although his father was an engineer, other close family members became dancers and played in the music halls of England. Martin von Haselberg, Routh's partner, was born in Argentina. His father was a doctor of philosophy and a writer, as well as a reporter for the Associated Press. He became an expert on Goethe and moved his family to Argentina to escape the rise of Hitler in Germany.

The Kipper Kids split up several times. The act also caused the breakup of both of their first marriages, because their wives hated the act and thought they were stupid for doing it. Each was divorced in 1980. The men agreed it was stupid at times, but they didn't want wives who would tell them that. However, both are remarried to new wives who support their zany endeavor.

Even though the Kipper Kids had said they were going commercial and Bette's Harry was studying to be a movie director at the American Film Institute, the two Harry Kippers continued to perform. They still seem committed to shock or performance art. Jim Sullivan, writing in the *Boston Globe* November 1, 1989, put shock art and performance art into perspective.

He said that the average person was not familiar with the world of shock art and performance art. There are always those who test the limits of the human body, spirit, or mind in modern art. The most familiar modern versions of shock art began in 1972 with rocker Alice Cooper, who would chop up plastic toy dolls that he had earlier filled with phony blood—red liquid or maybe chicken's blood—while singing the song "Dead Babies." Or he would undergo a fake guillotining of himself, with part of the group holding up the phony bloody head of Cooper afterward to show that the killer had been punished.

In Cooper's 1987 tour the central song was "Chop, Chop, Chop/Gail," glorifying a serial murderer who slaughtered women named Gail. There was the mincing up of plastic dolls and the decapitating of a woman in a scene that squirted make-believe blood twenty feet out into the audience. At the conclusion there was a fake hanging. "We've upped the ante," Cooper told the *Boston Globe* at the time. "And the pressure of the valves. I'm becoming the Stephen King of rock 'n' roll, which is not a bad place to be."

Shock art attempts to disturb, provoke, and entertain the audience by playing to the thrill of seeing the unseeable and experiencing horror while still safely seated in one's twenty-five-dollar seats. Extreme acts are more easily done in film, where they are carefully orchestrated by the special effects experts who create the illusion of something that doesn't actually happen. In contrast, when performed on the stage before a live audience, there is a high sense of reality. One dramatic example in Boston was the performance of Joe Coleman, who literally had fireworks explode on his chest, to the alarm of the audience. Shock art has also invaded the world of dance, and, of course, it is an integral part of performance art. For example, in the film *Mondo New York*, which was released in 1987, the dance troupe engaged in a series of masochistic and violent confrontations.

In some ways these acts mirrored what had been happening in film since the 1960s with many offbeat and violent movies, the most notorious of which were the early snuff films showing a woman being sexually abused and then murdered. There are many films showing mindless, amoral sex, violence, torture, and antisocial behavior for which there continues to be an audience. Director Wes Craven's latest film, *Vampire in Brooklyn* starring Eddie Murphy, continues the genre.

Critic Jim Sullivan traced shock art and performance art as it infused the music scene in America. "Rock 'n' roll, the traditional outlet for frustrated youth, has, in one form or another, operated outside the mainstream since its inception. At one time Elvis Presley, Little Richard, and Jerry Lee Lewis were shocking. But as they and their followers found, those who wanted to keep the shock quotient were moved to greater extremes—the Rolling Stones posing in drag, Screaming Lord Sutch being carried on stage in a coffin, and the late Frank Zappa singing tales of exploits with groupies. Rock and roll shock art hit the mainstream with Cooper in the early seventies, and thrived along the fringes with Iggy and the Stooges. Both Iggy Pop, whose act included cutting his chest with broken glass and smearing peanut butter on his chest, and Cooper, whose act included more theatrical bloodletting, were inspired by the Doors' Jim Morrison, infamous for exposing himself during a Florida concert, which would be mimicked later in a variation by the Kipper Kids."

As Sullivan wrote in the *Boston Globe*, "The heat was turned up a notch when the punk rock revolution began to take shape in 1976. The New York–based Plasmatics, fronted by nearly nude ex-porn-star Wendy O. Williams, wreaked havoc with chainsaw music, chainsaw props, violence, and sexual explicitness. John Cale bit the head off a live chicken during one show. The Sex Pistols' Sid Vicious sliced up his chest on their U.S. tour; Johnny Rotten blew his nose all over the stage. Scraping Foetus Off the Wheel forced stomach turning by simply choosing its name. Singer–performance artist Lydia Lunch, girlfriend of Foetus' Jim Thirlwell, has unveiled multiple tales of rape and degradation on stage, the intent being to hold up a mirror to what she perceived as the ugliness all around us.

"Although Ozzy Osbourne is well known for biting into a bat on stage—it was a mistake, he thought it was rubber—heavy metal's version of shock rock tends to be more theatrical and outsized: Hence, the dramatic, semi-comic fake bloodletting of acts such as Cooper, KISS, King Diamond, and GWAR, the latter of whom was at the Channel last Saturday. In metal, you'll find allusions to Satanism, general mayhem and inverted morality tales. The idea is to provide an outlet for the unspeakable, an escapist, cathartic fantasy."

The late Robert Mapplethorpe shocked many, including outraged conservative congressmen, with his Jesus photo immersed in urine and another one showing a man urinating into another man's mouth. Critic Jim Sullivan maintains the view that performance art is the epitome of shock art: "It's in the performing-arts field, though, that the going gets most gritty. The Kipper Kids, known for showering themselves and others with debris, have pelted audiences with eggs, paints and ink; Harry Kipper gleefully relates in 'Re/Search No. 11: Pranks!' There was horror, literal panic, people were tripping over each other trying to get out of the room."

Others involved with the Kipper Kids in perfomance art included Chris Burden, who once acted out a crucifixion while on top of a Volkswagen, and the omnipresent Karen Finley, who entertained audiences by shoving yams up her rectum. Alex Grey, the Boston-based painter of the work *Necrophilia*, the subject of which is sexual intercourse with the dead, is another such artist. The objective of all of this "art" was to keep pushing the limits and, as people became accustomed to something that once revolted them, to move on to the next extreme. Generally, Alice Cooper was regarded as a bit silly, Karen Finley as disgusting, and Joe Coleman as dangerous to both himself and his audience. Jan Stuart described a more recent incarnation of the Kipper Kids at Alice Tully Hall in Lincoln Center in her story of August 3, 1993, for *Newsday*:

"Two middle-aged men, fleshy, bald, and much too naked, stand in the middle of a boxing ring. Their privates are concealed by jock straps, while everything else is slopped over in baked beans, cranberry sauce, several pounds of flour, paint, ink, shaving cream and glitter."

This was the performance art of the Kipper Kids as they appeared in a Lincoln Center show called *Serious Fun!* Their first ex-

Bette performing with the Harlettes at the London Palladium, 1978. (*David Redfern/Retna*)

Bette Midler as the lead in *The Rose*, the story of Janis Joplin, 1979. (*Nancy Barr/Retna*)

Bette Midler with Home Box
Office president Michael Fuchs, in
1984. (*David McGough/DMI*)

Bette with Gloria Steinem, 1984.
(*DMI*)

Bette with Andy Warhol, 1984. (*David
McGough/DMI*)

Bette Midler gets her own star on Hollywood Boulevard. (*Kevin Winter/DMI*)

Bette performing onstage with Jack Nicholson in the Live Aid concert in Philadelphia, July 1985. (*J. L. Atlan/Sygma*)

Bette helps open the new Disneyworld–MGM Studios in Lake Buena Vista, Florida along with Disney president, Michael Eisner. May 1989. (*P. Chauvel/Sygma*)

Bette, Mickey Mouse, and Disney president Michael Eisner in Florida at Disneyworld–MGM gala, 1989. (*O. Abolafia/Liaison*)

The All Girls of Bette's
All Girls Productions in
1990, the year they did
Hocus Pocus. Left to right:
Margaret Jennings
South, Bette Midler,
and Bonnie Bruckheimer
Martell. (*Michael
Grecco/Sygma*)

Bette receiving a Grammy in
Los Angeles, 1990. (*Frank
Trapper/Sygma*)

Bette receiving a Golden Globe, 1992.
(*Frank Trapper/Sygma*)

Opening Night for a Radio City Music Hall concert. (*David Corio/Retna Ltd.*)

Bette attending the American Film Institute Awards honoring Jack Nicholson at the Beverly Hilton Hotel in 1994. (*Steve Granitz/Retna Ltd.*)

Bette performing in costume. (*Janet Macoska/Retna Ltd.*)

Performing with the Harlettes. (*Walter McBride/Retna Ltd.*)

Onstage performance by Bette. (*Nancy Moran/Sygma*)

Glamour head shot of Bette. (*George Hurrell/Sygma*)

posure, in every sense of that word, to the audience of *Serious Fun!* came when the two Harry Kippers broke through holes in a big black box on the stage and then showed off their genitals through little trapdoors, aided by spotlights and magnifying glasses. From this point, they rapidly launched into a satire of Harry Lauder, wearing cardboard kilts and trashing the song "Roaming in the Gloaming" while accompanying themselves with banjo, sax, and flatulent gas noises—one of their trademarks.

Their performance art continued with more messing around on the theme of bodily functions, which seems to be the adolescent obsession of performance artists, including playing with a brown, pasty substance that the *Newsday* reviewer hoped tastefully was chocolate pudding. Some in the audience clearly didn't intend to wait around to find out, and many left during the first act, while those who stayed were apparently mesmerized by the Kipper Kids' antics and their flouting of manners and good taste. Some may have stayed because they, too, had a childlike fascination with seeing something their mommies would have considered naughty. That was the theory advanced by one reviewer:

"The Kipper Kids are the ultimate vicarious vaudeville: They break the rules for us—stripping, destroying, defying Miss Manners—and take the punishment to boot. Instead, by the time they emerge as baked-bean ballerinas, we are captivated and grateful. We've had a naughty roll in the sandbox and don't even have to send off our pants to the dry cleaners. It's a weird way to spend a Friday evening. It's an even weirder way for two middle-aged men to make a buck."

Critic Stephen Holden wrote in the *New York Times* on July 30, 1993, "Kipper Kids (Martin von Haselberg and Brian Routh), both of whom call themselves 'Harry Kipper,' play overgrown adolescents whose messy theatrical pranks elevate the food fight into a primal ritual. Audience members in the front rows risk being splattered."

The Kipper Kids were trying to convey some deep and significant message, but very few people had a clue as to what it was. For most people, it probably communicated the idea that undisciplined minds like to make mud pies.

23

Outrageous Ruthless People
in Beverly Hills

It was from deep inside his memory that Paul Mazursky fished up a comedy story from thirty years before when he was twenty-four. He recalled it as a 1932 French movie by Jean Renoir. The movie, which Mazursky had seen at the New York Museum of Modern Art, was based, in turn, on an original play by René Rauchois entitled *Boudu Saved From Drowning*. It was an amusing tale of two unlikely elements of society thrust together and how they interact to create the comedy of incongruity. A similar theme drives the classic *The Prince and the Pauper*, which Touchstone, the grown-up movie division of Walt Disney studios, filmed with Dan Aykroyd and Eddie Murphy supported by Don Ameche and Ralph Bellamy, in a new version called *Trading Places*.

In *Boudu Saved From Drowning*, a bookseller saves a hobo from drowning and brings him home. The two begin living together, and both lives are changed from the melding of their anomalies. The original was rewritten by Mazursky and scriptwriter Leon Capetanos for an American audience by shifting the scene to contemporary times, changing the hobo to a homeless person and the locale from Paris to Beverly Hills. The result was a script they called *Jerry Saved From Drowning*. The main roles were a homeless man and a stereotypical wealthy Beverly Hills Jewish couple. Mazursky recalls,

"I started thinking about the film again and that it might be interesting to switch *Boudu* to the United States. We [Mazursky and Capetanos] decided to poke fun at Beverly Hills. To make fun of my own life, so to speak."

In the updated, Beverly Hills version, Jerry Baskin is the homeless street person who decides to end it all by drowning himself in the swimming pool of the wealthy, newly rich Dave and Barbara Whiteman. Dave is wealthy from the wire coathanger business and rakes in loads of money while his wife tries to spend the money as fast as she can. Dave saves Jerry from drowning and invites Jerry to stay with them until Jerry can get his life in order.

In the casting, Mazursky demonstrated imagination while adhering to the Disney formula of using over-the-hill actors. He selected Nick Nolte as the homeless man, Richard Dreyfuss as the husband, and Bette Midler as his wife. Of these three, Dreyfuss was the only first choice, and Mazursky connected with him immediately as Dave. Still, he didn't want to commit to Dreyfuss until he saw who would be playing the other parts, because these actors would not be functioning in a vacuum and would have to relate both as people off the set and as actors on the set. For the homeless man, Mazursky's first choice was Jack Nicholson, even though the latter was obviously a star at the time. Nicholson read the script and liked it, but was committed to another movie, *The Two Jakes*, and could not break free. Dreyfuss suggested Nolte, whom Mazursky says he also had in mind, and they concluded he would be right for the part.

He first thought about Cher or Dyan Cannon for the Beverly Hills matronly wife, but decided that Bette Midler was an even better choice, and when he consulted with the Disney studio, they enthusiastically agreed. Bette described her reaction to Paul Mazursky's telephone call: "It was like a call from the gods. It's like *I'll Cry Tomorrow*—it's so Lillian Roth I can't stand it."

Bette and Mazursky hit it off at their first meeting in spite of the fact that Bette was nervous because she hadn't been seriously considered for a picture since *Jinxed* and she had had such a traumatic experience with Don Siegel. "I thought I was going to meet some silver-haired Hollywood type, but Paul turned out to be an

ex-stand-up comic, a guy with whom I had instant rapport." Mazursky changed the name of the movie to *Down and Out in Beverly
Hills* before they started shooting on May 20, 1985.

Mazursky's sensitive directing style proved effective, and the
three egos sublimated themselves to the film. Bette was eager to
prove that she was not a temperamental prima donna and was grateful to Disney for giving her another chance at a comedy film. "I
have no real empathy for matrons who don't have a lot to do with
themselves. You know the type—so much time on their hands and
no real imagination. However, Paul showed me what was wonderful
about Barbara and how to make her amusing. Barbara Whiteman is
a soul in torment. The reason it's funny is that she really doesn't
have anything to be in torment about."

Beyond the character as written, Bette was also able to bring
some of herself into the role, seeing Barbara as cynical and angry
with her lot in life. Known for her salty talk on stage and her obsession with talking about and exposing her tits, Bette thought it
was ironic that she would be appearing in a Disney movie.

"I never tell people I'm working for Disney. Walt would roll
over in his grave! If I hadn't made my name practically taking my
clothes off and being bawdy, I'd be delighted to work for the straight
Disney guys. I grew up watching *Dumbo* and those movies. And
Hayley Mills: I was crazy about her."

John Broderick, the unit production manager on *Down and Out*,
was impressed by the way they all worked together and how Bette
impressed him. "It was a very upbeat cast," he said. "It was a good
movie. It was very professional and it was on target. So they all
did what they were supposed to do, and they all had a good feeling
about it."

Broderick came away with three impressions: Bette was not
pretty, but she was a terrific actress; he had to guard against drinking
by the three principal actors; and they had a fabulous wrap party
(the party celebrating the completion of the filming).

"I thought she was ugly. She is ugly. Bette Midler is not a pretty
woman. Other than that, you wonder what's going on and then you
find out she's playing the wife and she was sensational! She has
become an institution at Disney."

As for the drinking by the three principals in the cast, that was a problem Broderick had to monitor carefully. "Bette got a little drunk in doing the scene in the den," he said, "where she grabs Richard Dreyfuss and Richard's having this affair with the maid. When she [Bette] starts putting her legs around Richard at the bar, she was actually a little blotto.

"When the movie started, it was like sitting on a fucking volcano because Richard had had his problems, Bette had had her problems, and Nick Nolte had had his problems. The condition on them doing the picture was that they all stay clean. This is basically, if you look at it, it was kind of their comeback movie collectively. All three of them were in the throes of major habitual problems. That's why they worked so cheap on the movie.

"They did a tremendous job, but it was scary for Paul [Mazursky]. It was scary for everybody because one never really knew when they might make that little turn and go down that dark alley. I fired a driver because he was taking Nick Nolte out to a bar. Because these people are trying to stay close to the stars, trying to kiss the star's ass. They do that because they're powerful and they're stars and people want to get close."

This was a different Bette than before: more mature, more settled, and more sensitive to the fragility of life and success. The film turned out to have the intimate feeling of a stage production. Happily for Bette, after *Down and Out* finished in August 1985, the word spread through Hollywood that Bette Midler was funny, easy to work with, and a seasoned professional. Disney Studios liked her so much, they offered her another role as part of a three-picture deal.

Critic David Brooks in the magazine *Insight* summarized the film as "a comedy and a very enjoyable one. At the same time, *Down and Out in Beverly Hills* is exceedingly intelligent, a movie that mixes the hilarious with the true." The packed movie theaters around the country testified to the film's success.

In *Down and Out in Beverly Hills*, Bette played a role many actresses would have shied away from, and Bette herself said, "I was pretty shaken when I saw the movie. I didn't realize just how terrible I was going to look. I wouldn't have done that role five years ago. I would have thought it beneath me, because this was when I was going to be a great dramatic actress. And, yes, I would have cared too much to look like that."

Even before video rentals, the movie earned $60 million at the box office for Disney. It was a very important movie for Disney and its new management of Frank Wells, Michael Eisner, and Jeffrey Katzenberg as they worked to make Disney a profitable studio again. Jeffrey Katzenberg, the chairman of Disney Studios, said, "This lady is as smart and nailed-down as anyone I deal with."

Bette was recovering from her nervous breakdown and depression, and the career offers were coming in again: offers for concerts, proposals for tours, ideas for albums, and best of all, scripts for other movies.

The next script she liked came to her as a result of her appearing on *The Tonight Show* and singing a comedy song from her *Mud Will Be Flung Tonight* album, "Fat as I Am." Three Disney directors who saw her performance thought she was just right for a comedy they were developing, *Would Anyone Please Kill My Wife?* The directors were the brothers David and Jerry Zucker and their partner, Jim Abrahams, who were coproducers of a series of zany movies that had made them famous and rich. *Airplane!* was their first, released in 1980. Since the Zucker-Abrahams combination worked at Disney Studios as did Bette, that coincidence provided an additional incentive to send the script to her for review. When she first read the screenplay for *Would Anyone Please Kill My Wife?* Bette flipped. "The screenplay was as funny as anything I've ever read," she said later. She hastened to the phone to accept immediately.

Like many screenplays in Hollywood, the plot was "adapted," this time from O. Henry's classic "The Ransom of Red Chief," about a kidnapped brat who is such an irritating little twit that the kidnappers pay the parents to take him back. So *Would Anyone Please Kill My Wife?* followed that story line and depended on the usual comedy premise of switched circumstances producing unintended results when a man's annoying wife is kidnapped.

The character named Barbara (same name as the wife in that other adapted story, *Down and Out in Beverly Hills*) is a loudmouthed, overweight, rich wife who hectors her unhappy husband, played by

Danny DeVito. Danny is fed up with his wife and decides to get rid of her. He wants to have her money, however, and so divorce is out of the question. He plans to murder her, but before he can, a disgruntled ex-employee kidnaps her for ransom and demands millions for her return. As writer Dale Launer crafted the screenplay, Danny refuses to pay the ransom and hopes secretly that the kidnappers carry out their announced threat of killing their victim.

Meanwhile, the kidnappers, who are amateurs, do not have the guts to kill Barbara. She proves so irritating that they can't wait to get rid of her. They keep lowering their ransom demand so that Danny will pay and they can return her, but he refuses. While she is in captivity, Barbara, realizing she is close to death, undergoes a transformation. Her personality softens, she works out and loses weight and begins to build a friendship with her kidnappers. The only thing that outrages her is that her husband won't buy her freedom. The kidnappers keep lowering the ransom until it has dropped from millions to a mere $10,000, and she incredulously asks, "Do I understand this correctly? I've been marked down?" They confirm that is so, and she shrieks, "I've been kidnapped by K-Mart!" In the end, she has trimmed down to a more attractive figure and turns the tables on her faithless husband by getting the kidnappers to let her go and help her get revenge on him.

It was a good role for Bette, and she wanted it, but there was a glitch named Madonna who had impressed Disney executives with her acting in the 1985 hit *Desperately Seeking Susan*. They wanted to get Madonna on the Disney lot, and the only role they had available at the time was Barbara in *Would Anyone Please Kill My Wife?* The issue became moot when Madonna rejected that role and took one in another film, *Shanghai Surprise*, which was released in 1986 to a tepid response.

After Madonna was gone, the Disney executives, the Zucker brothers, and Jim Abrahams talked some more and finally offered the role to Bette. She embraced it and was on the lot shooting the film in January 1986, while they changed the name of *Would Anyone Please Kill My Wife?* to *Ruthless People*. Bette loved the part about the wife slimming down in captivity because, since her marriage, Bette had put on about twenty pounds which she wanted to lose.

She said, "My husband loves restaurants and I've never gone about eating with the gusto that he's taught me. I've been eating food from countries you didn't even know had food. Ten pounds is like blimp city for me [she is only five feet one and a half inches tall]. So I made a resolution to lose the weight. I went on a juice fast and I started working out. That was good because I have a whole exercise scene in *Ruthless People* where I have to do push-ups and sit-ups."

But *Ruthless People* was not the biggest production in progress. She announced in March of 1986 that she was carrying a baby Kipper.

Bette joked with the press about the baby and said that, just as her father was embarrassed about the kind of things Bette did in public, most likely her child would be embarrassed too. She declared, "Well, I'm going to put my baby in boarding school as soon as possible in a far corner of England—no, Scotland near the heather and the highlands—so my baby will never hear any of this!"

Reference to her father was poignant because as the new life within her was fluttering, her father was dying. He had been quite sick for much of the previous year, with two heart bypass operations, and was disheartened about his own prospects.

"He didn't want to go on," Bette said. "He really wanted to lie down and die. And I said, 'No, what's the point of doing that?' and I got him through it. I rose to an occasion that I didn't think I could rise to and I feel that a lot of that was because I had Harry in back of me saying, 'Yes, you can do it.' "

It was a comfort for Bette that she had never had before, having someone who had faith in her and who sustained her. Barry had been rough on her professionally, to their mutual benefit. Russo had jerked her around and kept her feeling dependent in order to feed his own ego. Peter had probably been the nicest man she knew. Harry was there to help her settle up with her father and to let them say "I love you and goodbye" to each other.

In June 1986 *Ruthless People* was released as a great tour de force for Bette, with industry raves for the success of her two comedies in a row. In fact, *Ruthless* was a showcase film for Midler. From these two box-office hits, Bette promptly slipped into the third picture of her deal with Disney. This one was with another comedienne, Shelley Long, who first came to wide public notice in her role as Diane Chambers in the TV series *Cheers*. This time the movie was called *Outrageous Fortune*, and it involved a man (Peter Coyote) leading a double life who is loved by two women in New York City. Each woman is convinced she is his true love, and when he suddenly disappears, they team up to find him and see which of them will get him. Their chase takes them across country and into the wilds of Arizona in pursuit of their mysterious lover, who is, unbeknownst to either of them, a secret agent also being hunted for more lethal reasons by the KGB, CIA, FBI, and assorted other heavies over whom the two women constantly stumble.

Bette is the tough, street-savvy lady, Sandy Brozinsky, and Shelley Long is the naive, cultured woman. The two are bound together in their pursuit of their common love for their runaway boyfriend and the need to stick together for survival in the process. It is, again, the humor of incongruous relationship, as was *Down and Out in Beverly Hills*. The shooting, under the direction of Arthur Hiller, began right after *Ruthless People* opened in June.

Hiller said that, while Shelley Long had already been cast, he and the others involved were undecided who would play Sandy Brozinsky. "When I came in [to direct the picture] Shelley Long was already attached. We [producers, studio, and writer] sat down and started talking about who could play the other role. And we bounced around a lot of names. And some of them were very good. So I said, 'Well, let me think about it.' Then the next day, someone at the studio said, 'What about Bette Midler?' We all said, 'Oh, that's perfect! That's perfect!' And everybody grabbed at it. It worked out very nicely."

They filmed first in New York City and then shifted to Newark International Airport and, finally, to Santa Fe. They were on location for six weeks with Peter Coyote, George Carlin, and John Schuck.

There had been rumors about friction between Shelley and Bette, but apparently the conflicts were resolved. Some disagree-

ments were inevitable. For example, Shelley was cast for the film
first and then Bette was hired. Every actor tries to get top billing in
the movie posters and marquee positions as a matter of pride and
business negotiation. Both Bette and Shelley had demanded first
position, and since Shelley had been hired first, she probably would
have gotten it. But the two actresses agreed on a compromise that
put Shelley first on half the posters and Bette first on the rest. The
two may not have become close friends while working together on
Outrageous Fortune, but both were determined to be professionals
about the project and their working relationships.

Peter Herald worked with Bette on *Outrageous Fortune* and said
it was interesting filming her while she was pregnant. First of all,
he immediately learned that the private and the public Bette were
two different people.

He recalled, "I first met Bette during preproduction. It struck
me that she looks all different in civilian life than she does in the
pictures. Her screen personality is quite different, more outrageous.
She plays Bette Midler. I was surprised that she looked quite civi-
lized."

Beyond that, Herald found her a veteran performer. "I think
she's a trooper. She was pregnant, but she did the whole picture.
We staged it in such a way so that it'd be easier and used doubles
for scenes that could be dangerous. She was good about it. She never
brought up the fact that she was pregnant. She never said, 'I can't
do this because I'm pregnant.' She was very professional. Amazingly
professional.

"We photographed her so that the pregnancy didn't show. It
worked out fine. We started out in New York, went to Mexico and
ended up here, in Los Angeles. It wasn't shot chronologically, nor
was it shot where her scenes came last. We bent over backwards to
make it comfortable for her."

Beyond that, they had been assured medically from the first day
that the film was doable with her pregnant. Director Arthur Hiller
said, "I remember the first day we got together and read the script.
Well, I went in with impressions, needless to say, that she was a
wonderfully talented person, but I didn't know her. I do remember
worrying about the pregnancy. I spoke to her gynecologist and I

spoke to two other gynecologists, and they all said the same thing. Basically, she can do anything as long as there aren't any sharp impacts. One said she could even play tennis, which would be ridiculous. . . . We still worked very carefully on wardrobe to hide the pregnancy, but it wasn't too difficult because by nature we could put her in sweaters and things. But there was lots of mountain climbing and stuff like that."

Because of that mountain climbing and the two actresses' clambering around, there were some touchy moments. Hiller recalled, "I remember a scene where Bette and Shelley Long finally decide to become friends out in the middle of the desert, and they're hitchhiking out in the middle of nowhere and finally they see a big oil rig on the other side of the road. They decide to run across because they're willing to go in any direction. When we're filming and they start to run across [the road], Bette tripped and fell and the blood drained out of me because I thought, 'Oh, My God! I've just killed a child.' I just went into total panic. Shelley helped her up and grabbed her shoes that had flown away and then they got on the oil rig. That's when I found out Bette did it on purpose. She just suddenly got the idea that it would be funny if she fell, so she did a protected fall. She knew what she was doing."

The filming of the movie went well, but partway through, word came that her father's heart trouble was getting worse. It seemed to everybody, including Chesty Midler, that his remaining days were few. In spite of the differences between them, Bette and her father talked regularly on the phone and doubtlessly shared a certain closeness—though not the intimate relationship Bette wished. So when that depressing news came, she started to slip away from the production in New York or Arizona and fly to Hawaii to spend some of the little time her father had left with him. Her pregnancy made him very happy, as did her marriage, because that was the kind of thing that a regular daughter did.

"My father needed me and I think he was very, very happy that I came through. I think he felt that he didn't deserve any support because, when he was raising me, he didn't really pay much attention. But I just went ahead and gave him all the help I could. I guess he thought I wasn't so bad after all, even though I do stand up and tell dirty jokes."

Peter Herald recalls that time as a mark of the kind of performer and the kind of person Bette appeared to be:

> I remember when we were down in Mexico. I was in the production office, it was a Saturday, I believe, and the phone call came in that Bette's father was dying. That he had little time left. So we talked and sent her to Hawaii. She spent a few days with him while we shot around her.
>
> A few days after she came back to Mexico, her father passed away. I liked the fact that she had such an attachment to her family. She was in quite bad shape when she found out her father was as ill as he was. And nothing mattered anymore, she had to go to see him. We had four days that we could shoot without her, which we did. It must have been very hard for her [to come back] because I'm sure that she saw that her father was failing and recovery was questionable. But she was professional enough to come back and do the picture.
>
> I remember the day we got word that her father had passed away. I have a feeling that Bette was prepared for it. She wanted to see him once more and she did. She was quite brave about it. The crew liked her, respected her, and they all felt her personal loss.

She knew that she had been an embarrassment to her father because she hadn't grown up to be the simple hausfrau he thought was proper, or, lacking that, a respectable professional woman. "He wanted me to be a professional person and to have a stable job and not get into trouble, not make any noise, not have people look at me."

Bette was, in fact, a very successful professional entertainer, but that's not what Fred wanted. To him she was vulgar in a public way that brought unwanted attention to the Midler family, and Fred could never bring himself to acknowledge her genius because of that. "He wouldn't give me any reward," Bette said sorrowfully.

When she was pregnant, she hoped that it would encourage him to try to hold on so that he could be around when the baby was born. There was a softening of love between daughter and father, with the hope that Chesty Midler would live long enough to see his first grandchild. Bette fervently wanted that moment for him and for herself. Regretfully, it didn't happen, and one day Chesty Midler died in his beloved Hawaii. Bette sadly buried her father next to her mother and her sister. It was one of those dark moments of life, but this time Bette had someone she loved to comfort her and someone inside her to give her hope. Although the biological clock was ticking, Bette and Harry were so happy with the pregnancy that they dreamed of having several children. "I know I have to move fast," admitted the pregnant Bette. "My clock and all that."

Bette was proud of her acting work as her third film went into public release January 1987, to public acclaim. *People* magazine assessed *Outrageous Fortune*: "Bette Midler and Shelley Long bring out the bitchy, bawdy best in each other in this breakneck farce." And *USA Today*'s Mike Clark wrote, "Shelley Long and Bette Midler together could energize even the most witless writing, but that's not an issue in *Outrageous Fortune*. Newcomer Leslie Dixon's script is witty and zippy, casting the twosome in roles they've virtually come to define: WASP princess and tawdry street trash. Midler and Long are outrageously funny."

What was pleasing to Bette was that her three-in-a-row success led to a solid recognition of her ability as a comedy actress. Disney gave her her own production deal on the Disney studio lot as Jeffrey Katzenberg, then chairman of Disney Studios, announced, "Bette Midler is the single greatest asset as a performer we have."

The production deal was a delight to Bette. "Was it *Outrageous Ruthless People in Beverly Hills?*" she asked. "The films have certainly indicated a direction to stay in. The whole package is a surprise: to be a box-office success hand in hand with Disney. A real shocker. I mean, Walt Disney never would have hired me."

The new production deal gave her the power to select, produce, and direct her own films, with financial backing from Disney, who would then handle promotion and distribution. In the simplest terms, her production deal generally worked this way: The studio would give Bette and her staff offices on the studio lot and advance money to pay Bette's staff and the operation of her All Girl Productions, in addition to putting up the money for Bette and her main assistant, Bonnie Bruckheimer-Martell, to develop scripts, hire production crews and casts, and shoot films.

Disney, of course, had to approve how the money was spent and had to be convinced the film would be successful. For example, it okayed, or "green-lighted," in studio lingo, *Big Business*, but said no to *For the Boys*, which Bette and All Girl Productions took to Twentieth Century Fox studios to make.

Disney made a profit on the money it advanced to Bette and All Girl Productions and received a share of the income from theater box offices, foreign distribution, videotapes, and television. The studio often handled the distribution and promotion, and for this, too, it got a profit. In any event, for every person who gets a production deal as Bette did, there are scores or even hundreds who would like one, so it was a signal honor that Disney was willing to invest its money in Bette Midler.

Bette explained why she formed her own company, All Girl Productions, along with her colleagues, Bonnie Bruckheimer-Martell and Margaret Jennings: "I've decided to be as realistic about what I do as I possibly can be. And what I can be is very, very funny, which not a lot of ladies are right now, and I can also sing, which not a lot of ladies are doing. And very few of them sing and are funny in the same picture. So I've been inching my way toward that. I'd like to have a niche, a little piece of the pie where I can do what it is that I do and I don't step on anyone's toes and I'm not disappointed if I don't get their part."

Bette now felt she had found her role all by herself in making the film comedies that brought her such acclaim and pleasure. "You know, these kind of comedies, I'm happy that people like them and I'm happy that they make them. But you always want to do something more, something better. I guess I feel like I have to pay some dues and then I'll be okay."

24

The Real Baby Arrives

One of the most important moments in Bette Midler's life occurred on November 14, 1986—two weeks before she turned forty-one—with the birth of her first child. This infant was given the name Sophie Frederica Alohilani von Haselberg. Bette had joked about giving it a name like the one Bob Geldof had given his child, Fifi Trixibelle, but Harry said that could be an embarrassment to the child in later years, which makes one wonder what Harry thinks Sophie Frederica Alohilani von Haselberg will be.

Some people believed that Bette was following her mother's idea of naming her children after favorite entertainers and named her first daughter after Sophie Tucker. That is not so. Bette explained, "She is not named after Sophie Tucker, contrary to what people might think. The Frederica is for my father, Fred, and Alohilani is Hawaiian for 'Bright Sky.' "

The main concern of her life now was Sophie, who changed Bette and Harry's life from the minute she emerged into the world. "I was appalled," Bette said. "We both cried when she came out. She looked like a sixty-year-old stock broker: bald, wrinkled, and puffy." That, of course, all changed as Bette and Sophie grew and bonded together. And there were new things to learn, such as the business of breastfeeding. "Before I discovered the electric breast pump, it was agony."

Bette spent the early part of 1987 recuperating from the birth and slimming down from the weight she had gained while pregnant.

In spite of the weight gain, it had been a relatively easy pregnancy. "I haven't had any morning sickness or any of the stuff they keep talking about," Bette said. About the worst it got was shortness of breath and being unable to sleep on her stomach, in addition to developing a strong new craving for sweets.

After recuperating from the childbirth, Bette got involved in the first development deal that All Girl Productions was bringing into production. It was a team-up of Bette with another comedienne who had been enormously successful on her own, Lily Tomlin. The new script was called *Big Business*, and it featured the old plot of two infants being switched at birth.

In *Big Business*, Bette and Lily are two sets of identical twins separated at birth. Other characters include the Sheltons, a rich New York couple vacationing in a small southern town, Jupiter Hollow, and the Ratliffs, who are locals living in the community. Each couple has twins in the rural hospital, and a nearsighted nurse mixes up the twins, both dual sets of girls and both sets named Sadie and Rose. One of each set of twins is given to each set of parents. Years go by and we find that Sadie Shelton (Bette) is a hard-as-nails CEO of a major business conglomerate and her sister Rose Shelton (Tomlin) is an idealist with no interest in corporate life. The other set of mismatched twins consists of Rose Ratliff (Tomlin), a tough, hard-driving factory foreman, and Sadie Ratliff (Midler), a quiet big-city sophisticate. The four meet and the fun and confusion begin.

Director Jim Abrahams characterized Bette and Lily Tomlin working together: "I just knew the two actresses would have good chemistry—they'd have to in this situation. Their bodies seem to work with one another, there's a respect. Lily tends to think through her roles to the nth degree, working out every conceivable motivation. Bette, once she has the character in her head, wings it. You never know what she'll do from take to take."

To create the multiple images necessary for such a film in which one actor has to appear as twin characters in the same scene, Abrahams used a technique called motion control, creating a split screen utilizing a computer linked to the camera. One actor plays out each of the twins' parts, and the computer and split-screen camera mesh them together to create the illusion of two identical twins.

Once the film was done, Bette seemed to spend the rest of 1987 getting awards and working on a television concept. She received several American Comedy Awards in April 1987, as Best Comedy Actress in *Ruthless People*, Funniest Performance on a Record for *Mud Will Be Flung*, on which she worked with her husband, along with a lifetime achievement award for the totality of her concert, film, television, and stage work.

There were also offers from the publishers Little, Brown and Company, for a book on motherhood and from HBO for a comedy special. She agreed to the HBO special, but her main focus was still on Hollywood and the movie game.

For the HBO special, Bette came up with an unusual approach. She decided to perform those routines from her stage act in which she unmercifully satirized every sacred cow imaginable. She would do an Italian takeoff of how *The Tonight Show* might look on a low-budget, public-access cable channel, in which all of her guests would present what they believed was the best in entertainment, when actually it was dreadful. It was like the "Vickie Eydie's Global Revue: Around the World in Eighty Ways" satire she did on stage. The title for the show, which aired on HBO March 19, 1988, was *Beyond Mondo Beyondo*, and an added plus for Bette was the television introduction of her husband, Martin von Haselberg, in his performance-art role as part of the Kipper Kids.

Bette wore a dreadful looking dress that appeared as if its designer were insane, and she spoke to the audience in pidgin Italian while acting as Mondo Beyondo, the hostess of the show, and featured far-out and strange performers. Mondo Beyondo announced to the audience, "They think that if you make much money, you have no taste and must be a moral slimeball. Not true. Look at me. It proves you can be rich and still keep your integrity."

The engaging part of the show occurred when Bette did her patter between acts and then rolled videotape of the next zany act. But these were actual performances done by serious entertainers—not parodies made up for this HBO show. They were all earnestly performed avant-garde routines by artists trying to make a statement. Her lineup on the show included Luke Cresswell and Steve

McNicholas as the Yes/No People's Drum Town, who wander around a city drumming on rooftops, garbage cans, and whatever else presents itself; Bill Irwin, a baggy-pants mime-comic; Paul Zaloom in a comedy sketch in a New Jersey garbage dump, focusing on the delights of the way yuppies dine; and the La La La Human Steps, a dance troupe from Canada that performed in an empty swimming pool. The final act on the show was the Kipper Kids performing their wind-breaking flatulence number while wearing jockstraps and tires around their waists and spraying vegetable colorings and Reddi Wip on each other.

The irrepressible Miss Mondo Beyondo ended the special by urging viewers to demand that their local station managers bring back her program the following week after they (the viewers) have tended to other essentials such as going to the bathroom and baking pizza. With a "Ciao, for now, bambinis," she closed the show. *Newsweek* magazine would laud the special: "Midler as Mondo Beyondo continues demonstrating she is one of the most outrageous funny people on TV, a maximalist comedienne in a minimalist age."

Part VI

The Life of a
Movie Star Mother

25

1988—*Beaches* and Baby

By 1988, Bette was into two Bs in her life, *Beaches* and Baby. The material for the movie project *Beaches* had been known in the Hollywood studio circuit for a time, particularly by Bette because of the unusual circumstances of its creation.

The story that would become *Beaches* was originally an Iris Rainier Dart novel, but its creation as a book and then a movie was unusual, according to Midler. What made it so different was that the author of the novel didn't write it until she had spoken to Midler and then created it with Bette in mind.

"Before she wrote it," Bette said, "she called me up and she said, 'Look, you don't know me, but I have an idea for a book and you are the inspiration for this book and when I am done, I want you to read it.' So she sent it to me in galleys and I thought it was terrific. There were certain things about the character that I thought were a little rough for my taste, but she went on, she had a big success with the book. Then it went around the studios, and so actually I would have to say that ever since about 1980 I've known about it."

When Bette appeared on *The Oprah Winfrey Show* to talk about *Beaches* on December 14, 1988, she praised the story to the audience and urged them to see the film. "It's the kind of movie, I don't know how men feel about it, but you should get the tickets and you should take them and you should take your best girlfriend to see this movie. Oh, I'm telling you I was weeping by myself."

Beaches costarred Barbara Hershey, and its screenplay was by

Mary Donahue, who also wrote *Agnes of God*. The book and movie tell the story of the friendship between two girls as they grow into women and how they drift apart, then come back together because of the lifelong bond between them as one becomes a well-known singing star and the other remains out of the public eye. It was Midler's fifth movie for the Disney studios and featured the hit song "The Wind Beneath My Wings."

The other B in Bette's life was, of course, the baby, who made her enormously happy. "I love being a mother, but I have lots of help. I'm not out there carrying my baby twenty-four hours a day all by myself, you know. I mean I have a husband who gives me a lot of support. I have a nanny. Yes, my raising of my child I'm enjoying tremendously. I think if I were doing it by myself, I would probably be dead by now. . . . It exhausts you. It gives you like major folds in your eyes."

Still, Bette's life was filled with caring for her daughter, and there were some things she would not or could not let others do for her. Even though her husband, Harry, was supportive enough to get up in the night with the child, he could not feed her, since Bette was nursing her. Bette said, "There are certain things that I absolutely insist upon doing because I don't want to miss. I take her to the gym and swim. I go to the play group. We make cookies. We read books and sing songs and stuff, and I put her on the john, feed her. I love to do the cooking because I like to make sure that she doesn't have too much salt, she gets good grains. She likes butter, and she'll just like grab the whole stick and put it in her mouth."

The little tot learned she could have her way about some things and could even make Mommy go away when she became annoying, as mothers sometimes do. That's when Sophie would give Bette a little shove and say emphatically, "No! Mommy." And Bette was convinced that "the Terrible Twos," which most toddlers go through, started early with her daughter, Sophie.

"I think she started at seventeen months. She said, 'No,' and she definitely has a mind of her own, but I just bite my tongue. I resist the impulse to shake her or to scold her. I'm just letting her live it out. I'm having a good time. Sometimes she has too many things because people from all over the country send her things. I mean it's beautiful stuff and I'm grateful for it, but sometimes she doesn't know where to look and I want her to cherish things. So a lot of the time, I'll just go through and weed out certain things."

Bette was so entranced with motherhood that even though she began having a family late in life, she still wanted to have two more children. She bragged that her gynecologist told her she had the insides of a thirty-year-old and that she could keep on having babies for a long time, which pleased her immensely. Unfortunately, the second try resulted in a miscarriage.

Part of the private side of Bette is her domesticity beyond motherhood. "I've always liked being in the house. I've always liked to read and I've always liked being semidomestic, sweeping and cleaning. I love to decorate and garden, to get out and dig in the weeds. I used to like to go out and not get drunk, but see what people were wearing at least and what the new dance steps were, and now I have no idea what they're doing. Basically you would go out to get laid and if you're getting laid at home, you don't even, you know—I mean, well, you don't really . . . that's why they made clubs, so people can meet each other and then go home and have babies."

The marriage between Bette and Harry worked well, and no one was exactly sure why, but it was probably that Harry and Bette were ready for marriage and that they were both determined to make it work. Bette clearly enjoyed her marriage and was amazed she had found such a perfect man for herself.

"My husband is quite eccentric and, of course, I'm quite eccentric. So our eccentricities are always like bumping into each other. 'That's my area. Get out of my way.' And you can't do that. You have to sort of say, 'Well, it's your turn now.' And it's interesting. You really have to mature. In order to give, you give your things up and then you gain and that's really the theorem or the axiom . . . because there's no director in the house [to tell everyone what to do.]"

In Bette's December 1988 appearance on *The Oprah Winfrey Show*, the two talked about what Bette did best. Bette said she still didn't know that she was really talented. Then they had the following exchange, which confirms that the one medium in which Bette thinks she has the most talent is the concert stage.

OPRAH: I've never seen you in concert.
BETTE: Oh, I'm fabulous!
OPRAH: Are you?
BETTE: Yeah. No, I'm fabulous. Just fabulous. Oh, I really am.
OPRAH: Are you really?
BETTE: That's my best thing.

When she described what was involved in her stage performances, Bette revealed something that critics and people in the audience didn't realize about the anxieties she endured. "First you have to heave a lot in the ladies' room beforehand, and then you're light enough to go out and dazed enough to go out and face them. Yeah, I tell you, if you're prepared, it's a lot of fun. If you're just thrown to the wolves, it can be truly, truly agony, because you freeze. Your brain freezes up on you, but if you're prepared, you have a foundation and then you can fly. If you have no foundation, then you can sink real easily. I mean, I found if you know what you're going to do, you know what you're going to say, you have an idea what you want to say, what your message is that evening, what songs you're going to sing, how you're going to move around the stage. If you have like a plan, then you're free. If you just go out and wing it, then you can have a lot of trouble."

Then Oprah displayed a film clip of the concert movie *Bette! Divine Madness*, which didn't do well in theaters even though the concert was the usual sellout smash when it toured the country live.

Bette told Oprah and her audience, "I was really sick. It was a horrible, horrible, horrible shoot. It was so horrible. The rains had come and we shot it in February. The rains had come into Los Angeles and we were shooting in Pasadena. It was like the streets were completely flooded, the water was up to here, we had to drive through the water in order to get there, and the basement of the theater was flooded and there was the danger of electrocution. I had like, I had pneumonia. Oh, it was . . . and I begged them, 'Please don't make me make this picture. I'll give you back all my fee.' [She was being paid $850,000.] They made me make that picture. They made me do it. So when I look at it, I'm not that crazy to look at it because it reminds me of all that horror."

During her Oprah appearance, Bette also gave some very private insights into the emotional upheavals she endured, such as the feelings she experienced on the movie *Jinxed* and how she worked her way through them. "Well, I think really the idea that I'd get out, the idea that there was light at the end of the tunnel, and you know what else is really good when you're really feeling bad? It's rage, anger. Rage works. To feel that what's happening to you is unjust and then you can get angry. That's a real energy booster, I've found. A nervous breakdown (which I had) is kind of lonely, kind of desolate, real desolate, gray, very gray. You know, when you cannot move. You can't get up. You cry all the time."

Oprah asked her if exhaustion played a role in the nervous collapse, and Bette replied, "That does play a big part in it. When you spend a lot of energy and, you know, things aren't going your way and you're unjustly let down or betrayed, that can trigger, but exhaustion actually does play a part in it."

The strain that produced the nervous breakdown also resulted in Bette's determination that someday she and Harry and their child would retire to Hawaii, where she had a home. She said, "I'm going to have to do it whether I like it or not. It's partly because in this business, you only have a certain amount of time and the camera can be very unforgiving. You can get a lift. You can add more light, but sooner or later you have to face the facts."

Of course, Bette could continue to write books, which she does well. "I'll tell you something. I wrote a book called *A View From a Broad* that's a fictionalized account of something that I went through, and I would like to make a movie of that fictionalized account, but I would never want to tell the truth about my life."

The Rose continued to be her favorite movie, in spite of the fact that her later comedies, such as *Down and Out in Beverly Hills*, *Ruthless People*, and *Outrageous Fortune*, were much bigger commercial successes.

But there was no question about which was Bette's favorite role. "I have to say of all the pictures I've made, I like *The Rose* the best. But I like this one [*Beaches*] too. I like the real characters."

26

1990—Stella Dallas: The Life and The Movie

Just as Bette rediscovered old songs and updated them as part of her repertoire, in 1990 she delved into an old story of a single mother and updated it as her next movie project. *Stella Dallas*, a novel by Olive Higgins Prouty about a mother's devotion to her daughter, had already been made into a movie twice, and it reminded Bette of her own childhood in some ways. It brought back memories of living in rural Aiea with the sugarcane fields as a backyard and a huge garbage dumpster as a nearby neighbor, lying like a giant whale beached on the red soil of Oahu.

When Bette first read the script, she said that every third page had her crying because she related the struggle of Stella to the hard times endured by her own mother, which she appreciated more now that she, too, was a mother. "I had a fabulous mother. She made me believe in myself and I used a lot of her in the film. She was not a single parent like Stella, but we were poor and she was that generation of women, almost all gone now, who always put their family ahead of themselves. She worked hard and kept nothing for herself, nothing. Never a new dress or new shoes. She adored me, my mom, and I still have nightmares about her, because as a grown-up I didn't give her the time I should have. Now that she's gone, I have regrets."

The Stella Dallas story was first screened in 1925 as a silent film, and the basic plot was about a working-class woman who becomes pregnant from a quickie affair with a rich playboy and strives to raise the child alone. Finally, she decides that the only thing she can do, although it is heartbreaking for her, is to surrender her teenage daughter to her natural father's family, who can take better care of her.

When Stella was filmed a second time, as a talkie in 1937, it made Barbara Stanwyck a star and put a different spin on the plot. In the Stanwyck version, Stella is a tramp who cunningly inveigles a rich man into marrying her and then dumps him and raises her daughter on the generous alimony she receives. In Bette's interpretation of Stella Dallas, she is an honest, decent, working single mother whose pride leads her down an honorable path and who is devoted to raising her daughter.

For Bette, Stella is the personification of her own mother. "My mother reigned indomitable. She believed in me and with no money, no help, four kids, and a difficult husband, she pressed on through the morass. Nothing got her down. Stella is deemed vulgar. Her poverty is beyond her control. She has no education, no social status, and she knows it. In one of the film's key scenes, she gives her daughter, Jenny, a birthday party and, humiliatingly, nobody shows up."

This moment brings Stella to realize she cannot provide for her daughter as she wants to do, and she agrees to let the rich and socially prominent family of Jenny's father have her. In the end, Bette was Stella standing outside the father's family home in a snowstorm, nosed pressed up against the window, while inside her daughter is married in a ceremony to which Stella was not invited.

It's a sad story about difficult times, and it was hard for Bette to shoot the film. "We shot for ten weeks in the ugliest place in the world, a warehouse in the east end of Toronto next to a sewage plant. Grim. Cold. Very dirty. I had to shower three times a day."

Bette was apprehensive as to how the critics would receive *Stella*, because it is a woman's movie just as *Beaches* before it had been. "*Beaches* touched a huge chord in women, but was reduced to tearjerker status by fifty-year-old male reviewers who feel they've been manipulated when they start to cry. I'm afraid that's what I'm up against on *Stella* too."

Bette was nervous about having a movie turn bad because of what happened in 1982 when the film *Jinxed* bombed and made her studio poison for four years in spite of her performance in *The Rose* three years before.

She also didn't like it that some Disney executives talked about how they had saved her from ignoble artistic extinction. "Disney always tells the press they found me face down in the gutter and dragged me out of it. So I've told Jeffrey Katzenberg to stop saying that. True, I didn't work for three years and was unjustly accused of sabotaging that terrible picture. Nobody wanted me. I had a nervous breakdown. It's a horrible thing to lose faith in oneself—a killer. I sat home crying, sleeping, and spent plenty of time getting drunk on Courvoisier. Finally, I went to a therapist and learned I wasn't to blame, that my feelings of persecution were correct. He told me to get busy."

So she did and came back stronger than ever and met and married Harry and had a child, all of which had now made her more serene and happy than she had ever been in her life.

For the January 1990 issue of *Ladies' Home Journal*, editor Cliff Jahr expressed the thought that by remaking *Stella*, Bette was taking one of the biggest risks of her career. After all, *Stella* was a melodrama, and Bette's forte in film so far had been comedy, except for her first starring feature role in *The Rose*.

Still, the biggest challenge for Bette in 1989 was not finishing the movie *Stella* or getting ready to do another one—*Scenes From a Mall*, with Woody Allen—later in 1990. For Bette the important goal was to produce a third birthday party for Sophie on November 14. She had gone to great lengths to make sure everything was just so, but she hadn't reckoned on one thing: Sophie had decided she wanted to be a brat instead of being three.

When Sophie woke up on her third birthday and found a paper crown her mother had made for her, she immediately ripped it off and began crying. At breakfast she tore the foil wrapping from her chair and announced that she hated being three; she hated the cupcakes Bette had baked for her classmates at school; she hated the party decorations; and she had no intention of having a good time or of becoming three! So there!

Bette was in tears. "Oh, I was so hurt. Oh, it was so horrible, horrible, horrible. Oh, I can't tell you how horrible." Bette was worried about the child growing up as a Hollywood kid and yet she did all the things that made Sophie a Hollywood kid. A few days before Sophie's birthday, they all went to the fourth birthday party of Candice Bergen's daughter, Chloe, who had her own built-in child's entertainment center at home with children's rides and video games.

At the same time, Bette was very strict about Sophie's environment, food, and clothes. She had the little girl eating lots of vegetables, fish, and tofu and tried to keep her out of trendy clothes. Most of all, she wanted to raise Sophie to be well educated and self-reliant so that she could survive rich or poor.

Now Sophie was the princess. "Oh, God, yes. I'm completely enchanted by my child. She's very affectionate though she wasn't for a long time. She'd say, 'No kisses, no kisses,' because she has a certain coldness too. She can turn it off just like her mother."

And, at three, Sophie became more rambunctious, which became a problem for Bette, who found herself in an anomalous situation. On the stage, she performed in a raucous and rebellious way, but now she was a mother with a little daughter who would sometimes also perform in a raucous and rebellious way. What was stock in trade for Bette Midler, stage performer, was not the order of the day or night for Mom Midler with baby Sophie. Her mother, Ruth, had been a disciplinarian, trying to keep four active kids under control without a lot of help from father Fred, and now the apple had not fallen far from the tree. Bette was now the family disciplinarian, and Harry thought she was a little too tough on the child and refused to join in disciplining her.

Bette tried to be the perfect mother and give her Sophie everything that Bette hadn't had as a child. Bette had her own strict rules for raising the princess Sophie: the three-year-old was not allowed to watch television, eat junk food, or stay up late. Bette described her regimen for the child: "I've got to say we're on the pompous side. At first I thought, 'Well, gee, everyone's going to think I'm a jerk.' And then I thought, 'I don't care what they think. I want her to have a foundation in things the world considers good and artful.' "

Bette doesn't like the violence on television programs or the sexuality of the commercials and leans toward parent and child just being together. "We just do stuff together. We do a lot of construction paper, a lot of drawing, a lot of chatting, a lot of dancing around and making up stories and games and stuff." Bette reflects on that whole brouhaha over the third birthday party and says she wanted a divorce so her husband would leave and take the child with him. Looking back on that basic motherhood experience, Bette learned something.

"I couldn't deal with it. I was reduced to being a four-year-old. She really pushed the buttons. And you know, it was true, I had done the wrong thing. I had never had a birthday party in my life until I was thirty-five or something like that, so I'm acting all this stuff out through her—at least this time I did. But I know better now. I did learn a lesson."

In February 1990, Connie Chung interviewed Bette, along with her husband, in her Coldwater Canyon home two months after Bette turned forty-four and the night after her sixth movie for Disney Studios, *Stella*, opened. It was an interview that divulged some very private glimpses of Bette. For one thing, her forty-fourth birthday made her reflect upon her professional future.

"I'm forty-four now, so I hope to keep going but you don't know what people—whether the people are going to stick with you. You know, sometimes they want to see a young face. So you don't know how you're going to fare, but that's okay. I can always do live shows, and I look fabulous in the spotlight."

The interview also allowed Bette to talk about her successful relationship with Disney Studios and how movies had lately been dominating her time and talent professionally, running from *Down and Out in Beverly Hills* to her latest in 1990, *Stella*. The first five movies made on the Disney lot grossed more than a third of a billion dollars. While she was focusing on movies—she hadn't done a concert in five years—music was not entirely neglected, particularly in a movie like *Beaches*, which nobody liked except the public. The critics panned it, but the public gobbled it up and the theme song, "The Wind Beneath My Wings," became a hit record—the first sung by Bette to become number one on the charts. It motivated her to create another album.

Bette's forty-fourth birthday hardened and softened some other views she had of life and the world. The death of her parents, her miscarriage in 1989, and the number of her friends dying from AIDS were sobering. "It's unbelievable. It's like I was in a war. I don't think those losses made me stronger. They've robbed me of love and happiness and laughs, so I try not to think of them."

On the death of her many show business friends from AIDS, she said, "I've lost everybody. I don't have any friends left—nobody to talk to. I know at least thirty-five men who have died from AIDS. Dear, dear friends, three of them my dearest. I miss them . . . the laughs. Our culture is cruel, its homophobia unconscionable. Makes me wish I wasn't in the human race. That's why I had to shut the television off. Well, I'll never make it past forty-five if I don't shut this off, because this is just too grim. It's very, very grim. I don't know. I do sound like such a star-joke, I imagine. I'm sorry. Usually I get naked."

Still, in spite of all the sadness and depression, Bette was happy in many other ways. She endured the trauma of the miscarriage in 1989, but was still determined to have another baby if she and Harry could. "My daughter says, 'I want a baby, I want a baby,' so we're trying. I have no fear about doing this at forty-four. And, y'know, people who want to have babies will do anything. I'm going ahead. We have our little kits. We even stand on our heads. So there I go, sometimes, standing on my head. It's a sight to see, I can tell you."

Seven days after Bette's interview with Connie Chung, she did an interview with KCBS Los Angeles reporter Steve Kmetko to hype her new movie *Stella* again. It was difficult because of the discord that erupted between the two of them. Finally, in exasperation she said, "God, the sound of my voice is really starting to give me a headache. You know that feeling? It's, like, so irritating. And this poor world has to listen to this for weeks on end. Oh, I'm sorry guys. Just go see the picture, all right? Why do you have to listen to this drivel?"

Kmetko came back at Bette with, "Why do you do this, then?"

Bette answered, "Well, I do it because I like my picture and I believe in my picture and I want people to see my picture. Unfortunately, you won't let me just come on here and say I made this wonderful picture. Can I—would I—you please let me address the American public and say, I made a very nice picture. I struggled with it. I had to be in a dark, dank room for many, many months and I've interviewed people and I wore ugly clothes. Please go see me. It's just—I have to come on and tell you about my sex life."

Looking back later, Bette felt that *Stella* had been unjustly savaged by the press, and it hurt her. "Nobody saw it because the press maligned it so terribly," she said. "It was slightly old-fashioned, but it wasn't badly made. And I was really good in it. You have to realize that with *Stella*, Jeffrey Katzenberg bought that for me and he paid an arm and a leg for it, because he really believed in it. He felt that maybe we were onto something new with *Beaches* and that maybe people wanted to see something slightly more sentimental than the usual fare.

At first Katzenberg could not get anyone to direct the film. Finally John Erman agreed to do it. Bette continued, "And by that time Jeffrey was already into it for a lot of money and he had to make the picture. And he had to eat it. Which is too bad. There were a lot of mistakes made, but I'd like to think that after twenty years I wouldn't live or die on one script. But it broke my heart when I was turning through *Premiere* magazine and saw 'A must to avoid' after *Stella*. I was really shocked."

Bette's mood in this period was revealed in an interview in September with Alan Petrucelli for *Redbook*, in which he asked Bette what makes her laugh. That is, what makes the entertainer who makes other people laugh, laugh? The question was more insightful than it might appear on the surface, because it motivated Bette to reveal a side few have seen.

Bette said she wasn't sure that she wanted to be funny anymore. She had lost too many friends to AIDS and she had the new responsibilities of married life and motherhood. "I'm not funny—I'm completely hysterically funny. When I'm inspired, I'm untouchable. No one can top me. But I don't find life funny anymore. Not with the hatred in this country, not with the terrible toll AIDS has taken, not with the amount of ugliness in the world. So I have chosen to live in my own little world, in which I'm up to my neck making records and movies, one after another. I wish I could find life funnier, but I can't . . . I just can't. The older I get, the more curmudgeonly I become. I guess I'm an old fart."

Petrucelli found that the zany Bette Midler he had known in 1980 had become the matured, married, and maternal Midler of 1990. Bette told him, "I have grown older and wiser. My priorities have changed. My career takes third, fourth, fifth place now. My husband and my child come first. Being a wife and mother is hard work—it takes up so much time and energy that I just don't know how those women with more than one kid do it. I guess they do it for the same reason I do it . . . for love."

27

Women in Movies

B ette was in two movies in 1990, John Erman's *Stella* and Paul
Mazursky's *Scenes From a Mall*. *Scenes From a Mall* was a curious movie in many ways and, gratefully, it disappeared from
movie screens all around America faster than ice cream at a kids'
party. The subject was not one that most audiences appreciated
since it centered around domestic discord in a Jewish couple's marriage with much of it filmed at what was supposed to be a multi-
level mall in a predominantly Jewish neighborhood in West Los
Angeles' Fairfax District called The Beverly Center.

Only the exteriors were shot there, however, since Woody Allen
hates Los Angeles and refused to spend more than a few days there
making the film. All the interior shots were done, to accommodate
Mr. Allen's Angelesophobia, at a mall in Connecticut. Bette said she
loved working with Woody. Woody has been silent on whether or
not he loved working with Bette, but the film was not a success for
many reasons. It is about domestic discord which most people have
enough of at home and aren't willing to pay $7.50 to see on the big
screen; it was very Jewish, which has a limited audience in most parts
of America; and, it was awkwardly done in spots. There is one scene,
for example, where Woody and Bette are supposed to be having sex
and it would be more exciting to watch a pit crew change tires at
the Indy 500.

Since much of her career was now focused on movies, she was
concerned along with other actresses about the male domination of

the film industry and good roles for actors, as well as how long her appearance and voice would prove acceptable to her audiences. She has frequently commented in recent years about how much crueler aging is to a woman, and particularly one in the public eye.

Interviewer Lawrence Grobel, talking with Bette for *Movieline* magazine, told her that Cher had said there were no great movie parts for women over forty, and Bette replied, "I don't feel that way. I feel like I can go on forever. People always want to see a funny little old lady, don't they? And if they don't, I'll make them. I still have the Sophie Tucker story to do yet. I don't have that fear. I also know that fear is something that they're all going through. I wonder if they're just catching it from each other, though. I mean, it's obvious that Cher can go on forever too if she wants. Her career is longer than God so far."

Bette's acting ability is attested to by important directors such as Mark Rydell, who directed her in *The Rose* and *For the Boys*, and Arthur Hiller, who directed her in *Outrageous Fortune*. Hiller said:

> Bette has an amazing talent. There aren't that many amazing talents. I don't know quite how to describe it. Except that you can teach any reasonably intelligent person to paint, but you can't teach them to be Picasso, and that applies to Bette. I mean you can teach people to act, and if they're intelligent and have some feelings, they'll be very good. But people like Bette, you can't teach that. It's a God-given gift. I'm sure that everything enters into it, but I swear, some people—they have to be born with it. That amazing talent I think would have been there no matter where they grew up. I'm not saying that background doesn't affect you or that a lot of people aren't groomed by their genes. When did Mozart start writing music, five? And, just like that, there are some actors that are born with a great talent.

In that context, 1990 was notable in the Hollywood film industry for the reemergence of the issue of Hollywood discrimination against women. Hollywood is sexist and unfair to most actresses, probably because there are too few women in executive positions where the decisions are made. Defenders of the current Hollywood production system say movies are expensive and production decisions are business moves and not creative ones. Movies are a business and not an art form for most producers simply because when they stop thinking about them as a business, they are quickly out of business. Since women are rarely big box-office draws or big money-makers, there is a scarcity of roles for women and actresses are paid less.

The Screen Actors Guild in August of 1990 released a study showing that actors got 71 percent of all the feature film roles and were paid twice as much. In fact, women over forty in Hollywood were cast in only 9 percent of the roles.

During the 1930s and 1940s, a new feminine ideal emerged: worldly types such as Bette Davis, Joan Crawford, and Barbara Stanwyck with strong appeal to women, who, for the most part, selected which movies to see. Perhaps half of the films released were "women's films," major vehicles for major female stars under contract to the studios. They portrayed the poor girl who, by dint of sex and other wiles, rose in society (Joan Crawford in *Possessed*), the career woman who succeeded through wit and style and grace (Irene Dunne in *The Awful Truth*), the Spider Woman luring innocent men to their doom (Stanwyck in *Double Indemnity*), the "kept" woman who fell in love with tragic results (Dunne again in *Back Street*). More upbeat images were provided by Doris Day movies, variations on the classic romantic comedies that featured Carole Lombard, Jean Arthur, and Claudette Colbert. About *Back Street*, one critic wrote: "Swell romance, a little tear-jerking and a woman's picture— which means a money production." Commercial success and female appeal were inextricably linked. The coming of television in the late forties, however, changed the face of the industry.

"Television, without question, cut off the older audience, and women lost control of the moviegoing dollar," says film critic and historian Richard Schickel. "The person deciding which film to see became a guy under twenty-five who usually headed for action films. Actresses were relegated to semisupporting roles or to prestige films which took aim at the Oscar nominations essential to their business. It became a very tough marketplace for them."

"Actresses have a much tougher time now. There aren't nearly as many good roles," according to producer Mark Johnson, who did *Rain Man* and *Avalon*. "In the forties, you had the great romantic comedies with strong women characters. Carole Lombard, Barbara Stanwyck, Bette Davis outdrew the men. In the fifties, Doris Day was as much of a draw as Rock Hudson. Elizabeth Taylor was enormous in the sixties and Streisand in the seventies. But for at least five years now, we haven't had a real strong female box-office draw." And that's what it's all about, "a strong box-office draw," when you are a production company that is putting thirty to forty million dollars on the line.

Beyond that, many of the studios have been gobbled up by bottom-line-oriented conglomerates who want profits on their inflated investments. The high prices paid for control of Universal, Columbia, MGM, Disney, and Paramount mean more profits must be generated to pay off the enormous debt incurred in buying those studios. For example, Bette Midler's production deals with Disney are affected by the fact that the Bass Brothers of Texas are the largest stockholders and are not interested in creativity as such, only in dividends and stock prices of Disney shares.

The new owners are not moviemakers, they are business investors; and the old-time moviemakers were never risk takers. They weren't risk takers then and they are not risk takers now. They want movies to make money, and to ensure that, they want actors with big box-office draws, and there aren't many women in that category. This profit-oriented mentality has existed in the movie industry from its beginning in various manifestations. For example, early filmmakers refused to put the actors' names on their films because they didn't want actors to become popular, because then they could demand higher salaries. That particular practice changed when Irving Thalberg started giving actors film credits, but the profit-focused mentality remained the same.

In a November 11, 1990, analysis of the situation in Hollywood for actresses, the *Los Angeles Times* summed up the prior decade in filmmaking: "Never known as risk-takers, in a era of escalating production and marketing costs, [Hollywood producers are] even more under the gun. Working with contracts that usually run [only] three years and with stockholders breathing down their necks, studio heads in the '80s began pandering to the youth audience whose repeat business held the hope of blockbusters. Playing to that undiscriminating age group meant a proliferation of formula films with costly special effects featuring the same handful of increasingly pricey male stars." The emphasis on box-office-generating male stars was echoed by Lisa Weinstein, who produced the hit *Ghost*: "Movies are so expensive that the studios want to hedge their bets. They go for the five or six big male names: Cruise, Stallone, Schwarzenegger, Eddie Murphy, Willis, to bring the audience in."

Underscoring the male actor drawing power is the Quigley Poll, which surveys theater owners about the habits of the American moviegoing public. In 1961 there were three actresses among the top ten box-office moneymakers (Elizabeth Taylor, Doris Day, and Sandra Dee), but by 1989 that list was down to one (Kathleen Turner). Still, Bette Midler and Barbra Streisand are strong draws in the minds of most Hollywood pundits in specialized movies such as musicals or comedies.

Aging is another issue affecting actresses, including Bette. The good old double standard applies to men and women in acting just as it does to men and women in many other fields. Sid Ganis, formerly president of Paramount Pictures motion picture group, says, "The older actresses are in a bind because the audience is fickle. It wants younger women. It thrives on new blood." When an actress gets to forty, she slams into the wall that divides romantic, sexual roles from character roles as the schoolmarm or the maiden aunt. Even when adapting European movies—a favorite Hollywood activity—the role played by an older female European actress is played by a young American actress half the age of the male lead.

Another factor that has become important for filmmakers is not one that might occur to most of us: The movie business has become more international, with forty percent of a film's income coming from overseas showings. This is even more important when one considers that some of the major film studios are essentially foreign-owned: Sony owns Columbia, and Universal is owned by Japanese industrialists and MGM was owned, until recently, by a French bank. What this means is explained by Mike Simpson, cohead of the motion picture department of the William Morris agency: "The pictures that travel best are those in which language isn't central [as it is with most female-oriented films]. That usually means action-adventure pictures, almost always with male leads. Third-world countries, in general, have a macho attitude toward films."

Shirley MacLaine, always outspoken, believes a different kind of theme is needed in some pictures. "The problem is less the number of roles available to women than the film industry's discomfort with projects involving relationships, feelings, communication—the kind of things women are more likely to go into than men."

She is supported in that view by producer Lisa Weinstein. "The issue is not just women, but allowing room for diversity. Studios don't know how to make small films now. If every studio made two or three $12 million movies a year, there'd be room for a different kind of story."

Actress Rachel Ward agrees that it is the male-dominated psyche that determines women's position in most films. "I've read twenty-five-odd scripts in the last five weeks and in all of them the women were there so they could get fucked on page 50. . . . Producer Joel Silver said that the only way he wants women in his pictures is either naked or dead. Unfortunately, he reflects a lot of what other people think and is just pig enough to say it."

Lisa Weinstein said that Paramount finally decided to make her film, *Ghost*, because it had been producing a lot of action male-oriented movies and thought it ought to drop in a woman-oriented film. She added, "Patrick [Swayze], after all, is a guy women find very attractive. Women came and took their boyfriends. And their boyfriends told their friends about it. There's an ingrained belief that it's easier to get women to 'men's films' than vice versa, especially among the under-twenty-fives."

How does all this relate to Bette Midler? Well, she faces the same problems in getting films approved, and two of her most appealing movies for women, *Beaches* and *Stella*, took poundings from studio executives, with one of them commenting, "They were the worst kind of women's movies—sloppy sentimental, no reality."

The critics don't often like sentimental films because they think being emotionally moved by a film makes them less professional.

Nevertheless, the audiences do like these films, and that's what ultimately matters. Bette's reaction to the critics' reaction was, "They got kind of nasty with 'You're manipulating us' reviews, but it must have touched people in a way that they wanted and needed to be touched."

Regardless of how some of the movies Bette made turned out at the box office, if they were musical and allowed her to display her talents as a singer, they offset disappointments at the movie theater with successes at the record store. The song from *Beaches*, "The Wind Beneath My Wings," became a big hit record and garnered three Grammy nominations.

In the summer of 1990 the first National Women's Conference was held by the Screen Actors Guild. One of the speakers, Meryl Streep, half-seriously predicted that the steady erosion of women's roles in film would lead to women being eliminated from movies entirely by the year 2010. Today probably every studio in Hollywood can claim to have at least one movie in production that has a female lead, but the fact is that there has never been a time in Hollywood's history when there have been fewer major female roles being cast. At the time of the first National Women's Conference, Julia Roberts was acting in *Dying Young*, produced by Sally Fields; Cher, Winona Ryder, and Christiana Ricci were being featured in *Mermaids*; Demi Moore was in *The Butcher's Wife*; and Meryl Streep and Shirley MacLaine had leads in *Postcards From the Edge*. But all of this was quite modest compared to the number of roles available for men.

Richard Mestres, president of Hollywood Pictures, admitted there was always pressure to put two or more actresses in costarring roles bolstered with a strong male lead to broaden audience appeal and to protect the producer's investment. But the idea of a single woman star carrying a film, as Schwarzenegger, Cruise, or Willis can, is not thought possible. As actress Rachel Ward sees it, "In Hollywood, you're not an actor but a commodity. I realize we are talking about 'show business' and not 'show art,' that there's a capitalist philosophy at work. But it's a perpetual dilemma being an actress. Had I known what I was heading into, I would never have become one."

Bette Midler is one of the few actresses who can pull in a full house with a comedy film on the first weekend or two or a film's showing, which is regarded as a critical kickoff by the industry. In contrast, even hot, young, and pretty actresses such as Meg Ryan and Julia Roberts are problematical by themselves. Older actresses like Jane Fonda, Sally Field, and Glenn Close are also older women and, while respected, are less likely to be cast. The sexist, unpleasant, but undeniable truth is that the public likes them nubile, not necessarily seasoned. This seems to be a uniquely American prejudice, because mature European actresses continue to do reasonably well in romantic roles even after they pass forty.

Would *Total Recall* have been successful with an actress in the role played by Arnold Schwarzenegger? Some women in the industry think so, but the question is probably moot; to get the movie made, Carolco Pictures covered the film's $60-million-plus budget by preselling its rights in U.S. and foreign markets based on Schwarzenegger's box-office appeal. No one believes that could have been pulled off with a female star. Anyhow, in the minds of many, women and action just don't mix. "The studios don't want actresses in nontraditional roles," says one production executive. "The conventional wisdom is that *Aliens* would have done twice as much business if Sigourney [Weaver] were more traditionally 'feminine.' I don't agree, however."

Supporting this theory are examples of action movies starring women which never took off in public acceptance, including thrillers such as *Blue Steel* with Jamie Lee Curtis and *Fatal Beauty* starring Whoopi Goldberg. Hollywood increasingly employs a "more is more" attitude when it comes to violence and keeps remaking the same movie over and over again, such as *Die Hard 2, RoboCop 2, Another 48 Hours,* and *Beverly Hills Cop III.*

"In the end, Hollywood reflects the sexism and racism of society in general," says Susan Tarr, vice president of Isis Productions, Cher's production company. "Wealthy white males run the industry. There's a spate of violence and action covering the map—the product of male thinking and sensibility." The tenor of the times doesn't help. "Films mirror what's going on around them," says William Morris's Simpson. "In the seventies, the feminist ideals were firmly entrenched. Then the [feminist] movement tailed off and the public—and the movies—followed suit. At the end of the day, studios are interested in making money, not in carving out a new social path."

Overt examples of discrimination against actresses are hard to document, but the signals come through loud and clear. "Producers want their films to be made," says Weinstein. "When they receive the implicit message that studios aren't interested in films starring women, that at the end of the road there may not be a green light, they're less likely to try."

Women in the industry, recognizing what they face, are increasingly turning to self-help approaches by having their own production companies, as Bette Midler, Dyan Cannon, Cher, Jodie Foster, and others have. Jodie Foster's Egg Productions is, in fact, one of the major operations in Hollywood. It has a development deal with European backers that gives Foster $100 million to use for filmmaking, and she plans to produce and direct—not necessarily always act in—two films a year, with *Nell* as the first one and *Home for the Holidays* with Holly Hunter as the second.

Ron Meyer, president of Creative Artists Agency and an agent who represents such talent as Jessica Lange, Goldie Hawn, Jane Fonda, and Cher, says that the self-help movement has been in place for a while now. "Recognizing that they won't be in pictures with doors being kicked down, actresses aren't sitting around bemoaning their fate. Most have their own development companies to generate material. Incidentally, actresses aren't the only ones tired of the leaning, both here and abroad, towards men kicking ass. Every macho man wants to do something sensitive and meaningful."

Money is a major factor in the sex discrimination currently in vogue. Throughout the early history of Hollywood, actresses' salaries kept pace with those of men. Adolph Zukor paid Mary Pickford $10,000 a week in 1916 and guaranteed her half the net profits from all her films. Gloria Swanson received about $300,000 a film in the late twenties—as much as Douglas Fairbanks—and a weekly salary more than double that of Buster Keaton. At one time, Mae West and Barbara Stanwyck were the highest-paid women in the country.

Today the belief that only male stars can be trusted on marquees dictates the terms of salary negotiations. In an interview in December 1993 with the *New York Times*, Streep complained, "I make half of what Dustin [Hoffman] makes, half of what [Robert] Redford makes, half of what Jack [Nicholson] makes. There are different rules for men and women . . . and I think it stinks." She elaborated on the issue later in the *Miami Herald*: "If there are four good roles a year and sixty women are beautifully qualified to play them, they'll go to the first one and try to get her cheap, and if they can't, they'll go on to the next one. We all cut our salary demands. And that's a happy economy for the people who pay us."

Sigourney Weaver, who is reportedly receiving $4 million plus a percentage of profits for *Alien III*, told an interviewer that, while she is well paid, she must make five pictures to equal the amount her male costars make in two. Raising the possibility of a boycott by actresses if the situation isn't remedied, she charged: "It's just sexism. Pure and simple."

Nonsense, says producer Mark Johnson. "The truth is that it all has to do with the market. More people go to see Jack Nicholson in a movie than Meryl Streep in that movie." Rachel Ward agrees with Johnson. "We don't appeal to the same number of people, so we have to take the whole scale down a bit," she says. "Anyhow, who needs $11 million? It's just ego and a power trip. Women should take the lead and take less to make the pictures we want to make. You can't take risks on a big budget. We can't have it both ways."

If principle won't turn the industry around, the bottom line might. The industry can't afford to ignore story lines appealing to more than 50 percent of the population. Besides, the line of the moment is that "feelings sell." "The current situation has less to do with women than with the machine," says Kate Ginsburg, who has a production company with Michelle Pfeiffer. "Box office has less to do with quality than with merchandising—the ability to buy a T-shirt. When a movie starring a woman does $15 million on opening weekend, things will change."

According to Roger Birnbaum, president of worldwide production for Twentieth Century Fox, that's not an impossibility. "These days the big numbers are $100 million, and the right actress with the right material can blast through that."

"If you have a good female-driven story, people will go see it," concurs Gordon Crawford, senior vice president of Capital Research Company. "It was Julia Roberts and not Richard Gere who carried *Pretty Woman*. As usual with Hollywood, reality and perception are often miles apart."

One highly placed studio executive forecasts that, just as teen flicks were replaced by cop/buddy movies, they, too, will be edged out by the growing market for adult films. "Women as attractions in movie theaters can come back because women make up at least half of the audience. Whether that will happen this year or three years from now, however, I can't say."

Small consolation, however, for the current crop of actresses. "For those of us over thirty, it's fairly frustrating," says Rachel Ward. "I've talked with other actresses and the big issue is: How much are we prepared to compromise? It's always a risk. If we get too precious and stick to our standards, we don't get to work. We're frightened that we won't have the opportunity to fulfill our potential. Our time might be past by the time the pendulum swings back."

Building on the theme of women over forty in Hollywood, at the end of 1994 Bette had in development with Bonnie Bruckheimer-Martell, at All Girl Productions, *Show Business Kills*, which follows the lives of four women in the entertainment business in Hollywood who are over forty and how they deal with their lives and their careers. *Show Business Kills* is based on a novel of the same name released in early 1995 and written by Iris Rainer Dart, who wrote *Beaches*. In the story, the forty-plus women—a screenwriter, a soap opera star, a studio executive, and an actress wife of a TV star—each try to hang on to their success in various ways.

And that is the sort of concern that worried Bette as she approached her fiftieth birthday in 1995.

28

1991—Mark, Bette, and *For the Boys*

Bette's major debut as a film actress was in *The Rose*, directed by Mark Rydell, and they were teamed again in *For the Boys*. The plot as described by the *Washington Post*:

"Midler plays Dixie Leonard, a girl singer (that's what they called them then) in an Andrews Sisters–style trio. She's tapped for an overseas USO Christmas show thanks to her uncle Art, who happens to be a shtick-writer for premier song-and-dance man Eddie Sparks (James Caan). So Dixie wings her way to London, and the moment her platform pump touches the runway, she's hustled on stage with Eddie. They take an instant dislike to each other offstage, but they share a catch-fire comic chemistry under the lights, and the boys go wild for Dixie's red hair and blue comebacks."

The story takes the pair though three wars, with Bette's husband dying in the first one—World War II—and her son getting killed in the last one, Vietnam. The *Washington Post*'s reviewer obviously loved Bette in the role as she flaunted and flounced her way through the film, tapping everyone's sexual desires with the song "Stuff Like That There," and their romantic longings with the Beatles' "In My Life."

For Caan the movie was a major step on the comeback trail after his private and professional life descended into the pits during the 1980s. During that period, Caan's two marriages collapsed. He made bad career choices and suffered a deep depression exacerbated by personal and money problems, along with the premature death of his beloved sister, Barbara, from leukemia. His comeback was in contradiction to the F. Scott Fitzgerald observation that there are no second acts in the lives of Americans.

In *For the Boys*, Caan plays the role of Eddie Sparks, an insecure, frightened, but talented performer who becomes a legend working with Bette's Dixie Leonard character. He is on the flaky side morally: He is unfaithful to his wife regularly and, at one point, betrays a friend to the McCarthy witch-hunters. The film was produced by Bette's All Girl Productions, and she didn't have Caan in mind in the initial casting, but the director, Mark Rydell, insisted on him.

"I was skeptical [about Caan]," Bette said. "I remembered him from *The Godfather* and *Gardens of Stone* and *Misery*. Real tough. Then I looked at *Funny Lady* and *Harry and Walter Go to New York*. He was hilarious. Mark told me that Jimmy was the most underrated actor in America. I said okay."

To build rapport between his stars before the shooting began, Rydell required Bette and Jimmy to learn tap dancing together. They did so, eight hours a day for the next four months, although Bette resisted the idea because she didn't want people to see her making mistakes and looking ridiculous. "It was torture," Bette said. "Both of us were overweight. We both lost twenty pounds. I was ashamed of the way I looked. I was so self-conscious in leotards. I looked horrible. Yeah, it was a binding experience."

The tap-dancing lessons Rydell put them through were a mark of his style in directing, because it took a master to pull together Midler and Caan. According to Stephen Rebello, writing in *Movieline* magazine, both Bette and Jimmy have the reputation in Hollywood of being very difficult. Rebello wrote, "The gifted stars who play USO song-and-dance troupers in the $30-million-plus, four-decade-spanning dramatic musical love story are two of the stormiest actors in town. Other directors might sooner face amputation of a favorite body part than mess with *either* Bette Midler or James Caan. Director Mark Rydell, who introduced Midler to movie audiences in *The Rose* and has directed Caan twice before, admits only to some 'times' on the movie."

The CBS entertainment reporter Steve Kmetko interviewed

Bette about *For the Boys* on *CBS This Morning* on November 29, 1991. Kmetko asked what she would think if the movie were called a Bette Midler movie.

Bette replied, "I would be so flattered. I would be thrilled. I made it for myself. I had a lot of help. I had tremendous, tremendous support. But the idea was to be able to do everything that I could do and I think this movie does allow for all that."

Kmetko said it seemed *For the Boys* connected to Bette days in Radford High School in Hawaii. It was reminiscent of h first all-girl group, the Calico Three, that toured military bases round the Hawaiian Islands back in the 1960s. Bette told Kmetko nat she and her All Girl Productions staff actually began planning *For the Boys* right after *The Rose*, which doesn't ring true since A Girl Productions didn't exist then, but it may be that Bette a d some of her colleagues in what became All Girl Productions ad talked about something like *For the Boys*.

Bette said, "I wanted to do something about entertainers in Vietnam because it was such a—I wanted to nake a war movie in the worst way, and I couldn't imagine how possibly could unless I played an entertainer in that time. It's really terribly exciting, and women don't really get to be in really exciting, rambunctious movies as the hero or the heroine."

Then, Kmetko tried to characterize the role Bette played in *For the Boys* and asked what description title she liked best.

MIDLER: Thank you, I think I like singer best of all. I mean, I like being an actress and I do . . . I like mom—mom and mogul, I like. That's my new favorite combination.

Then, Kmetko wanted to know what were the perks of being famous that Bette liked best of all.

MIDLER: It's a whole life. It's not just one thing. The perks are very nice but, if you're making stuff that you don't like, with people that you hate, it's—everything's a grind and everything looks black so the best thing to do is to find stuff that you really love to do, with people that you love to do it with and then the whole thing just falls into place—like me!

*   *   *

Bette had demonstrated her feeling about AIDS in a moving appearance that year at the awards ceremony for AIDS Project Los Angeles (AIDS PLA) along with Robin Williams. She told the audience at the Universal Amphitheater:

"The last ten years I have worked on behalf of people with AIDS because I couldn't stand idly by, twiddling my thumbs, pissing and moaning while people I loved shriveled up and died. I began my career in 1965 and I am not lying, I do not exaggerate one minute, when I tell you that nearly everyone who I started out with is dead."

She went on to name them, one by one—almost fifty friends, collaborators, and mentors who were gone—as three thousand people in the audience listened in tearful silence. "I never thought that at such a relatively young age I would be on such intimate terms with death." She punctuated her sad remembrance by singing the Beatles song "In My Life" for her adoring audience.

Bette doesn't make many public appearances anymore because she has concentrated her life on her home and family, with her career being mostly in the movies. "I really have decided that the outside world doesn't have a lot to offer. You have to make your own heaven in your own home. How many after-hours bars can you go to? How many vodka gimlets can you drink?"

Married seven years by this time, Bette and Harry admitted to some rough times adjusting to marriage in the early years because of different upbringings and different personalities. She is a yeller like her father, and Harry is quiet like his father. She felt she had married the best person she knew who wanted to marry her.

His view was comparable. He said, "Even though I didn't know her at all [on our wedding day], I remember consciously making the decision that no matter what happens I'm going to keep working at this to make it work."

Focusing on film work is another way of working within a carefully controlled environment, away from the thousands of fans she used to entertain in clubs, concert halls, and amphitheaters across the country and around the world. The film medium is once removed from that reality and one of the most cocooned mediums for artists. She has done well at it for herself and for her partners at Disney Studios. But even the relationship with the studio is not that important anymore. She has done seven films in her Disney deal, but that was out of eighty that she presented for consideration. Moreover, she had to take *For the Boys*, the sentimental movie that she wanted to produce, to Twentieth Century Fox. "We asked [Disney Studios]. We brought it to them," Bette said. "It was one of the things we had to offer them when we first came [to the studio] and it was not their kind of picture."

It is also common gossip around the Disney lot that many of the Disney people do not respect her abilities and perpetuated the story that Disney rescued her from movie oblivion with *Down and Out in Beverly Hills*. Jeffrey Katzenberg, until recently chairman of Disney Studios, would go out of his way to counter that kind of talk. "One of the things that upsets me about our partnership," he told Kevin Sessums of *Vanity Fair*, "is that we somehow made a star out of Bette Midler. That's nonsense. The only person who made a star out of Bette Midler is Bette Midler. . . . I've wanted to say this for a long time, because I've gotten tired of people somehow or other accrediting her success to us. It's just incredibly inappropriate and unfairly diminishes her."

That is the same sentiment echoed by Mark Rydell, who directed her in *The Rose* and, more recently, in *For the Boys*. In *The Rose*, Rydell felt he was directing a girl, and in *For the Boys*, he directed an adult woman with a talent that he believes is similar to Katharine Hepburn's.

29

1992—The Lawsuits

I f Bette had been waiting a long time to bring the USO entertainer's story, *For the Boys*, to the screen, so had Margaret Theresa Yvonne Reed—better known by her stage name, Martha Raye.

After the release of *For the Boys*, Martha Raye sued Twentieth Century Fox and Bette Midler on the grounds that the film was her life story and it had been stolen by Bette and Twentieth Century Fox. The complaint contended Martha Raye had registered the original movie treatment with the Writers Guild of America under the title *Maggie* in 1991. She claimed that she then showed the film treatment to executives at Fox and there were a series of meetings to explore Fox producing and distributing the film. At the time, she offered Fox the rights to her life story for $1 million out front plus a percentage of the film's gross income.

Furthermore, Raye claimed that in 1985–86, she had met with Bette Midler and talked about Midler playing Martha Raye in the movie. Raye said that Bette was very interested and kept a copy of the treatment so she could study it and decide if she wanted to do the movie. Then, around 1990, according to Raye, Bette and Fox went ahead with the movie that became *For the Boys*. Raye said that when she complained to Fox, the studio answered that *For the Boys* was "inspired" by the life story of Martha Raye, but was not "based" on her life story. Instead, Fox maintained that the concept of *For the Boys* was dreamt up and developed by Bette Midler and, therefore, the studio did not have an obligation to pay Raye anything.

Raye sued in September 1992 on the grounds that she had been defrauded and sought $5 million in damages.

Richard Ferko, Martha Raye's attorney, spoke with me and said that he knew they would have trouble with the case. They submitted the fifty-three-page treatment to the court for comparison with the script that was used in *For the Boys*. The court found that there were similarities and concluded that the treatment was the story of Martha Raye's life but did not parallel the plot development used in *For the Boys*. The film portrayed a fictional character different from what Martha Raye had been. For instance, in the film, the leading character, Dixie Leonard, has a son who plays an important role in the film. Martha Raye has a daughter.

The ironic part is that Martha Raye's life story is actually more interesting than the fictional story portrayed in the movie *For the Boys*. It seems probable that Fox and Bette took the concept of Martha Raye's life story and used it as the inspiration to create a story set in the same time and place and featuring a girl singer, but avoided paralleling Raye's life too closely. Also, it is possible that the $1 million price tag Martha had put on her story was too high.

There were a number of sad aspects to the trial. First, Martha Raye admired Bette a great deal. When, in Raye's opinion, Bette and Fox stole the story and Bette played the role, they robbed Raye of credit and money she sorely needed in the fading years of her life. Second, by the time the case came to trial, Martha Raye was an old and broken woman whose health had deteriorated so badly that she could not come to court and testify on her own behalf. So it came down to Bette Midler, charming and respected, giving her side in court against the absent plaintiff. Even if Martha Raye had physically managed a court appearance, it is doubtful she would have been coherent and more than likely that she would have humiliated herself. Beyond that, one of Raye's key witnesses had died, and so Midler and Fox won the case. Soon afterward Martha Raye had a stroke and died in 1994.

Ironically, there was an earlier lawsuit that would be related to the Martha Raye–Bette Midler case. On March 23 of that same year, 1992, the U.S. Supreme Court affirmed a judgment awarded to

Bette Midler against the advertising firm Young and Rubicam. Back in 1985, Young and Rubicam created a television commercial for the Ford Motor Company designed to sell their Lincoln-Mercury Sable and used the song "Do You Wanna Dance?" written by Bobby Freeman in 1958, which Bette had made popular in her first album for Atlantic Records, *The Divine Miss M*, in 1972. Young and Rubicam initially went to Midler's agent and asked if she would sing the song for them, and the agent turned them down, which motivated Young and Rubicam not to give up the idea, but to search for a Bette Midler soundalike.

They found her in the person and voice of Ula Hedwig, who had been a Midler Harlette for some ten years. Ula did her Bette Midler imitation and recorded the song for Young and Rubicam, who aired the commercial approximately sixty times. Bette's reaction to the commercial was, "She sounds more like me than me. The congas are the same, the piano is the same, the 'aahs' are the same. It's a ripoff."

The similarities not only outraged Bette against Ula for singing the song, but drove her to sue Young and Rubicam and Ford for $10 million in Los Angeles federal court in 1986.

On July 20, 1987, U.S. District Judge Ferninand F. Fernandez said he thought Young and Rubicam and Ford had committed an ordinary theft, but he couldn't find any legal precedent he believed bolstered Bette's claim for damages and dismissed the case out of hand. Not willing to let it go at that, Midler had her attorneys appeal the case to the Ninth Circuit U.S. Court of Appeals, where Judge John T. Noonan reversed the lower court and said that the defendants had pirated Midler's identity. Specifically, Judge Noonan wrote, "We hold only that when a distinctive voice of a professional singer is widely known and is deliberately imitated in order to sell a product, the sellers have appropriated what is not theirs and have committed a tort in California." He sent the case back to the lower court for trial.

On October 26, 1989, U.S. District Judge A. Wallace Tashima decided that there really wasn't any case against Ford, even though they had approved the commercials before they ran, and he agreed to drop them from the case while allowing Bette and her attorneys to proceed against Young and Rubicam. They called an expert witness, Steven Carbone, who said that at the time the commercial was aired, Bette had become an extremely popular artist and could have easily commanded up to $2 million for such a commercial. Robert Callagy, the attorney for Young and Rubicam, countered with a December 1984 *Time* magazine article in which Bette was quoted as saying that her career was in the dumps and that she was giving up on her singing career. In rebuttal, Bette testified that she must have been blue at the time of that magazine interview and that, soon after, she started her successful movie career with Disney and Touchstone Studios.

Peter Laird, Bette's lawyer, played her recording of "Do You Wanna Dance?" for the court while Bette swayed to the music and testified it was her first hit song and boosted the success of her career. She said that she didn't know about the commercial until friends telephoned her to inquire how much she had been paid for making it. Moreover, she was angered because she didn't do commercials.

She said the commercial damaged her reputation. "I don't do commercials," she testified. "I don't believe in it. I resent people looking at the commercial and thinking that's me. They think I sold out. It doesn't matter if I win or lose this trial, the damage is done."

Then Laird turned to the matter of whether or not she would have ever considered a commercial for the Ford Motor Company, and Bette emphatically said she would not because she disliked their products. "I think they're cheap," she declared. "I think they're poorly made. I think they fall apart after a year. I do have my standards. They're low, but I do have them. If you don't believe in a product, you can't stand with it."

Callagy then attacked on behalf of his client, and Bette responded defensively as he questioned her about ads she had done for both *McCall's* and *Us* magazines, as well as producing a 1984 advertising contract Bette had signed to promote liquor on Japanese television. She snapped back that she had signed the contract but had no intention of going through with it. "I don't want to see a bunch of drunken Japanese on my conscience," she said.

"You mean you sign contracts with no intention of going through with them?" Callagy asked.

"Only occasionally," Midler replied.

Then Ula Hedwig testified that before she recorded her imitation of Bette, the Midler version of the song on record was played for her several times and she was instructed "to sound as much as possible like the Bette Midler record." To which Callagy responded that Young and Rubicam was not trying to have Hedwig imitate Bette Midler, but to imitate the recording of Bette Midler, which, he claimed in the wonderful fine-line logic that comes naturally to attorneys but eludes most common folk, was not the same thing as what the plaintiff, Midler, was charging. Three days later the jury awarded Bette $400,000.

Naturally, the losing side appealed to the Ninth Circuit U.S. Court of Appeals and claimed that the jury instructions were inadequate; that Midler's claim was preempted by U.S. copyright law; and that Midler had failed to prove that Young and Rubicam deliberately tried to imitate Bette's voice. However, the appeals court upheld the award to Bette of the $400,000 (*Midler v. Young & Rubicam*, 9th Cir., Nos. 90-55027, 90-55028) because Ula Hedwig had testified at the trial that when she had originally been contacted by Young and Rubicam, they told her to send in an audition tape on which she was instructed to sound as much like Bette Midler as possible.

The only victory Young and Rubicam won out of its appeal was that the judge ruled Bette had not proven Young and Rubicam had "evil motive" in what it did and therefore wouldn't grant punitive damages. Young and Rubicam had not used Bette's name or likeness in the commercial, and the court refused damages on the claim of copyright infringement. However, the court's ruling was based on the fact that Young and Rubicam "did appropriate part of her identity."

The judge ruled that Midler's style was a possession under a California law that had originally been passed to protect the rights of dead celebrities and was also based on a 1974 case, *Motschenbacher v. R. J. Reynolds* (498 F. 2nd 821 [1974]). In that instance, famous race car driver Lothar Motschenbacher sued the R. J. Reynolds Tobacco Company because it ran a television ad in which Motschenbacher's racing car could be seen and which led some people to believe that he was endorsing the tobacco products of R. J. Reynolds.

Bette Midler's success in what has become known as a "misappropriation of identity" suit has subsequently inspired other public figures such as Patti Page, Vanna White, Mitch Rider, and Carlos Santana to file similar misappropriation identity suits against advertising agencies and advertisers. The irony about all these legal actions is that Bette Midler will now be legally identified with having sued and won against someone who misappropriated her identity. There are those who wonder if that wasn't exactly what she was guilty of herself when she did *For the Boys* and misappropriated Martha Raye's identity.

30

1993—*Hocus Pocus* and
Radio City Music Hall

Whatever one thought of Bette in the misappropriated identity case, in 1993 she assumed the identity of a long-dead character in the movie *Hocus Pocus*. This provided an opportunity for the *Ladies' Home Journal* to do another of its annual stories about one of its favorite ladies, and it sent seasoned writer Sally Ogle Davis to cover the making of *Hocus Pocus* for its July 1993 issue.

When Davis arrived at the Disney Studios on Buena Vista Street in Burbank, it was a beautiful, warm spring day, but the whole atmosphere was transformed the minute she stepped inside Soundstage 2 to a different time and place.

She later wrote, "It's fall in New England, a dark and stormy night. The scene is an ancient graveyard, all crumbling headstones and lichen-covered statuary. Crew members are wearing surgical masks for protection from the dust created by eighteen tons of dirt mixing with the fog machine's clouds of gloom. But at least one member of the cast is having a good time. In flaming red Medusa curls, artificial buckteeth, a high-collared green-and-purple dress, striped green-and-black leggings and black shoes with curled-up toes, Bette Midler is literally sailing above it all."

Bette was attached to a tether line suspended from a small crane being maneuvered under the instructions of the director. *Hocus Pocus* is a fairy tale revolving around the concept of what would happen if three authentic witches, the Sanderson sisters, were summoned from seventeenth-century Salem, Massachusetts, on Halloween night.

The plot has a teenage boy whose family has just moved to Salem. He is stuck with taking his kid sister trick-or-treating on Halloween. Along the way, he runs into his new girlfriend from school. They all go to a dark museum, where the boy accidentally releases the three Sanderson sisters—the three dead witches—from death. Winifred Sanderson, played by Bette, is the cruel one; Mary Sanderson, played by Kathy Najimy, who was in *Sister Act* with Whoopi Goldberg, is the crazy witch; and Sarah Sanderson, played by Sarah Jessica Parker, is the dumb, boy-crazy witch. Released from death for the time being, the three witches have to suck the life out of the children of Salem by dawn or they will be dead forever. Meanwhile, the teenage boy and the two girls rush around trying to undo what they did and get the witches dead again.

Bette's first appearance takes place when she crashes a Halloween party, and everybody thinks she is just another of the adult guests. At this point, she mounts the stage and sings "I Put a Spell on You." This is the one part that the reviewer for *People* magazine, Tom Giatto, loved—unlike most of the rest of the movie. "It's a great scene," he wrote. "Would that there were more of them in this cluttered muddle of a movie. *Hocus* can't make up its mind whether it's a campy vehicle for Midler and her witchy siblings, played by Najimy and Parker, or a thriller aimed at kids, about how three plucky children foil this evil sister act."

Brian Lowry's review for *Variety* wasn't quite as critical: "With Bette Midler and her on-screen sisters shamelessly hamming things up, it looks as if those involved in making this inoffensive flight of fantasy had more fun than anyone over twelve will have watching it. Still, the blend of witchcraft and comedy should divert kids without driving the patience of their parents to the boiling point, leaving a chance to conjure up a little box office magic among that contingent before the pot tips. *Hocus Pocus* suffers from inconsistency, careening aimlessly between a sense of menace and a comedic sort of Three Stooges on broomsticks."

Duane Byrge of the *Hollywood Reporter* was the most laudatory of all the reviewers. "Eye of newt, toe of frog, voice of Bette. Ala-kazamm! Stir it together in a percolating cauldron full of black cats, graveyards and special effects and, *Hocus Pocus*, you've got a bubbling children's feature from Disney. While it may take downright sorcery to conjure up another box-office winner amid the current bulging batch at the box office, this perky release will be a Halloween-in-July for Buena Vista. It's a veritable bagful of box-office treats."

Hocus Pocus represented a $6 million investment by All Girl Productions in a try at coming up with a winning movie to offset the three weak efforts that had preceded, *Scenes From a Mall* with Woody Allen, *For the Boys*, and *Stella*, which had been given a bad time by some critics, to Bette's disgust. She said, "They call them weepies, tearjerkers, women's pictures. Well, so what?"

In a way, that comment reflected Bette's frustration over not having her career back in the times when women had a strong on-screen Hollywood presence. "Sometimes I think I'm in the wrong era. Yet I know I'm lucky to be where I am because then [in the twenties and thirties] I would never have made the cut. I don't have the face for it, and I don't have the body. I don't have anything they required except the enthusiasm and the drive."

Even though All Girl Productions had about ten projects in development at the end of 1992, insiders told me that *Hocus Pocus* was actually dumped into their lap by the Disney Studios people after Disney had done much of the development. Part of Bette's production deal with Disney was that the studio had to offer her a certain number of movie projects and Bette had to take some of them or the production deal was off. Among the staff, there was a lot of tension because of the on-again-off-again wavering of Bette and some of her close advisers about film projects offered to her and even those that were not offered to her but that she wished were.

In many respects, Bette became obsessed with being a movie star whom Hollywood had passed by. Some projects were rejected by her attorney, who told her she was a big star and didn't have to take just anything. And she was haunted with indecision, afraid of making the wrong kind of movie and rejecting the right kind of movie and not being sure which is which until after the film is made.

Hocus Pocus, for example, was not one that anybody really wanted to do. In the end, it might have been better if they hadn't made it.

Two things struck reporter Sally Ogle Davis about her *Ladies' Home Journal* interview with Bette on *Hocus Pocus*: The first was how small and restrained Bette is in person. "In real life," Davis wrote, "she favors subdued Armani suits, glasses, subtle makeup and no jewelry except a thin wedding band." Second was the rift that there seemed to be between Disney and Bette at the moment.

Speaking of Bette's All Girl Productions company, Davis said, "Their motto: 'We hold a grudge.' Last year, the grudge appeared to be mostly against Disney, which chose not to back *For the Boys*, the bouncy big-band musical about star-spangled [USO] entertainers. . . . The movie, which ended up being a Twentieth Century Fox project, was a labor of love for Bette . . . and hardly anyone went to see it—which probably accounts for her current attitude about the movie business."

Davis's comment reflected what Bette said to her about the film business in Hollywood; "I've been through a lot in the last months. It's been a lot of stress. It made me doubt everything. There are people whose fortunes wax and wane from picture to picture. I am one of them, and I can tell you, your stock is up one day and down the next."

It was in such a fit of depression that Bette swore never again to make a movie musical, "because people are not interested in them. They want a thrill a minute. They want violence. They want to be overstimulated."

Despite her depressing views about her work, Bette was very happy with her husband and her daughter, who were the main focus of her life now. One of the sunbeams that triggered Bette's inner spirit was when her husband or, more important, her daughter, Sophie, showed up on the set, which one or the other did almost daily. The reaction was electric, as director Kenny Ortega describes it, and the star on the set was instantly Sophie—not Bette. "When Sophie would walk onto the set, Bette would just light up. I mean it was like klieg lights went on."

It was in one of these upbeat moods that Bette decided to reassert her positive side and do a TV movie version of *Gypsy* for CBS during the holiday season in December 1993, plus another set of stage concerts—her first in a decade—ending at Radio City Music Hall.

Davis was clearly one of Bette's greatest fans, as is movie director Mark Rydell. Davis said, "She looks happy, healthy—and terrific. In fact, her photographs, despite being taken by the best in the business, never do justice to her lovely skin, her apricot coloring and her amazingly warm smile."

And Mark Rydell adds, "What can she not do? She's a miracle. Sure, she's not conventionally beautiful, but when the light goes on, have you ever seen anything as attractive in your life as her? She's like the Grand Canyon—a national treasure."

In July 1993, *Hocus Pocus* was released, and regardless of how it did, Bette enjoyed playing the role of the wicked witch. "She's very, very funny and I could play her—I'd be happy playing her the rest of my life. She gets to do everything, you know. She's completely demented. She's—she can be quite evil, but most of the time she's very funny. Of course, she doesn't know how funny she is. But she can be quite wicked."

What Bette didn't know at the beginning of the film was that both her colleagues in *Hocus Pocus*, Sarah Jessica Parker and Kathy Najimy, were big Midler fans, with Kathy saying Bette was on the top of her Christmas tree. Bette only found out when they started shooting *Hocus Pocus*. "It turned out that Kathy Najimy was an old fan of mine and that she had come looking for me once when I lived on Barrow Street in New York City. She had left a letter and a picture for me or something like that. And she reminded me of all this. Of course, I had to say 'Kathy, I was unaware at the time.' But she took it well."

Sarah Jessica was a different kind of a fan who had sung in the musical *Annie* and had the same voice teacher as Bette at the time. Bette told NBC's Katie Couric when she appeared on the July 16, 1993, *Today* show to hype *Hocus Pocus* about how she first met Kathy Najimy and Sarah Jessica Parker. "We were singing that song, 'I Put a Spell on You,' and I walked into the studio. They had their microphone and, of course, I had my microphone because they were singing the background part. Well, I started to sing and I looked over at them, and their little knees were like [shaking]. They were totally freaked out. They came to me afterward and said, 'We couldn't believe we were standing there singing with you.' "

In a way, that must have made Bette feel semiancient, since these two young women viewed her as some kind of legendary figure. It probably stirred some of Bette's concerns about growing older and whether the crowds would still want to see and hear her when the crow's-feet took over. It would continue to be a growing concern.

Another major Bette event of 1993 was reported by *New York Magazine* when it said that happy days were here again because Bette was back in concert for the first time in ten years, starting September 14. She was slated to open at the Radio City Music Hall for an unprecedented six-week engagement with her new version of *Experience the Divine*, which she had been perfecting on the road.

Reviewer Richard Davis Story wrote in *New York Magazine* on September 13, 1993:

> At 47, Bette Midler still has the appetite. She's done the cabaret route, won four Grammys, a Tony, two Emmys, and a couple of Oscar nominations. She's got the husband, the kid, the big house in Beverly Hills, even her own production company. Yet she also has such terrible stage fright that she throws up before every show. "The only performers," she says "who don't get sick are sick."
>
> *Experience the Divine* is three hours of best Bettes, including old Bette, new Bette, AM-FM Bette, and a brand-new Broadway Bette doing "Everything's Coming Up Roses." There's an eight-piece band, a new slew of Harlettes, and a visit with old friends like Delores DeLago, the lounge singer with the electric wheelchair, mermaid outfit and palm tree. There's vamp and camp, wisecracks, platform heels and, as Bette herself puts it in one old song, "pretty legs and great big knockers."

That was a vastly different assessment than the cutting John Simon review that appeared in the October 11 issue of the same magazine. Clearly, Simon didn't like Bette's performance, but he admitted the audience did.

> There is the tacky scenery. Then the tacky costumes and lighting. And finally the tacky star herself . . . She descends on the huge Radio City Music Hall stage like a one-woman infestation of locusts: Bette Midler, or the triumph of the middling. Yes, she can sing, but her songs, except for a couple of standards, are mushy or manic and, either way, pall quickly as she drags them out in an aural drag act. The audience, true worshipers all, emitting orgasmic grunts and hysterical laughter at the Divine Miss M's least twitch (although few of her twitches can be characterized as "least"), could not be more presold: Miss M is screeching to the converted.
> She delivers her comedy routines with expert timing. But the material is horribly hit or miss, and often leads up to a frenzy of tastelessness. Her cavortings and gyrations merely underline her unsightliness, which she hurls at us as if it were an aphrodisiac. The crowd is in ecstasy: The rewards of vulgarity are infinite.

Simon continues in the same vein, savaging the cast, the star, the production, the management of Radio City Music Hall, and, most of all, the audience, concluding that, while they come up for a standing ovation, the only thing that comes up for him is his dinner. Not a pretty thought.

Entertainment Weekly reviewed the same performance more as if reporting on a cocktail party or baseball game. It noted that this was Bette's first concert tour in ten years and that the opening was followed by a reception at the Metropolitan Museum of Art. Celebrity attendees included mega-agent Mike Ovitz, Barry Diller, Diane Sawyer, Mike Nichols, k. d. lang, and Lauren Bacall. Reporting the statistics of the opening as one might report the opening game of the baseball season, *Entertainment Weekly*'s Melina Gerosa told her readers that 113 bouquets were delivered to Bette's dressing room;

176,220 people would see and hear her thirty sold-out shows; Bette would gross $11 million; and it took thirty hours to prepare the five hundred handmade, gold-dusted chocolate roses served at the reception. And, of course, there were favorable reviews of the performance by both Bruce Weber and Stephen Holden of the *New York Times*.

In the 1980s, Bette had focused mostly on movies and did well with some and not so well with others. She started her roll at Disney Studios with the successful *Down and Out in Beverly Hills*, *Ruthless People*, *Outrageous Fortune*, and the sentimental *Beaches*. The not-so-good movies that followed, *Stella*, *Scenes From a Mall*, *For the Boys*, and *Hocus Pocus*, made her think she had better check out who she had become and where she was professionally. Concerts and clubs were always the things she loved best, for, among other reasons, they provided live contact with her adoring audience.

She also has some words about what has happened to popular culture in recent times, with attacks on Amy Fisher and Geraldo Rivera, who mauled her during a groping session in the bathroom. "Everything's tabloided out these days! And the violence! Oh, my God, the violence! There's a proliferation of pedophiles and freaks that didn't exist ten years ago."

Geraldo's autobiography, *Exposing Myself*, consists of three parts that he tediously repeats: (1) He has been to lots of geographical locations—the chapters are mostly place names; (2) he is an insatiable stud whom no woman can resist; and (3) he is a great journalist.

Here is how Geraldo describes meeting Bette for an interview at her home in Manhattan's Village: "She had great tits and a personality to match. We were in the bathroom, preparing for the interview, and at some point I put my hands on her breasts. She loved it and we fell into a passionate embrace, which segued immediately into a brief and torrid affair. Bette had an enormous sexual appetite in those days."

Then, he said, he followed her to Oklahoma City, where she was doing a concert, and she demanded sex from him again and again until he finally had to beg off exhausted. "She was wild and hungry and one of the few women who were just too much for me to handle," he concluded. He wants us to know there aren't many women he can't handle.

Bette's version of the liaison is, predictably, different. "He's such a toad! He has the nerve . . . he's such a user. He'd just come off his Willowbrook thing. He was really hot. He wanted to interview me, but I forget what channel it was for. This was twenty years ago! He came to my house and he and his producer pushed me into the bathroom and they broke poppers under my nose and started to grope me. I hadn't even said hello. I was completely shocked. Completely stunned. I didn't know what to do. Then I recovered and when we did the interview he started telling me about Maria Schneider, [the actress in Bertolucci's *Last Tango in Paris*] and how he must have jumped on her. This guy was insane. It was interview rape. Well, this was no rape. He didn't rape me, but it was pretty shocking. What a slimeball! I'm really appalled. I'm sure he doesn't give his own measurements. I'll repeat. You call that little thing an affair?"

Bette did not need the tour to prove that she was a star. And at forty-seven, she had achieved a lot in her lifetime. Personally, she was fulfilled, with a wonderful, but eccentric, husband; her daughter, the headstrong Sophie; and a wonderful Beverly Hills home. She did the tour because she felt "out of touch with my audience. I mean, who is my audience these days? A lot of the old fans from the [early days] are gone from AIDS. But then a lot of the really young girls who loved *Beaches* are going to see the show out of curiosity." Moreover, Bette was a performer, and audiences are her life and her energy source. She needed to draw power from their presence and interaction.

One of the reasons Bette needed to do the show was to reassure herself that her live audiences still loved her. It was the old fear that festered inside her. She had worked very hard to make it big in the entertainment business, and she never felt completely secure with her success. She realized that success—particularly in show business—was ephemeral and could slip away as quickly as it came.

31

A Different Rose in *Gypsy*

In her most recent mass media triumph, Bette coincidentally played the role of Rose again, except this time it wasn't the Janis Joplin image. It was the Gypsy Rose Lee story, with Bette playing Mama Rose.

The genesis of the television film, which has the trappings of becoming a holiday classic, was symbolic of the turmoil within the Midler movie production operation. When the idea first came to Bette's attention, her attorney was absolutely set against Bette, while Bette's vice president for development, Judy Dytman, saw it as a great role for Midler and advocated Bette taking the role. The project was on-again, off-again for weeks. Deadlines were missed and set again and missed again because Bette and her close associate Bonnie Bruckheimer-Martell were indecisive. This indecisiveness was a common characteristic with Midler and Bruckheimer-Martell.

Their hesitancy on *Gypsy* was due in part to it being a movie made for TV; many feature movie producers regard TV movies as inferior. If she did *Gypsy*, Bette thought it would be an admission she couldn't make successful feature movies anymore and had to stoop to television. Still Judy Dytman was convinced that this was a consummate role for Bette and, in her frustration, decided to make a move that would force the decision—she leaked word of the project to the press.

The press reported Bette was going to do *Gypsy*, and there was immediate favorable reaction from the public as the telegrams poured into the show business trade magazines and newspapers, calling the casting of Bette as Mama Rose a great move—a stroke of genius. Flowers began arriving and with them predictions of a great hit and notes saying it would be the sensation of the year. Judy knew she had sold the concept when, all of a sudden, the idea of Bette playing Mama Rose was no longer her idea. It suddenly became Bette and Bonnie's idea and the project went ahead.

Everybody agreed that *Gypsy* was not the sort of program that most networks are willing to air. The director, Emile Ardolino, said, "Everybody realized that this was unique material. [It's] something you don't find in the usual stream of television fare." Something unusual is exactly what appealed to executive producer Robert Halmi, Sr., about the *Gypsy* project, because he liked television and thought too many movie people thought films were superior to television programs. Halmi says:

> Television is so much better than bad movies. And there are so many more bad movies. I mean, out of all the movies that Hollywood produces, there's a handful that are dealing with quality—that are artistically good. I'm not talking about *Jurassic Park* or special effects, I'm talking about movies.
>
> I like TV. I can do much more—six hours, eight hours, ten hours, as long as it takes. I can do *Gypsy*, which is three hours and a musical [which is regarded as risky these days].
>
> I did *Lonesome Dove* and everybody said, "Westerns are dead. Long miniseries are dead." So I did a Western that was eight hours long and I reestablished Westerns. It's tough to generalize. You do what you think you really like and satisfy yourself and you do it well and smartly. Look at *Scarlett*. Everybody knocked the hell out of me on *Scarlett* and *Scarlett* did incredibly well and I'm proud of it. So just because other people think it's bad, who cares? I do what I want to do and I do it well and it usually pays off.

That's Bette's theory. At least you're proud of your work. You're not ashamed of it. You know in your own heart you did the best you could do. That's it. I don't care who says what. Bette's a performer and I'm an entrepreneur and there are very few of us around who really believe in their own self.

That was the attitude that got *Gypsy* made for television. The story is the true saga of the ultimate stage mother, Mama Rose, who propelled her daughter from vaudeville to burlesque. It was the subject of a 1959 Broadway smash starring Ethel Merman singing the songs written by veteran songwriter Jule Styne with words by a neophyte lyricist, Stephen Sondheim. It is a story that appeals to audiences because it is the tale of the impossible dream fulfilled through perseverance and hard work. Not unlike the story of Bette Midler's life.

Then it was made into a disappointing movie starring Rosalind Russell as Mama Rose and Natalie Wood as Gypsy. Bette realized that they were trying to follow theatrical giants in re-creating the story for television. But Bette and director Ardolino, who did *Dirty Dancing* and *Sister Act*, worked to make this a first-class production, including shooting all the songs, such as "Everything's Coming Up Roses" and "Let Me Entertain You," live and not lip-synched. "Nothing was skimped on," Midler says, "except my salary."

Bette was forty-eight when she did *Gypsy* and she still delivered a high-octane performance. Linda Hart, who worked with Bette various times as one of the Harlettes, told *USA Today* (December 12, 1993), "She has incredible energy. She sets a tone for everyone. You look forward to working with her again." Linda appeared in the production as Miss Mazeppa, the stripper who knows how to "bump it with a trumpet."

When producer Craig Zadan first pitched the idea of Bette re-making *Gypsy* for CBS television to the then-programming chief Jeff Sagansky (he is now executive vice president of Sony pictures), his reaction was instant: "If you can get Bette Midler, you have an on-the-air commitment." Zadan finally got Bette to agree, and most critics thought that Mama Rose would have heartily approved.

Gypsy aired on CBS December 12, 1993, in what some thought was a risky venture but which, to paraphrase one of the hit songs from the show, came up roses for the network. The three-hour musical beat the competition in every segment, with a 28 share of the audience, against *E.T.* on NBC, which garnered a 14 share, and ABC's *National Lampoon's Christmas Vacation,* which came closer with a 21 share. The share number is the percentage of television sets turned on at that time tuned to the program. So Bette's 28 share meant that 28 percent of all the televisions turned on were watching her.

People magazine said this about Bette's performance in Gypsy: "Bette Midler was born to play the role of Mama Rose, the shameless, smothering showbiz mother." Bette's presence and poise in the role transformed her into the pushy, loud stage mother of Mama Rose and, as such, brought a greater verity to the character than had either Ethel Merman, who appeared on Broadway in the role or Rosalind Russell, who played it in the early film version. *People's* split-personality review ended up loving Bette in the role, but hating the whole concept of musicals on television.

Variety's Jonathan Taylor was enthusiastic about the show and predicted a long life for this version as a holiday TV perennial. He said it was not easy to put on a musical that would play on the small screen or to overcome the image of the Mama Rose role that was stamped out by the original, Ethel Merman, but Bette did it:

> Bette Midler [is] in a role she was born to play. Midler as Rose is explosive, riveting and impossible, yet impossible not to love. Younger and feistier than Merman's Rose, with much of the insanity that marked Tyne Daly's 1989 stage revival, Midler presents a stage mother who loves and tortures her two daughters with equal vigor.

Still, the story of the impossible dream sought after by the unsinkable spirit fascinated Bette, and she loved the music. Bette says they were all conscious of the giants each of them was following in their respective roles. "We all have shadows in this show. Those are the shoes of giants."

Bette was particularly proud that none of the songs were lip-synched but were sung live. "That's something that's hardly ever done anymore," she said.

Robert Halmi, Sr., the executive producer on *Gypsy*, said it was an experience for him to work with Bette:

> She's talented and did a fantastic job for me and was a big pain in the ass to work with. You have to interpret it with this kind of loving sauce. She's a perfectionist, and for a producer it can be extremely difficult. But the end result kind of qualifies all that. She's tough to work with but then you figure out that it was worthwhile.
>
> I met her during rehearsals. She was a feisty little woman who really was running everybody around, including the director, the producer, and her own staff. She's very single-minded and very tough and maybe that's why she's so good. A lot of people have feelings about the way she works, but when the work is being done, I never saw so much energy per square inch in anybody.
>
> I also met her during production. I remember she came to me and didn't quite realize what I was doing (or who I was) and started to bad-mouth the producer, about how cheap he was. She was trying to get another thirty or forty thousand dollars for the set. It was a railroad scene. She said, "I don't know how the hell to get it, this guy is cheap." And I said, "Well, it's me, so you might as well get it."
>
> When she told me that the producer was cheap, at first I thought that she was pulling my leg, but then, when I found out that she didn't know who the hell I was, I thought it was funny. Bette just laughed and laughed and told everybody, "Hey, look what I did. I did a stupid thing and it paid off."

32

The Irrepressible Aaron Russo

For seven critical years in Bette Midler's career, following her early success at the Continental Baths and the small-club circuit in the 1970s, Aaron Russo came into her life and took charge of making her a star. It was standard fare in the stories told about the two that Bette demanded that Russo make her a "legend." Bette said later that the stories weren't quite on the mark:

> I didn't tell him to *make* a legend. I said I wanted to be one. I said I didn't want to be nothing. What's the point of being in something that you love so much and only being a cipher in it? I wanted to be a phenomenon, I didn't want to be just a schlepper. He was into it. He really wanted to do the same thing because success is a game. It's a big game. It's like everybody's playing and playing to win. And everybody wants to be a winner. So you're constantly jockeying for position. And constantly looking for a way to get ahead of the other person. Until you grow up enough to know it's not really very satisfying.
>
> The thing that's satisfying is your relationship with your God, your planet, your family, your friends and how you see beauty and how you see the world. You come down from that perch a little bit and give that up. You can't eat your newspaper clippings. And you can't take your newspaper clippings to bed. It's really not that satisfying.

In any case, they loved and hated, fought and worked until, as Bette said, she couldn't take the mind-fucking anymore and Aaron Russo became history in her life.

Paranoid, clever, mean, love-obsessed, bright, funny, nuts—all of those adjectives can apply to Aaron's persona when he was with Bette. Many hated him, some appreciated him, and no one loved or understood him—not even Aaron himself. Yet, along with Fred Midler, Barry Manilow, and Harry Kipper, Aaron Russo was one of the four important men in the life of Bette Midler. These four were a significant influence on what she is today. So, what happened to Aaron after Bette sent him packing?

First, he worked through the grief and trauma of the separation, and then he ended up in the movie business, like Bette. He already had credit for the production of *The Rose*, and from that, he parlayed his nerve and talent into becoming a Hollywood producer with reasonably good credentials, to the surprise of some, and was involved in the production of *Partners* and *Trading Places*. In 1983, Russo produced the Nick Nolte film *Teachers*, which was shot at Central High School in Columbus, Ohio. Nolte played a disillusioned teacher who regains his desire to teach.

In 1985 Aaron produced *Wise Guys*, a comedy directed by Brian De Palma with Joe Piscopo and Danny DeVito as two down-on-their-luck hoods who tangle with a mafia boss. Russo had a deal with MGM/UA for a time as a producer, which gave him access to the lot and the studio's marketing services, but such arrangements can also prove frustrating because the studio can control what pictures you make and where and how you make them. That is the kind of deal that Bette would have with Disney Studios. Finally, in 1986, Russo left that arrangement and decided to move to Purchase, New York, with his wife and two kids to set up his own studio. He said that life in Hollywood wasn't for him and that it was a daily irritant to have to fight with the people in the studios all the time. "To be happy, you have to like who you are. I wanted to make movies the way I wanted to—without the anguish. Being a producer for someone else is like being a crippled executive."

In his new venture as an independent film producer he was able to raise $70 million for film production and another $60 million for the advertising and marketing of the films he produced under the corporate name of Aaron Russo Entertainment. Along the way, he made deals with Vestron for distribution of videocassettes of his movies, HBO for cable exposure, and Orion Studios in Hollywood to take care of distributing his films in the United States. He planned to focus his operation on New York.

"I want to work with New York talent and New York people," he said. "I hope to become an oasis in New York for the talent here, New York writers, actors, directors, etc. I'm really trying to build a movie studio in New York. Not the physical plant, but the production and distribution facilities. I think New York is an untapped source, and I want the New York film community to know that there is an entity in New York now that can finance films—hopefully as many as possible that can be made right here."

The first Russo project was to feature Cheech without Chong in a movie about two hippies who run away to Guatemala in the sixties, then return to the United States on the eve of a U.S. invasion of that country to find help among their former buddies to stop the military operation. The movie was initially called *The Guatemalan Papers*, but someone wisely changed it to *Rude Awakening* because that's what it was for Cheech and not-Chong who find out their hippie buddies have become yuppies who don't care about social issues anymore—only making lots of money.

The November 6, 1988, *New York Times* review described *Rude Awakening*: "Eric Roberts and Cheech Marin play Fred and Hesús, peace-loving hippies who flee from a menacing F.B.I. agent in 1969 to Central America. When they return to New York 20 years later, they are astonished to find a society obsessed with brand-name water, walk-in closets and remote-control track lighting. Even worse, their ex-commune buddies, Sammy and Petra, have both sold out."

Russo himself nostalgically recalled the revolutionary days of the 1960s, when he had the Psychedelic Electric Circus nightclub in New York: "It really was a time of love and peace. You went to Central Park, and there'd be thousands of people on your same wavelength."

Early in 1988, Russo made a deal with the Showscan Film Company to produce three feature-length movies using the new Showscan filming process. Showscan was stuck, like the developer of every other new system, in that theater owners do not want to spend the money to install the new equipment unless there are films to show on it and movie producers do not want to make movies using a new system unless there are theaters where they can be shown. The Showscan system used seventy-millimeter film that was shot at sixty frames per second and shown at that same speed. That's twice the size of ordinary film, which is shot and run at about a third of that speed.

"Mr. Russo is the first major filmmaker to commit to Show-scan," said Roy Aaron, the president of Showscan. "His enthusiasm, financial backing, and commitment for three pictures has impressed us." Films were to come on line at the end of 1989 and have one more produced every year after that.

At the end of 1989, Russo announced another film project, this one involving pop star Cyndi Lauper. According to Russo, *Paradise Paved* was a comedy thriller. Meanwhile, in September 1989, *Rude Awakening* appeared and David Anson at *Newsweek* gave it a mixed review. "This promising satirical premise, a kind of Rip van Winkle fable, yields wildly erratic results. There's a hilarious cameo by Andrea Martin, and Cheech is a hoot. But when it gets speechifyingly in earnest about saving the planet you may want to crawl under your seat and hide. Best wait for the video, when you can fast-forward to the good parts."

A review by Thomas Maier for *Newsday* was a bit tougher. "Putting it politely, the nation's film critics are not enamored of the new movie, *Rude Awakening*. In fact, most say it stinks. Gene Siskel and Roger Ebert, the Chicago critics, each gave the comedy a thumb's down. It's a spoof about two '60s hippies who come back to America, a land of yuppies in the 1980s, after years of living underground. Ebert suggested the film may be one of the worst films of the decade."

Worse was the lawsuit that the film generated. Russo had hired David Greenwalt to direct the film for a fee of $125,000 and a 5 percent cut of the gross profits. As soon as Russo saw the first day's film, or "dailies" as they are known, he knew he had trouble. Greenwalt appeared inept to Russo, Russo fired Greenwalt, and a lawsuit resulted. In the legal papers, Russo said, "The very first day of filming revealed that Greenwalt had little or no ability to design and shape the basic ingredients of a motion picture scene." At the same time, the star, Eric Roberts, said that Greenwalt was the worst director he had ever met. In the end the suit was dropped, and Russo and Greenwalt shared director's credit.

What was even worse, the movie placed fourteenth among all pictures that opened that weekend in August 1989, when *Rude Awakening* was first released. Not a good showing, and it could have meant trouble except that Aaron was solvent. *Crain's New York Business* for August 19, 1989, described Russo's position as strong in spite of the poor showing of his movie. It noted that, first of all, he had done other movies that were successes, such as *The Rose* with Bette Midler and *Trading Places*. This record, combined with his feat at raising $100 million to underwrite his new film projects and with the stature of his business partners, Home Box Office, Viacom International, Rank Organization, and Cineplex Odeon Corporation, projected the image of a solid base for Aaron Russo Entertainment. Added to the past record and present financial strength, Russo enhanced the future prospects of his company by announcing six new film productions for the next two years.

"This company is Aaron," says Steve Scheffer, HBO's executive vice president of film programming and home video. "And this is a business where you bet on people."

Mr. Russo was betting on himself. "I want to build a movie studio from scratch. If the product is good enough, consistently, you'll have no problem building a studio."

The *Crain's* story outlined Russo's career, from his humble beginnings designing bikini panties for the family lingerie company to running rock clubs in New York and Chicago. After that, he became Bette Midler's guiding light in 1971 and through to the end of the decade with his first produced movie, *The Rose*, which won four Oscar nominations and, more important, grossed $60 million. After being dumped by Bette, he picked himself up and worked out a project producing *Trading Places*, starring Eddie Murphy and Dan Aykroyd. This film became the second-biggest grossing movie success of 1983, grossing $100 million.

After completing two more movie projects, *Teachers* and *Wise Guys*, Russo decided to move back to New York to establish his own production company. This suited Russo best, because he loved the exciting atmosphere of his hometown of Manhattan, and he worked best when he was the boss. Others saw the talent Russo had in organizing and directing a complicated enterprise such as the filming of a movie, and they backed him with their money—which was very unusual in the cutthroat movie business. It was particularly rare in Russo's case, because the people who put up the money let him have complete creative freedom to make the film as he thought best instead of hovering over him and demanding a say in every minor decision, as is usually the case with financial backers.

William Bernstein, the executive vice president of Orion, said his company went for the deal with Russo because he showed up on their lot with enough money of his own to shoot the films, take them through post-production, and market and advertise them. Bernstein noted, "There are not many guys who came to the door with that kind of offer."

And everybody along the way was willing to support or connect with Russo, because he displayed the kind of savvy business strategy that he used so successfully during the 1970s to promote the success of Bette Midler. He designed his films to be in the $8–15 million range, which was relatively cheap even then during the 1980s, and he went for limited creativity. "I'll try to make commercial films that have some intelligence, not a *Meatballs*, but not a real highbrow film like *Chariots of Fire*." As for the critics of his movies, Aaron had a simple view: "A movie is a critic's movie or an audience movie. Ours is an audience movie."

The following year, in 1991, Russo produced *Paradise Paved*, which was renamed *Moon Over Miami*, with Cyndi Lauper. In addition, Aaron hired songwriter Marvin Hamlisch to write the score for a comedy he was developing that would star Eric Idle and Lauren Hutton, called *Missing Pieces*. He also commissioned the theater critic of the *New York Times*, Frank Rich, to do a script, *Everyone's a Critic*, to be ready in the fall. That was all in the early part of the year, but then something happened.

Most people are not sure what, but in the September 30, 1991, *Newsday*, columnists Anthony Scaduto, Doug Vaughan, and Linda Stasi reported that Aaron had sold his house in Purchase and moved to Tahiti in the South Pacific.

In 1992, Orion pictures went bankrupt, owing a lot of people money, including a third of a million dollars due Russo. The next year witnessed a new industrywide financial problem involving Russo and others in the business.

In simplest terms, making movies is a very expensive investment for those who are producers and the studios that back them. Millions of dollars are at stake, and there are many things that can jeopardize that investment: a natural disaster during the shooting, such as a hurricane, earthquake, or flood, can disrupt a production. A sick or temperamental star can also delay filming. These disasters and problems cost money because the expenses mount every day regardless of whether any film is shot.

To protect their investment, studios and producers take out insurance policies, just as the Ladd Company did when it was filming *Divine Madness* with Bette Midler at the Pasadena Civic Auditorium. The insurance companies who write these policies spread the risk with other insurance companies. This practice is called reinsuring. One of the biggest companies that reinsures is Lloyd's of London, and about this time, Lloyd's was in a lot of financial trouble and began pulling out of the reinsurance market, which affected a lot of producers, including Aaron.

The *Daily Variety* of July 21, 1993, reported, "In the wake of massive losses worldwide, sources said Lloyd's would not grant reinsurance for films with budgets in excess of $20 million. The instability at Lloyd's led some entertainment lenders to no longer lend against Film Finances [a movie bonding company] guarantees." The result was that, since studios and banks who had advanced money for films couldn't obtain completion bonds or liability insurance to protect their investment, they tried to get their money back from the film producers. HBO had advanced $14 million to Aaron for two films, and now they wanted that money back.

Doris Toumarkine, reporting in the May 24, 1993, *Hollywood Reporter*, revealed, "In an effort to avoid a lengthy trial regarding its year-old legal claims against Film Finances [a film bonding and insurance company], HBO filed a summary judgment motion Friday afternoon in Los Angeles Federal Court hoping to recoup over $14 million advanced toward two Aaron Russo films. In accordance with a 1988 licensing and financing contract, HBO advanced $7 million apiece to Russo's *Off and Running* (also known as *Paradise Paved*) and *Missing Pieces*, both produced for the theatrical market. To minimize its risk, HBO, paying two premiums of $140,000, purchased guaranty bonds for both films, which were to be delivered by specified dates—Nov. 15, 1990, in the case of *Off and Running*, and June 1, 1991, for *Missing Pieces*. Claiming that neither film was delivered on time, HBO, hoping to recoup its advances plus interest, decided to call the Film Finances guaranties in July 1991."

The *Hollywood Reporter* story said that Russo had retired from films and was living in Tahiti. He had issued a statement that Tahiti was the kind of place for raising a family as contrasted with the gang-ridden streets of America's cities. However, the irrepressible Aaron Russo was not one to walk off and never be heard of again.

He returned to Hollywood and, on September 13, 1994, announced to the world through *Daily Variety* that he had founded a new political party, the Constitution Party, to reform America. Given the elections of November 8, 1994, he may be on to something. Here is what he told *Daily Variety*:

"You have to understand the premise," Russo explained. "If you and I walk down the street and we see a poor person lying there, do you have the right to stick your hand in my pocket and give money to those people? That's exactly what the government does. If you eliminate income taxes and downsize government, the economy would be so good that jobs would be created and the small amount of people in need of welfare could use charities. People can do whatever they want to do, but they can't stay sleeping on the sidewalk for long if there's no welfare. They'll get jobs or they'll die. You can't bring down a whole country to save a few people."

Under his Constitution Party, the federal government would no longer legislate moral or personal choice issues, which means adults engaging in consensual behavior regarding sex, gambling, drug use, or assisted suicide wouldn't be lawbreakers. Russo hasn't yet tapped support from Hollywood, but he plans to. "I wanted to start it away from Hollywood, build a constituency, then try to build support." Russo, once rumored to have had tax troubles himself, will make movies with government-related themes. One of those projects is purportedly about a man tormented to death by the IRS, being written by screenwriter Paul Haypenny. Russo wouldn't comment on any other development projects, but it is clear that Aaron is back.

33

Bette in Disney's World

Bette's life today orbits around her home and movies. She went back on a concert tour with *Experience the Divine* in 1993, but that was the first one in ten years, and she hasn't made a significant recording outside of her movie sound tracks in the last decade either.

Movies are essentially the center of her creative life, and that is based on the Disney Studios lot in Burbank with her All Girl Productions. So it is worthwhile to examine who Bette is today in the context of her life in Disney's world of movies.

Her relationships with the Disney executives—almost all male—have been frustrating. "I think she saw herself as a person," said Judy Dytman, one of All Girl Productions' former executives. "I think the main issue for Bette on being a woman was trailing against the Boys' Club. I don't think it was an issue of, 'Oh, I'm a woman and how can I get in these ranks?' No, she was a larger-than-life person and more like, 'I can play ball with any of these people.' But I think the main issue about being a woman was the anger and frustration of this rock block of the Boys' Club—about material and perception and this kind of old Hollywood—how the male establishment sees women in what roles. But she was always making fun of them for being the 'good old boys.' I think sometimes she felt very powerful and other times she felt powerless."

Some of those around Bette in the movie world think she is very emotional and ascribe Bette's behavior to serious insecurity. They say Bette would often call people up and apologize for saying something insensitive. Bette would say that she didn't understand herself at times and that she just got out of control. She is a pulsating bundle of energy and moodiness and often gets very depressed about sad news that she hears. She tends to react with the sweeping gesture like wanting to fire everybody and start anew as she did after completing the stage production of *Divine Madness* before moving to Los Angeles to shoot the film.

Bette, her close friend and associate Bonnie Bruckheimer-Martell, and their staff are known to have animated discussions about the disastrous state of the world, with Bette supplying facts and details from her vast readings, amazing those with more advanced formal education but less comprehensive command of the facts and history. She admires intellectuals and seeks them out when she can. She is a notorious but selective penny-pincher, which probably relates to the frugal habits of her parents. She will demand money from Disney to redecorate her offices lavishly, but will deny someone on the secretarial staff a minor raise because that comes out of Bette's budget. People who ask for raises know they have to fight for them. Bette will tell them they do not need the money and that she can hire some really talented people to replace them for a lot less money and that they should be grateful they have a job.

One former All Girl Productions executive who spoke only on the promise of anonymity told the author what it was like working there with Bette and Bonnie:

> Bette had exquisite taste that ranged from the very highbrow, things she was fully aware were uncommercial, to slapstick. She has a great appreciation for musicals, for every genre, and an appreciation for the genre in itself and, I think, a real studied knowledge of the genre. And so I wouldn't say that Bette is closed-minded to anything. She was very open-minded. But she did want things intelligent and with strong characters, obviously. There was definitely a conflict with Disney over this because she had a different perception of things. Although there were many things in which we were all very in sync.
>
> But on some of the things that they would offer her, I

think she just felt that they were simplistic. Disney, I think, came to see her as the "housewife heroine," as some used to call Bette. They'd throw a lot of soap opera material her way, and this is a big generalization, but just characters that didn't really feel to her like herself. And so there was usually a conflict between All Girl Productions and Disney. A conflict among friends.

The relationship between Bette and the Disney executives was cordial, but they didn't understand each other. They were like two lovers who didn't speak the same language, in that each appreciated and thought he or she understood what was pleasing and right for the other person. However, each was wrong. Disney executives like simple, wholesome plots which are very carefully scripted and micromanaged from the executive suite. Bette wanted to do stories that were more complex and had the texture that would allow her to grow as a performer by making her stretch her talents.

Beaches confirmed in the Disney people's mind that Bette's main appeal was to the middle-class, middle-aged female audience. Bette, while feeling good about *Beaches*, wanted to do other things, such as the story of Lotte Lenya and her open marriage with Kurt Weill, but such themes made the blood drain out of Disney executives' faces in the interminable meetings Bette would have with them. Even *For the Boys* wasn't acceptable to Disney, because of the controversial scenes about McCarthy-era witch-hunts and the Vietnam War. In short, films done under the Disney logo not only had to be commercially sound but had to be Disney commercially sound.

"Meanwhile," said Judy Dytman, "we had many things in development with them. Sometimes we'd get into conflict over the direction of a script—they would want to water things down. An interracial love story would always be a big controversy. They would perceive stories as controversial while we saw them as interesting and challenging. But this is something that you hear from every production company in those years they had a deal with Disney. Far worse, Bette made an exclusive deal with Disney and, when you're exclusive to anyone, you're stuck in their perceptions of things. Tom Hanks had the same problem."

Bette had an exclusive-producer deal with Disney, but it was an arrangement she would grow to dislike, as have others. Like Bette, David Bombyk, who coproduced *Witness* and *Explorers*, was one of those who agreed to exclusive deals at Walt Disney Productions when Michael Eisner and Katzenberg took over the reins there. Bombyk was never able to produce a single film while he was at Disney and ultimately became president of the Geffen Film Company. "Because you can only take projects to them, you are almost a part of the staff," Bombyk said. "It's to their advantage to use your talents, and in this case they made me feel like part of the family."

Sometimes the producer has a deal allowing him to take his movie projects elsewhere if his home studio does not want it, but that's not always good either. As Bombyk experienced it, "Inevitably, what happens is you wind up spending 20 percent of your time in meetings and 80 percent of your time driving between the various lots."

Beyond that, each studio has its own culture. In a September 11, 1986, *Los Angeles Times* analysis of the industry, Robert Friendly noted what it was like on the Disney lot, where Bette had to function. "At Disney, part of the problem, according to insiders, is that executives prefer to make movies from ideas they have conceived or discovered. These producers go in and pitch [suggest stories] over and over again, and they [the creative executives at Disney] don't say yes to anything," said one recently departed Disney production executive.

One producer offered ideas for thirty different films, none of which have been approved. Disney took on these producers but did not always trust their judgment. "The Disney philosophy is, you're going to do what we want to do. That kind of attitude frightens off a lot of veteran producers who think they have accomplished what they have by trusting their own creative instincts," one producer stated.

The way Bette's old confidant and chief factotum, Aaron Russo, saw these exclusive-producer deals was the way that Bette would ultimately wind up viewing her arrangement at Disney too. Russo said, "The problem with exclusive deals is, at the core, you are little more than an employee of the studio. The only real benefit is picking up a weekly paycheck, and for that you don't need the movie business. For that you can sell your soul."

As the *Los Angeles Times* analysis concluded, "The biggest problem for producers like Russo [and like Bette] is that, under these deals, the studio always has the final say. If it doesn't want to make the producer's movie, the film is not only out of the game at that studio, but it can't be made anywhere else. 'It's hard to like yourself if you don't respect yourself,' said Russo."

Another producer, Brian Grazer, who did *Splash* and *Night Shift*, has avoided these kind of exclusive studio deals for the simple reason that, as he says, "if it works on creative, communicative and emotional levels, then you are the recipient of a lot of money, which is a good thing. If it doesn't work, then you are trading everything you own—your creative powers—for freedom and money."

Judy Dytman was with Midler's All Girl Productions through the middle of Bette's second deal—a five-picture arrangement—with Disney. "At the time, Bette was the most highly paid actress in Hollywood—unprecedented at the time. They guaranteed her five pictures and it looked fabulous. These are people she had become very friendly with—people who really resuscitated her film career: Jeffrey Katzenberg and Michael Eisner. But I think she had a lot of trepidation that maybe they wouldn't let her do the pictures she wanted. This is a woman who had a rough, up-and-down film career and was now riding high and had just been offered an unprecedented amount of money. Disney said sincerely, 'We're going to try and make this work with you and do the pictures that you want to do.'"

Sister Act was a good example of the kind of pictures Disney wanted Bette to do that Bette didn't want to do. The plot involves a woman who is witness to some mob activity and becomes a murder target to keep her from testifying in court. Because of some corrupt cops who keep revealing her hiding places, a police detective places her in a convent where she pretends to be a nun and, while there, revitalizes the moribund institution. Disney executives thought this idea was a riot and perfect for Bette. On the other hand, Bette didn't like the script and was nervous about making fun of Catholicism after the *Divine Miss J* incident in New York when Russo had come to her rescue. She thought, "Does a Jewish pop singer really want to make fun of the Catholic Church?" So she backed away from it, and it went to Whoopi Goldberg.

Next, the Disney executives wanted Bette to do a remake of an old Jane Wyman melodrama playing a nanny and Bette turned that down too. Then there was the script that had Bette as an aging showgirl who ends up at a small Texas college and transforms its cheerleader squad into a glitzy production team that dazzles everybody.

As Dytman saw it:

Frankly, Bette is such an unusual, such an outrageous talent that, let's be honest, how many people can sit down and say, "Oh, I know what's right for Bette Midler. I can come up with an original Bette Midler project." Because Bette is a genius. She's brilliant, she's funny, and I think very few people have a grasp as to what story could be done with her. Also, she fell into the same pitfall as any woman in her early forties. Most of the people out there in Hollywood are men in their late twenties writing action pictures.

We'd also have a lot of meetings through CAA [Creative Artists Agency], who was Bette's agency. We'd have a lot of meetings with top writers and, to be honest, it's not like there were these amazing projects that people were pitching, and Bette's a very hard person to develop for. Bette was fabulous with script material and writers. If anything, Bette has a directness that is certainly disarming to a lot of people. I always loved it and found it refreshing. She cut through the bullshit and said things how they are. A lot of times sensitive writers would get hurt by that, but they really shouldn't be. It was never intended to be personal. You'd come in and there would be a script and she'd go, "You know, I hate the first part, but I love the second part." And the writer would be sitting there going, "Oh my God, no one's ever talked to me like that." She's incredibly astute, a remarkable gut sense of story and character.

There was nobody smarter. The reason I'm talking [about Bette] is because I have such a deep respect for her.

I think that a lot of her mercurial behavior can dilute some
of that. I don't think it's important. What's important is the
essence of her, her shining intelligence. She has such a gut
sense of entertainment, of a story, of what's funny, of what's
not, of what's dramatic, of what's not. She's always open and
loves any kind of discussions. We would discuss for hours
how a character should do this or the repercussions of that—
she loves the intricacies of story. Bette's the classic self-
taught person, she's got a stack of books everywhere. She
devours books on any subject. She likes anything from architecture to the history of China to sociology to Emile
Zola.

Harry, her husband, said, "She's always been frustrated with the
slowness of film development and with the collaborative committee
process, which absolutely breaks the spirit of something, because
she's so spontaneous. Things are done fast. She's used to live performance. I think she's completely stifled by the process of putting
together a film script, and it was particularly agonizing at Disney in
the sense of the committee and watering them down.

"I think that once her agreement runs out [with Disney], she
most likely would be unaffiliated with a studio or would have something where she had a first-look deal and had the ability to set
things up."

And, with Disney a studio that is undergoing much executive
turmoil now, it might be better for a strong, talented Bette to have
greater control over her cinematic destiny.

34

Bette at Fifty

What is the *real* Bette Midler like, and where is she going as she approaches fifty? The answers come from different people who have been with her at different times in different places. One who has known her all her life is her sister Susan, who remembers it all, including the so-called tough childhood. "Bette *says* her childhood was unhappy, but I don't think so. You know why? Because she comes back [to Hawaii] and does the same things with her child [Sophie] that she did as a child."

For example, Bette has a thirty-eight-acre estate on the island of Kuaui, where the movie *Jurassic Park* was filmed. She bought it two years after her father died. Susan, who used to have a lingerie shop near the Mauna Loa Shopping Mall and then went to work for the New York State Mental Health Department, has her own theory about Bette's memories of her childhood.

"She buys Sophie shaved ice. They go boogie boarding. They go to swimming classes and have summer fun. Bette ate shaved ice when she was a child. Bette went boogie boarding. Bette had summer fun. And just the other day she bought Sophie some of that Japanese rice candy. That's why she returns [to Hawaii] once a year—she wants to bring the memories back.

"What she means to say is that growing up is hard on everyone, including herself. You get disciplined, people don't like you. But not that growing up in Hawaii was especially hard on her."

Who is the real Bette Midler: the flamboyant, outrageous

Divine Miss M or the moving blues singer or the shy, reclusive hausfrau and bookworm or the funny, generous movie actress? According to her sister Susan, "She's all of the above. She's very, very different." And that's probably the closest and most accurate answer we'll ever get about Bette Midler. For all the negative stories about Bette and Hawaii, Susan thinks, "A lot of people don't understand that she has a very demanding work schedule and all these commitments. I think what she's able to do, she does. She budgets her time well. I'm very proud of her for that."

Film director Arthur Hiller, who worked with Bette in the movie *Outrageous Fortune*, has a view of her as a person and an actress:

> She's a very warm, caring person. Performance people have a potential for brashness, but you wouldn't realize that with Bette. I'm not saying that she doesn't have her moments, explosions and stuff, but we all have that. She basically is a real pleasure to work with, and I keep coming back to the fact that her talent really just oozes out. She makes it look so easy. She's quite smart and I think sometimes she portrays brash characters so that people don't realize that she is acting. She herself is not the brash character. She has a great mind and she's very aware of what's going on in the world and she manages to keep her awareness while she's working. Sometimes performers get so caught up in their roles that they lose touch with the rest of the world, which is okay, too, but to be able to be in touch with your character and still be in touch with the world around you is a neat trick. Bette does that.

One of many projects considered as 1995 arrived was a movie based on the very popular British TV series *Absolutely Fabulous*, with Bette playing Patsey, the Jennifer Sauders part, and Goldie Hawn in the role of Edina, played by Joanna Lumley in the TV series. Another movie would feature Bette and Eddie Murphy and would be produced at Paramount Studios. It is based on the true story of Florence Greenberg, the housewife who founded a record label and discovered the Shirelles. They wanted the group EnVogue to play the Shirelles, one of Bette's favorite girl singing groups. They are known for "Dedicated to the One I Love," "Soldier Boy," and "Will You Still Love Me Tomorrow?"

In 1994, Disney went through a tumultuous year, which must affect all the people on the lot because no one is certain which way things will go until the new executives are settled. A mark of the continuing turmoil at Disney was the resignation of Disney motion picture president David Hoberman on January 9, 1995. Hoberman had headed up both Walt Disney and Touchstone Pictures since 1988. The multilayered management levels at Disney Studios proved frustrating to Hoberman, and he worked out a five-picture production deal that will let him make movies and stay on the Disney lot without getting involved in the complicated management structure. "I feel liberated," Hoberman said.

This move came about when Joe Roth, the new motion picture group chairman, took over after Jeffrey Katzenberg left Disney. Roth felt the Disney organization was too complex and that it kept him too far away from the actual moviemaking process. "I need to be involved in the trenches of production day-to-day as opposed to being the last guy to hear about ideas. Everybody was frustrated at having to deal through a structure set up for a different kind of studio."

Joe Roth immediately made his style of management felt on the lot. He apologized to Robin Williams for Disney's misuse of the star's voice to hawk *Aladdin* merchandise, instead of dragging the issue through the courts and generating a lot of bad publicity; he signed Sharon Stone for $6 million to perform in *The Last Dance*; and he offered $3 million for the novel *The Horse Whisperer* as a vehicle for Robert Redford. All of this seemed to demonstrate that he is a take-charge executive who knows what he's doing and where he's going.

However, where he's headed may not be helpful to Bette, because Roth plans to produce fewer movies than Disney. That means fewer opportunities for Bette and others on the Disney lot. On the plus side, Disney has a reputation in Hollywood as being an unfriendly place for actors and filmmakers. The Disney people were said to be tightwads with money and to constantly interfere with production. Roth says he is trying to change that way of doing things.

The executive ranks of the Disney studios sustained another shock when Gary Galkin, one of its top marketing men, died from AIDS. Galkin was the main driving force behind marketing many of Disney's animated hits and also Bette's breakthrough hit, *Down and Out in Beverly Hills*.

However things sort out in the reorganized Disney studios, All Girl Productions has a number of projects in the mill, some of which will end up on the movie screen and some of which may wither away, as often happens in the film business.

Among the projects that All Girl Productions has in some stage of development in 1995 are several comedies which they are trying to get ready for filming, including *Accidents Will Happen, Extra Baggage, Phony Farm, Queen of the Boiler Room, That Old Feeling, Traps*, and *A View From a Broad*.

Other films also in development include *Dr. Joyce Wallace*, a comedy-drama true story about a doctor who works with New York prostitutes; *Lenya*, a musical biography and drama about singer Lotte Lenya and her unconventional marriage to composer Kurt Weill; *Miss Baba*, an animated film featuring the voice of Bette Midler with a story about a poodle who runs an orphanage and is also a detective; and *Show Business Kills*, the story of four different show business women over forty and their lives, adapted from the book of the same name written by Iris Rainer Dart, who also wrote *Beaches*.

The only film All Girl Productions had wrapped up at the end of 1994 was *Man of the House*. With a cast that includes Chevy Chase, Farrah Fawcett, and George Wendt, the film tells the story of an L.A. lawyer who joins a father-son group so he can learn about creating a better relationship with the son of the woman he loves. Bette is not in the cast. It was released early in 1995.

One aspect of Bette that needs to be understood is her long-term disaffection from contemporary lifestyles. Little has ever been said about this before, but Bette has always felt more at home in an earlier era. Judy Dytman saw that side of Bette and said:

Tragic is too strong a word for what it is. But there's a certain tragic element. You almost feel as though she's forty or fifty years too late. I think she was also very intrigued with Europeans and liked it better than what was going on here. I think she would have loved to work with European directors. She has an amazing range of taste. She'd be a great college professor. She's an incredible teacher and speaker.

I don't think anybody comes into a meeting with an actress and expects the kind of brilliance that she really had. I'm really talking from the heart. Writers would always walk away from a meeting and say to me, "My God, I had no idea she was that well read, so educated, so articulate." She talks like a professor. You don't meet anyone in Hollywood that talks like that except for a few development people. Studio executives don't talk like that . . . they're more like politicians.

Bette likes to garden, both flowers and vegetables. She loves to travel. She's very interested in architecture and design but also very interested in history. Reading and gardening are her big hobbies. I could never decide whether she was really complicated or simple, clear-cut.

Many people think that Bette Midler, the brassy, trashy, insecure, sentimental extrovert-introvert, is mellowing with time. "I think I am too," she says. "I'll tell you why. I don't think I'm anywhere near as crazy as I used to be. I used to be capable of quite serious rages. I'm not anymore. I'm really much more thoughtful. I like what I'm turning into. And I like the fact that I'm growing up, that I didn't arrest myself at age thirteen. One of my big things is to learn and to keep growing. It's hard sometimes, because things pull away. But that's basically my direction and I think it's positive."

She is open about who and what she likes and dislikes. It has hurt her occasionally, but not stifled her. Woody Allen she loves. Geraldo Rivera she thinks is a slimeball. Barbra Streisand she admires, but can't quite warm up to her, and "Bruce Springsteen is another stiff." Bette needed a song for a record and asked Bruce Springsteen's producer, Chuck Plotkin, if she could sing one and he gave her "Pink Cadillac." "He said, 'Oh yes, sure.' So I went into business, he became my producer and I cut that record and then Bruce wouldn't let me have it. I spent like $25,000 on the track and then he said I couldn't sing it: 'It wasn't a girl's song.'

"I can't talk about Madonna. I have nothing to say about Madonna. I have no opinion about Madonna. I certainly couldn't put her in the vast cosmic picture. I can't say anything without sounding like a jerk. You can't talk the truth and I don't want to lie. My views are my own, I don't want to slander the girl. She works hard. It's nobody's business what I think of Madonna."

She adores her daughter, Sophie, and she is deeply in love with her eccentric but very supportive husband, who does only one thing that drives her nuts: shaving his head from time to time. Bette is astonished about motherhood and keeps talking about having more children. About Sophie, Bette says, "She's a lot like me. So it's comforting, and also horrifying."

Producer Robert Halmi, Sr., who worked with Bette in the television film *Gypsy*, noted that the von Haselberg family unit was close and private. "Her daughter was on the set all the time," he said. "Her husband is a very private man and he doesn't want to interfere. Their marriage is rather private and stays at home."

Halmi confirmed that there is little pretense about Bette in her business and personal relations. He observed, "Bette has no hesitation, gets straight to the point, says what she wants. She's very straightforward. That's what she wants, and sometimes the problem is that she's just not going to give in anyhow."

In the working relationship between the two of them, Halmi said of Bette, "So at least I knew up front that I was going to lose, so I gave in. Why prolong the agony? Bette not only knows exactly what she wants, but she also knows that's good. I trust her completely.

"Bette has a very brash, New York attitude. Some people will be pissed off, the way she presents things. I don't. I love it. I like that kind of attitude. I'm pretty much the same way, I guess, when I want something. This is ego. In this business, everybody has an ego and everybody thinks he knows better and it's not true. If I find somebody [like Bette] who knows better than me, then I would be really stupid not to go along with them. It's knowledge and trust and taste."

Her life and her life focus have changed sharply since she married Martin von Haselberg, a.k.a. Harry Kipper, in 1984. From 1965 to 1984 she was completely self-absorbed and totally focused on her career, stealing occasional private time for her two favorite things, gardening and reading. Since her marriage she has become very involved with decorating her home, cooking, and sewing, and she guards her privacy. She is horrified by the AIDS epidemic and the many injustices and terrible things going on in the world today and tries to shield her daughter and herself from being exposed to them.

As for the present state of her career, she is no longer as tense about it as she used to be. She likes being on the Disney lot, even with its frustrations. Going on tour and to the Radio City Music Hall was an invigorating experience because it had been so long since she was regularly facing a live audience. She missed the excitement, but not the tension and exhaustion that accompany it.

In an interview with Myrna Blyth of the *Ladies' Home Journal*, she said, "I've learned how to make deals. I've learned how to negotiate and that some things are more important than others. In order to get what you want, you have to choose what's important. You have to find the point past which you would never go. I've learned how to take responsibility for what comes on my watch. You know the old expression 'It happened on my watch'? Well, you have to take responsibility. And I've learned where to buy my bras."

The story of Bette Midler is a saga of amazing achievement that brought the brash, salty Divine Miss M and the private, insecure, bookworm Bette from obscurity in a poor suburb of Honolulu to the Hollywood–New York star she is today.

Bette's performances tell anybody who's been made to feel inferior that they are okay. Bruce Vilanch, former *Chicago Tribune* reporter and longtime friend and colleague of Bette's, explains her universal appeal: "The key to Bette's success is that she touches a chord in anyone who's ever felt like they didn't belong. There was a world out there of people that she was touching which crossed all kinds of lines."

We love her because she is us and we are her.

Milestones in Bette Midler's Life

1945   Born December 1 in a suburb of Honolulu, Hawaii

1963   Graduated from Admiral Radford High School, Honolulu. She was class president and sang with a folksong group called the Pieridine Three, but was also known as the Calico Three

1963–65   Attended the University of Hawaii, toured military bases in Hawaii with the Calico Three, and worked in a pineapple cannery.

1965–66   Obtained a bit part as missionary's seasick wife in the movie *Hawaii* and moved briefly to Los Angeles to finish the movie.

1966   Moved to New York and worked as, among other things, a typist at Columbia University, a glove saleswoman at Stern's Department Store, and a go-go dancer at a club in Union City, New Jersey.

Got her first stage part in *Miss Nefertiti Regrets*. Successfully auditioned for the chorus in *Fiddler on the Roof* and, in February 1967, was chosen to take over the role of Tzeitel in the show and stayed three years. Off hours she performed at clubs around New York, including Hilly's and the Improvisation.

1968   Judy Midler, Bette's oldest sister, was killed when a car shot out of an underground Manhattan garage and smashed her against a wall as she was walking to meet Bette after a performance of *Fiddler on the Roof*.

1970   Obtained a role in the off-Broadway musical *Salvation* and, after that closed, returned to being a go-go dancer in a Broadway bar. Then began appearing at the Continental Baths, a gay spa and club, where she met and teamed up with a rising pianist named Barry Manilow.

1971   Signed a contract with Atlantic Records to do an album. Went to Seattle to perform in the Who's rock opera, *Tommy*.

1973   Won a Grammy as Best New Artist.

1974   Won a special-category Tony for adding luster to the Broadway season.

1975   Helped create and starred in *Clams on the Half Shell*, a New York stage review that sold out.

1977–78   Awarded an Emmy for Outstanding TV Special for *Ol' Red Hair Is Back*.

1979   Starred in another of her stage reviews, *Bette! Divine Madness*. Went on to star in the film *The Rose*, a story patterned after the ill-fated life of Janis Joplin.

            Won two Golden Globe Awards, as Best Actress for her starring role in *The Rose* and as Best Newcomer to Film.

1980–82   Did the stage show, album, tour, and movie *Divine Madness*. Fired her entire musical troupe after the end of the stage tour and was successfully sued by members of the cast, mostly the Harlettes, for $2 million. Made the movie *Jinxed*, which was a traumatic experience and turned into a bomb and soured the Hollywood community on her for the next four years.

            Won a Grammy for Best Pop Vocal—Female for her work in *The Rose*, 1980. Also, awarded a Grammy for the Best Recording for Children, *In Harmony/A Sesame Street Record*, done in association with other artists.

1984   Did an HBO concert, *Bette Midler: Art or Bust*. This was her debut as a TV producer. Married Martin von Haselberg, a.k.a. Harry Kipper of the Kipper Kids, in December.

1986   Signed a contract with Walt Disney/Touchstone studios for her first film in four years, a comedy, *Down and Out in Beverly Hills*.

1987   Sophie Frederica Alohilani born to Martin and Bette von Haselberg.

1988   Produced and starred in the feature film *Beaches*, the theme song of which, "Wind Beneath My Wings," was an award-winning hit that was number one on pop music charts. Did the voice of Georgette in the animated children's feature *Oliver and Company*.

1989   Formed her own company, All Girl Productions, in a studio deal with Disney's Touchstone Pictures. Colleagues in the operation are Bonnie Bruckheimer-Martell and Margaret Jennings South. About this time, she won a $400,000 lawsuit against an ad agency that appropriated her musical style using one of the former Harlettes, Ula Hedwig, without her consent.

1991   Awarded a Golden Globe for Best Actress, Musical or Comedy, in recognition of her work in *For the Boys*. Appeared as a special guest on the final Johnny Carson *Tonight Show*, for which she later won an Emmy.

1993   Did her first concert tour in ten years, *Experience the Divine*, ending with a record-breaking thirty-night stand at New York's Radio City Music Hall. Received the Golden

Partial List of Those Contacted
in Connection With This Book*

Jim Abrahams, director of *Ruthless People* and *Big Business*

Diane Carter Anderson, personal friend

John Broderick, unit production manager, *Down and Out in Beverly Hills*

Anita Busch, film critic, *Variety*

Wally Chappell, classmate at University of Hawaii

Judy Dytman, former vice president of development, All Girl Productions

John Erman, director, *Stella*

Charles Fink, head of Animation, Walt Disney Studios, worked on *Oliver and Company*

Whitney Green, unit production manager, *Hocus Pocus*

Robert Halmi Sr., executive producer of *Gypsy*

Peter Herald, unit production manager, *Outrageous Fortune*

Arthur Hiller, director, *Outrageous Fortune*, and president, Motion Picture Academy

Andy Hill, Music Department, Walt Disney Studios

Bruce Humphrey, assistant director, *Big Business*

Fugie Kajikawa, friend and actress with Bette in Hawaii

Irv Lichtman, *Billboard* magazine

Lena Logan, assistant to Ahmet Ertegun of Warners-Electra-Atlantic Records

---

*Many with whom we spoke insisted on not being identified because they are fearful it might hurt their relationship with Bette or hurt their careers—particularly in Hollywood.

Daniel McCauley, member of crew of *Jinxed*

Irwin Malzman, classmate at Radford High School, Hawaii

Lillian Malzman, close friend of Bette's parents in Hawaii and
  New Jersey

Edward Marley, unit production manager, *For the Boys*

Dick Mason, teacher at University of Hawaii

Sarah Jessica Parker, actress with Bette in *Hocus Pocus*

Bill Pullman, actor with Bette in *Ruthless People*

Peter Riegert, former lover and costar in *Gypsy*

Jack Roe, unit production manager, *Divine Madness*

Benjamin Rosenberg, assistant director, *Beaches*

Aaron Russo, one of the four most important men in her life;
  manager who made her rich and a former lover

Adam Sandler, music critic, *Variety*

Cynthia Sherman, staff, All Girl Productions

Evelyn Trapido, staff member of University of Hawaii Drama
  Department, who worked with Bette

Joel Trapido, one of her drama instructors at University of Hawaii

Jim Tyson, costume supervisor, *For the Boys*

Jim Van Wyck, assistant director, *Outrageous Fortune*

Partial List of Sources

Magazines

Advertising Age

"U.S. Supreme Court" (column) (Decision on award stands for Bette Midler against Young and Rubicam), March 30, 1992, p. 57. (1)

American Film

Peter Rainer, *"Stella"* (video recording review), September 9, 1990, p. 60.

Business Week

Ronald Grover, "Orion Is Still Star-Crossed," in LA, March 4, 1992, p. 37.

Commonweal

Paul Baumann, "Scenes From a Mall" (review), April 19, 1991, p. 260.

Cosmopolitan

1. "Beaches," April 1989, p. 52.
2. Marjorie Rosen, "Trashy, Torchy, Bette—A One-Woman Show: 'Bette Midler,' June 1989, p. 168.
3. "Siblings Speak: Famous Women Talk About Their Sisters and Brothers," September 1990, p. 272.

Crain's New York Business

Linda Moss, "Who Needs Any Raves? Producer's Got Bucks," August 21, 1989, p. 3.

Dance Magazine

"Everything's Coming Up Bette," December 1993, pp. 84–86.

Entertainment Weekly

1. *"For the Boys,"* January 10, 1992, p. 68.
2. *"Hocus Pocus,"* July 23, 1993, p. 45.
3. *"Experience the Divine,"* July 30, 1993, p. 58.

4. "Divine Gladness," October 1, 1993, p. 12.

5. *"Gypsy,"* December 10, 1993, p. 60.

6. "Not Their Cup of Tease," December 10, 1993, p. 61.

7. "Return of the Living Dead," December 31, 1993, p. 74.

Financial Times

1. Nigel Andrews, "Ghostly Encounters: Cinema," March 22, 1990, p. 21.

2. Alastair Macaulay and David Vaughan, "Serious Fun," August 13, 1991, p. 11.

Forbes

Lisa Gubernick, "The Hottest Thing Since Cinerama," September 4, 1989, p. 70.

Good Housekeeping

Vernon Scott, "Bette," March 1991, p. 64.

Jet

"Eddie Murphy to Make Movie," August 16, 1993, p. 63.

Ladies' Home Journal

1. E. Sherman, "Leading Ladies: Bette Midler Can Get Serious," January 1989, p. 58.

2. Myrna Blyth, "Bette on Bette," January 1992, p. 82.

3. Sally Ogle Davis, "A Sure Bette," July 1993, p. 96.

Library Journal

Randy Pitman, "Scenes From a Mall" (video recording review), September 15, 1991, p. 128.

Life

"A Day in the Life of a Screen Goddess Starring the One and the Only Bette Midler With Martin Von Haselberg as Everyone Else," April 1989, p. 114.

Los Angeles Business Journal

Jay Pinkert, "Showscan Shakes Things Up With Super Film, Really Big Screens and Even Chairs That Move," April 25, 1988, p. 18.

Los Angeles Magazine

"Gypsy," February 1994, p. 114.

Maclean's

1. *"Beaches,"* January 9, 1989, p. 45.

2. P. Young, "Trouble for Copy Cats," November 20, 1989, p. 92.

3. Brian D. Johnson, *"For the Boys,"* December 2, 1991, p. 86.

Mother Jones

Editor's Note ("Bette Midler, Political Activist"), January–February 1991, p. 8.

The Nation

1. A. Kopkind, *"Down and Out in Beverly Hills"* (review), March 1, 1986, p. 251.

2. Stuart Klawans, *"Scenes From a Mall"* (review), March 25, 1991, p. 391.

National Review

1. John Simon, *"Down and Out in Beverly Hills"* (review), March 28, 1986, p. 63.

2. John Simon, *"For the Boys"* (review), January 20, 1992, p. 64.

The New Republic

1. Stanley Kauffmann, *"Stella"* (review), March 5, 1990, p. 27.

2. Stanley Kauffmann, *"Scenes From a Mall"* (review), March 18, 1991, p. 32.

New Statesman and Society

1. Suzanne Moore, *"Stella Dallas"* (review), September 14, 1990, p. 27.

2. Suzanne Moore, *"Scenes From a Mall"* (review), April 19, 1991, p. 27.

New York Magazine

1. David Denby, *"Stella"* (review), February 12, 1990, p. 64.

2. David Denby, *"Scenes From a Mall"* (review), March 4, 1991, p. 73.

3. David Denby, *"For the Boys"* (review), December 2, 1991, p. 158.

4. Richard David Story, " 'Experience the Divine' at Radio City Music Hall—Six Weeks of Best Bettes," September 13, 1993, p. 72.

5. John Simon, "Bette Midler" (Radio City Music Hall concert review), October 11, 1993, p. 86.

The New Yorker
1. Terrence Rafferty, *"For the Boys"* (review), December 16, 1991, p. 117.
2. Brendan Lemon, "Vivat Divina!" September 6, 1993, p. 33.

People
1. Jim Jerome, " 'Lords' Spells Stardom for David Keith, a Tennessee Boy Turned Big-City Bachelor," March 14, 1983, p. 113.
2. Andrea Chambers, "Midler Has Been the Bette Noir of Showbiz, but Now She's Baby Divine to the Literary Set," November 14, 1983, p. 115.
3. C. Wallace, "Happy at Last? You Bette," February 3, 1986, p. 92.
4. S. Haller, *"Down and Out in Beverly Hills"* (review), February 10, 1986, p. 12.
5. "Bette Midler," Mail section, Anna Klaczynska-Mees, February 24, 1986.
6. Eric Levin, "The New Look in Old Maids," March 31, 1986, p. 28.
7. "Take One: Bette Midler," May 26, 1986, p. 29.
8. S. Haller, *"Ruthless People"* (review), July 14, 1986, p. 10.
9. "Bette Midler" (25 Most Intriguing People of '86), December 22, 1986, p. 38.
10. Peter Travers, *"Outrageous Fortune"* (review), February 16, 1987, p. 10.
11. "Chatter," May 4, 1987, p. 150.
12. "Tots in Tow, the Stars Turn Out for Snow White's Semicentennial," July 27, 1987, p. 57.
13. Peter Travers, *"Big Business"* (review), June 13, 1988, p. 14.
14. Brad Darrach with David Hutchings, "First Ladies of Laughter Double Up," June 20, 1988, p. 76.
15. "Bette Midler (Big Business)," August 1, 1988, p. 19.
16. "Bette, Robin and 1198 Others," October 24, 1988.
17. *"Oliver and Company,"* November 21, 1988.
18. Peter Travers, *"Beaches"* (review), January 9, 1989, p. 12.

19. "Mayim Bialik Who Strolls *Beaches* as Baby Bette Midler," February 6, 1989, p. 63.

20. Ralph Novak, *"Stella"* (review), February 12, 1990, p. 12.

21. "Holding Her Own Against the Divine Miss M," February 26, 1990, p. 58.

22. Susan Schindehette, Sue Carswell, Vicki Cheff, and Robin Micheli, "Waking Up Late to the Biological Clock," August 20, 1990, p. 74.

23. Ralph Novak, *"Scenes From a Mall"* (review), March 11, 1991, p. 14.

24. "Star Tracks," December 2, 1991, p. 11.

25. Leah Rozen, *"For the Boys"* (review), December 2, 1991, p. 30.

26. Kim Cunningham, "Vocal Hero," December 6, 1993, p. 158.

27. *"Gypsy"* (review), December 13, 1993, p. 13.

28. "Still Eager Divas, Barbra Streisand and Bette Midler Reconquered the Stage," March 7, 1994, p. 90.

Playboy

1. *"Down and Out in Beverly Hills"* (review), April 1986, p. 21.

2. *"Ruthless People"* (review), October 1986, p. 25.

3. *"Outrageous Fortune"* (review), April 1987, p. 22.

Redbook

1. Delia Ephron, "Talking With the Private Bette Midler—A Big Surprise!" March 1989, p. 28.

2. Alan W. Petrucelli, "What Makes Bette Laugh? Bette Midler," September 1990, p. 76.

Reuters

"Showscan in Film Production," April 11, 1988.

Rolling Stone

Peter Travers, *"Scenes From a Mall"* (review), March 21, 1991, p. 84.

Sight and Sound

1. Philip Kemp, *"For the Boys"* (review), February 1992, p. 44.

2. Leslie Felperin, *"Hocus Pocus"* (review), November 1993, p. 43.

The South Florida Business Journal

Alina Matas, "Hollywood Takes Added Liking to Local Filming," April 9, 1990, p. 5.

Stereo Review

Alanna Nash, *"Some People's Lives"* (album review), January 1991, p. 113.

Time

1. Richard Schickel, *"Down and Out in Beverly Hills"* (review), January 27, 1986, p. 64.

2. "Expecting, Bette Midler," March 31, 1986, p. 73.

3. Richard Schickel, *"Ruthless People"* (review), June 30, 1986, p. 86.

4. "Born to Bette Midler," December 1, 1986, p. 24.

5. Richard Corliss, *"Outrageous Fortune"* (review), February 2, 1987, p. 73.

6. Richard Corliss, "Bette Steals Hollywood; The Divine Miss M Is a Movie Star at Last," March 2, 1987, p. 64.

7. Denise Worrell, "Marriage Vegas Style," March 2, 1987, p. 69.

8. Richard Corliss, *"Big Business"* (review), June 13, 1988, p. 77.

9. Richard Schickel, *"Scenes From a Mall"* (review), February 25, 1991, p. 77.

10. Richard Schickel, *"For the Boys"* (review), December 2, 1991, p. 86.

11. Richard Corliss, "Bette Midler: Experience the Divine" (review), October 4, 1993, p. 83.

12. William A. Henry III, *"Gypsy"* (review), December 13, 1993, p. 86–88.

13. "The Most Unusual Crowd Ever at a Bette Midler Concert," January 10, 1994, p. 14.

TV Guide

C. Dreifus, "The Gypsy in Bette," December 11, 1993, p. 10–17.

U.S. News and World Report
"A U.S. Patent on Famous Voices," November 13, 1989, p. 19.

Video Magazine
"For the Boys" (review), June 1992, p. 62.

Vogue
Jonathan Van Meter, "A Fashion Fairy Tale Extravaganza" (Bette Midler interview), December 1991, p. 202.

Newspapers and News Wires

Boston Globe
1. Jay Carr, "Awakening: Go Back to Sleep," August 16, 1989, p. 79.
2. Jim Sullivan (contribution by Christine Temin), "When Shock Art Goes Too Far: Fear and Loathing in the Audience," November 1, 1989, p. 75.

BPI Entertainment News Wire
"Film Briefs," November 6, 1990.

Business Wire
1. "MGM/UA: Financial Results," July 9, 1985.
2. "Mr. Blackwell, Mr. Schmackwell," September 16, 1994.

Calgary Herald
James Muretish, "Furnaceface: The Quirky Quartet Has 'Matured,'" September 18, 1994, p. B-8.

Chicago Tribune
1. Nina Darton, " 'New York, New York' Is Producer Russo's Theme," June 18, 1987, p. 15, zone H.
2. Leslie Rubenstein, "A Sure Bette Midler Charges Full-Tilt Into Her Next Role," June 5, 1988, p. 6, zone C.
3. Dave Kerr, " 'Rude' Crude, but Works as '60s Film," August 16, 1989, p. 3, zone C.
4. Glenn Plaskin, "Bette's Back on Track, Midler May Play the Fool but at Heart She's a Survivor," January 28, 1990, p. 4.

Communications Daily
1. September 13, 1988, p. 4.
2. "New World Rejects Bid," July 19, 1989.

Gannett News Service

   1. Jack Garner, "Rude Awakening," August 11, 1989.

   2. Jack Garner, "Capsule Reviews of '89 Films," December 21, 1989.

Los Angeles Times

   1. Henry Weinstein, "Is Motion to Seek Evidence in Simpson Case Too Broad?" July 29, 1994, p. A1.

   2. Michael London, "Film Clips: All Tri-Star Rumors Lead to Saganski," January 11, 1985, Part 6, p. 1.

   3. Michael London, "Film Clips: MGM/UA: Two Guys Working on a Script," February 8, 1985, Part 6, p. 1.

   4. Michael London, "Film Clips: Youth Calls the Shots in 'Blue City,' " February 15, 1985, Part 6, p. 1.

   5. Martin Halstuk, "The Seduction of Hollywood: States Are Going All Out to Get Movie Makers to Run Away," September 22, 1985, p. 18.

   6. Suzanne Muchnic, "The Art Galleries: La Cienega Area," June 6, 1986, Part 6, p. 16.

   7. David T. Friendly, "First Look at the Studios: Exclusive Producer: Top Gun?" September 11, 1986, Part 6, p. 1.

   8. Lawrence Christon, "Stage Watch: L.A. Theatres Are Singing the Holiday Blues: 'Long Day's Journey Into Night,' Journeys to TV," December 11, 1986, Part 6, p. 5.

   9. Jennifer Foote, "Power Pack: Female Reps of Female Super Stars Have the Clout," August 23, 1987, Cal. p. 20.

   10. Zan Dubin, "Art News: 'Silent Bid Auction' to Benefit AIDS Victims," September 6, 1987, Cal. p. 96.

   11. "People: President of Arts Agency," September 10, 1987, Part 9, p. 2.

   12. "L.A. Beat: Indignities From the East Coast," March 13, 1988, Cal. p. 96.

   13. Lawrence Christon, "Comedy Column: Kipper Kids Seek a K.O. on Cinemax," July 31, 1988, Cal. p. 5.

   14. Kevin Thomas, "Movie Reviews: 'Rude Awakening' for Anachronistic Hippies," August 16, 1989, Part 6, p. 9.

   15. Stacy Jenel Smith, "Outtakes: If at First. . . ," December 17, 1989, Cal. p. 45.

16. Pat H. Broeske, "Jim Morrison: Back to '60s, Darkly: The Storm Still Swirls Around a Generation's Bad Boy as Oliver Stone Prepares to Bring His Story to the Screen," January 7, 1990, Cal. p. 6.

17. "Names in the News: Midler Junks TV for Daughter," Times Wire Services, February 1, 1990, Part P, p. 9.

18. Henry Weinstein, "Isgro Claims He's 'Fall Guy' in MCA Probe," April 17, 1990, Business p. 2.

19. Kirk Honeycutt, "Cinefile," September 2, 1990, Cal. p. 37.

20. Jube Schiver, Jr., "Judge Abruptly Ends Payola Case Against Three," September 5, 1990, p. A1.

21. David Pecchia, "The Movie Chart," October 14, 1990, Cal. p. 42.

22. Kathy Curtis, "Tasty Tape: At 'Choice Encounters,' the Videos Steal the Show," December 31, 1992, OC Live p. 4.

23. Henry Weinstein, "Judge Charges Justice Department Misconduct," December 24, 1993, Metro p. 1.

24. Ronald J. Ostrow, "U.S. Prosecutor Gets Reprimand in Payola Case," May 5, 1994, Metro p. 1.

25. Bill Higgins, "R.S.V.P./Into the Night: Pay-back Time," September 21, 1994, Life and Style p. 5.

26. Shari Roan, "Square Pegs? Being Rejected by Peers Is not Only Hurtful, It Can Cause Emotional Problems," September 28, 1994, p. E1.

27. Chuck Phillips, "EMI Hires Controversial Promoter," Cal. p. 1.

Newsday

1. Marvin Kitman, " 'Beyondo' Variety With Bette Midler," March 18, 1988, Part 2, p. 11.

2. Marvin Kitman, "After 'Python,' What Next?" August 7, 1988, TV Plus, p. 5.

3. Stephen Williams, Leo Seligsohn, Ronnie Gil, Elizabeth Wissner-Gross, David Friedman, "Performance Artists Get Punchy," August 7, 1988, TV Plus, p. 6.

4. Michael Fleming and Karen Freifeld, contrib. by Christie

Marshall, "Inside New York," August 7, 1989, News p. 9.

5. Michael Fleming and Karen Freifeld, contribution by Scott Ladd, "Inside New York," August 14, 1989, News p. 11.

6. Terry Kelleher, "A Bad Trip Back to the '60s," August 16, 1989, Part 2, p. 9.

7. Thomas J. Mair, "Rude Times During *Rude Awakening*," August 29, 1989, Business p. 45 (other edition City p. 41).

8. Michael Fleming, Karen Freifeld, and Linda Stasi (edited by Linda Stasi), "Inside New York," October 6, 1989, News p. 11.

9. Michael Fleming, Karen Freifeld, and Linda Stasi (edited by Linda Stasi), "Inside New York," December 27, 1989, News p. 11.

10. "People," February 2, 1990, News p. 8.

11. "Play a Few Bars, Marvin!" April 28, 1991, News p. 8.

12. Anthony Scaduto, Doug Vaughan, and Linda Stasi, "Inside New York," September 30, 1991, News p. 13.

13. Jan Stuart, "Take That, Miss Manners," August 3, 1993, Part 2, p. 47.

14. Susan Shapiro, "A Happy Ending—At Last," October 13, 1993, Part 2, p. 53.

New York Times

1. Chris Chase, Bette Midler (interview), January 14, 1973, Section 2, p. 3.

2. Janet Maslin, "Film: 'Teachers,' With Nick Nolte," October 5, 1984, Section C, p. 10.

3. Janet Maslin, "At the Movies," March 8, 1985, Section C, p. 8.

4. Walter Goodman, "Screen: 'Wise Guys,' " April 18, 1986, Section C, p. 8.

5. Thomas O'Conner, "Bette Midler Is Up and In in Hollywood," June 22, 1986, Section 2, p. 21.

6. Aljean Harmetz, "Hollywood Ambivalent as Film Trial Nears End," April 20, 1987, Section A, p. 15.

7. Nina Darnton, "At the Movies," June 12, 1987, Section C, p. 6.

8. Stephen Holden, "Avant-Garde Antics for Fearless Audiences," February 5, 1988, Section C, p. 1.

9. Jeannie Park, "When '60s Meets '80s, It's a 'Rude Awakening,'" November 6, 1988, Section 2, p. 24.

10. Vincent Canby, "Review/Film: Arousing the Old Populism for a New Antiwar Protest," August 16, 1989, Section C, p. 19.

11. "Films That Are Shooting," September 28, 1990, Section C, p. 5.

12. "Summer Festival: Dance," compiled by Gwin Chin, May 19, 1991, Section 2A, p. 10.

13. Stephen Holden, "Laughter, Music, and Dance, Seriously," July 12, 1991, Section C, p. 1.

14. Stephen Holden, "Sounds Around Town," July 30, 1993, Section C, p. 16.

15. Stephen Holden, "Cabaret Review: Karen Acres' Classically Controlled Pop," September 26, 1994, Section C, p. 14.

PR News Wire

1. "News Advisory," May 7, 1986.

2. "Showscan Film Corp Enters Into Agreement With Aaron Russo Films," April 11, 1988.

3. "Shows," November 30, 1988.

Seattle Times

Misha Berson, "Today's Top Shows Have a British Beat—For a Preview of Broadway Hits, Try a Tour of London's Stages," September 25, 1994, Arts and Entertainment p. M7.

Sunday Telegraph

Candida Crew, "People: Crash, Bang, Wallop—A Smash Hit! Candida Crew Meets a Man Who's Made a Show Out of Bashing Bins," October 27, 1991, p. 102.

Times Literary Supplement

Hugo Williams, "*Scenes From a Mall*" (review), April 26, 1991, p. 16.

United Press International

"*Teachers*," October 25, 1983.

USA Today

Mike Clark, " 'Rude': Ill-Mannered Attempt at Humor," August 16, 1989, Life p. 4D.

USA Weekend

Richard Price, "Best Bette Yet: Mommy Imperfect," February 4, 1990, p. 4.

Village Voice

"Are You Experienced?" October 5, 1993, p. 71.

Washington Post

1. Marylouise Oates, " 'People' Power: Barbra's Million-Dollar Bash," September 8, 1986, Style p. C1.

2. Rita Kempley, "Soporific 'Awakening,' " August 16, 1989, Style p. D10.

3. Hal Hinson, Rita Kempley, Richard Harrington, "New on Tape," February 1, 1990, Style p. C7.

4. Paul Noglows and Matt Rothman, "Film Finances on the Mend: Bonder Sees Solid Future in New Lloyd's Pact, Hogan's 'Jack,' " July 21, 1993, News p. 6.

Washington Times

Buzz McClain, "Elfman's Magic Lives in Both His 'Serious' Music and Rock," September 18, 1994, Part D, p. D1.

Vancouver Sun

"Insight Lite," September 17, 1994, p. B1.

Trade Publications

Back Stage

1. Richard Miller, "Bianchi to Close Shop to Direct Upcoming Feature: Ed Bianchi, 'Paradise Paved,' " November 10, 1989, p. 1.

2. David Sheward, "NY Filming Is Crisp for Fall: Feature Films and Television Programs," October 5, 1990, p. 1.

Back Stage Shoot

Lauren Sanders, "Get Me Someone Who Sounds Like . . ." October 18, 1991, p. 33.

Billboard

1. Paul Grien, "Bonnie Rates Top Honors at Grammys," March 3, 1990, p. 1.

2. Chris Morris, "Author Greenfield 'Presents' Bill Graham, Showman," October 17, 1992, p. 13.

3. Melinda Newman, "Divine Miss M Makes Tour News: Bottom Line on Baerwald's Message," May 29, 1993, p. 16.

Cineman Movie Reviews

"*Rude Awakening*," December 31, 1989.

Daily Variety

1. Kevin Zimmerman, "Singers May Say 'No', but the Sound Remains the Same," January 10, 1990, p. 3.

2. "*Stella*" (review), February 7, 1990, p. 30.

3. Will Tusher, "Musicals, Even an Actioner, on Midler Slate," November 19, 1990, p. 12.

4. Amy Dawes, "*Scenes From a Mall*" (review), February 25, 1991, p. 48.

5. Amy Dawes, "*For the Boys*" (review), November 18, 1991, p. 30.

6. Derek Elley, "Off and Running," June 16, 1991.

7. Bruce Harring, " 'Elly May' vs. Whoopi, Bette," June 21, 1993, pp. 4–5.

8. Brian Lowry, "*Hocus Pocus*" (review), July 26, 1993, p. 29.

Hollywood Reporter

1. Doris Toumarkine, "HBO Savors Savoy Slate: Largest Home Video Output Deal Pegged at $500 Mil for Four Years," June 16, 1992.

2. Doris Toumarkine, "HBO Files for Russo Millions," May 24, 1993.

Books

R. Warwick Armstrong, ed., *Atlas of Hawaii*, (University of Hawaii at Manoa, Honolulu, 1983).

Maxene Andrews and Bill Gilbert, *Over Here, Over There: The Andrews Sisters and the USO Stars in World War II* (Zebra Books, New York, 1993).

Dr. Alan Axelrod and Charles Phillips, *What Every American Should Know About American History* (Bob Adams, Publishers, Holbrook, Mass., 1992).

Mark Bego, *Bette Midler: Outrageously Divine* (NAL Dutton, New York, 1987).

DeSoto Brown, *Hawaii Goes to War* (Editions Limited, Honolulu, 1989).

Gilbert Chase, *America's Music* (University of Illinois Press, Urbana, 1987).

Ace Collins, *Bette Midler* (St. Martin's Press, New York, 1989).

Current Biography (H. W. Wilson Company, New York, 1973).

Clive Davis with James Willwerth, *Clive: In the Record Business* (William Morrow & Co., New York, 1975).

Editors of Time-Life Books, *This Fabulous Century: 1940–1950* (Time-Life, 1970).

———, *This Fabulous Century: 1950–1960* (Time-Life, 1970).

———, *This Fabulous Century: 1960–1970* (Time-Life, 1970).

———, *This Fabulous Century: 1970–1980* (Time-Life, 1970).

Bill Graham and Robert Greenfield, *Bill Graham Presents: My Life Inside Rock and Out* (Doubleday, New York, 1992).

William Knoedelseder, *Stiffed: A True Story of MCA, the Music Business and the Mafia* (HarperCollins Publishers, New York, 1993).

Dan E. Moldea, *Dark Victory: Ronald Reagan, MCA and the Mob* (Viking Press, New York, 1986).

Ann Rayson, *Modern Hawaiian History,* (University of Hawaii, Bess Press, Honolulu, 1984).

Sidney Shemel and M. Willima Krasilovsky, *This Business of Music* (Billboard Publishers, New York, 1979).

James Spada, *The Divine Bette Midler* (Macmillian Publishing Co., New York, 1984).

Anthony Storr, *Music and the Mind* (Free Press, New York, 1992).

Television and Radio Scripts

The Oprah Winfrey Show #588, December 14, 1988.

Saturday Night with Connie Chung, February 3, 1990.

CBS This Morning, February 8, 1990.

CBS This Morning, November 29, 1991.

CBS This Morning, December 8, 1993.

The Today Show, July 16, 1993.

GEORGE MAIR has been a journalist for over thirty-five years with CBS, the Los Angeles Times Syndicate, and Time, Inc.'s Home Box Office, and has served as press secretary to the Speaker of the U.S. House of Representatives. He has written thousands of broadcast scripts, newspaper articles, and syndicated columns and won thirty-two awards for writing. This is his thirteenth published book. His other books include *Inside HBO, The Jade Cat Murders, Family Money, Lethal Ladies, Bridge Down, Star Stalkers,* and *Oprah Winfrey: The Real Story.*

Index